Learning in a digitalized age

Edited by Lawrence Burke

A John Catt Publication

First Published 2014

by John Catt Educational Ltd,
12 Deben Mill Business Centre, Old Maltings Approach,
Melton, Woodbridge IP12 1BL

Tel: +44 (0) 1394 389850 Fax: +44 (0) 1394 386893
Email: enquiries@johncatt.com
Website: www.johncatt.com

© 2014 John Catt Educational Ltd

ISBN: 978 1 909717 084

Set and designed by John Catt Educational Limited

Printed and bound in Great Britain
by Ashford Colour Press

Contents

About the contributors

Lawrence Burke is an experienced international educator of 25 years. In the 2011/12 academic year the Higher Colleges of Technology, Al Ain Men's College awarded him Teacher of the Year. Prior to working in the Higher Education sector he was Deputy Head-Academic with The British International School in Jeddah, and Acting Head of Secondary with The International School Suva. He has held leadership posts with St George's College, Quilmes, Buenos Aires, and The Overseas Family School, Singapore. His leadership roles in international schools include school counselor, careers guidance counselor, Head of Year, Head of Department and coordinator of external international curricula. He blogs at http://www.lawrenceburke.org and has a professional website at http://lawrenceburke.net.

Dr. Burke's writings, publications and research have appeared in *The International Schools Journal, International School* magazine, and *The Journal of Imagination in Language Teaching, The International Educator, Curriculum Perspectives*, HCT Publications, TESOL Arabia publications, and *Quadrant* magazine.

Andrew Callaghan is an IB English literature teacher and Theory of Knowledge Co-ordinator at one of India's leading Cambridge and IB Schools, The BD Somani International School Mumbai. He has over 20 years experience teaching overseas including the British Council Singapore, company training in Indonesia and most recently six years as Head of Year, IB teacher and staff trainer at the British International School of Jeddah. He loves teaching at the BD Somani International School because his IB students love technology but they also love books.

Lisa Martin is a veteran educator of 20 years, having taught in the United Arab Emirates, Malaysia, the USA, and currently Jordan. She is the founder/director of the world's first online Model United Nation's program, O-MUN. Lisa has spent the past two years developing the O-MUN program. When not glued to her computer, she loves to read old fashioned books, garden, and explore, with her daughters and husband, the interesting country of Jordan she currently calls home.

Dr Patrick Dougherty is a professor of International Liberal Arts and director of the English for Academic Purpose program at Akita International University in Japan. His research interests are in teacher development, the use of creative writing and student heritage in the EFL/ESL classroom, and use of technology to provide access to education. When not at work, he travels with his wife and two daughters, goes scuba diving, and writes short stories and poetry.

Josephine Butler is a faculty member of Liberal Studies at Abu Dhabi Women's College delivering Research Methodology courses to undergraduate female students. She is currently pursuing her doctorate in Education from Deakin University, Australia. Her interest is in using technology to provide innovative solutions for program delivery.

Gregory Vrhovnik is from the US and, after time in Europe, Japan and Thailand, is now living in Abu Dhabi where he teaches at the Higher Colleges of Technology. His speciality focus is Business Communication and research in distant learning methodologies. When not academically engaged he enjoys photography and long distance cycling.

Serge Morissette is a Canadian teacher who has been working in the Middle East for over ten years. In his previous career, Serge was an elementary school teacher, a secondary school principal, and an education officer for the Ministry of Education of the province of Ontario, Canada. He presently teaches at the Faculty of Education at Al Ain Women's College (AAWC) in the United Arab Emirates. He is a strong advocate of the Learning By Doing concept and to the Whole Student approach in education.

Tanya Tercero is a first-year PhD student in Second Language Acquisition and Teaching at the University of Arizona in Tucson in the US. Her focus is on L2 Use and CALL. She is currently a Graduate Assistant in Teaching for freshmen composition in the Writing Program at the university.

Dr Michelle Rogers-Estable and **Dr Roudaina Houjeir** are educators with the Higher Colleges of Technology in the United Arab Emirates and have a keen professional interest in educational technologies and teaching and learning.

Diane Evans has lectured in business and office technology for 30 years in the UK, Canada and, more recently, the UAE. She collaborated on research into electronic portfolios and investigated evaluation of e-learning in part fulfilment of an MBA in Educational Management. Diane has returned to the UK and would like further opportunities to research the evaluation of e-delivery.

Ieda M Santos holds a PhD in Education from the University of Warwick, UK. She is an Assistant Professor at Emirates College for Advanced Education in the United Arab Emirates. She teaches Educational Technology courses and supervises students during their practicum and internships in schools. Her research interests include online learning, technology integration, and mobile learning.

Yasemin Allsop has been working as an ICT Coordinator in primary schools in London for almost 10 years. She is currently employed at Wilbury Primary School in London, UK. She has MA ICT in Education from the London Knowledge Lab, University of London. She is also an MPhil/PhD student at Goldsmiths, University of London, focusing on children's thinking and learning when designing digital games. Prior to her teaching career she worked as a child psychologist for many years. She is the editor of an online magazine called *ICT in Practice* where educators from around the world share their experiences of using technology in education.

Dawn Seddon is on the faculty with the Higher Colleges of Technology in Al Ain. Dawn is a talented artist, and is pursuing further research into how students learn using iPads.

Professor Clyde Coreil is a distinguished educator. He is editor of *The Journal of the Imagination in Language Learning*. Professor Coreil teaches at New Jersey City University, New Jersey 07305, USA. His main efforts have been in the areas of creative writing, linguistics and editing. His most ambitious undertaking in the last-mentioned field is the anthology *Multiple Intelligences, Howard Gardner and New Methods of College Teaching* (2003) and the seven volumes of *The Journal of the Imagination in Language Learning and Teaching*. He holds an MFA from Carnegie

Mellon University and a PhD in Linguistics from the City University of New York.

Yasmine Salah El-Din teaches linguistics at Cairo University and academic reading/writing at the American University in Cairo. She has a Master's degree in TEFL and a PhD in Contrastive Pragmatics. Her areas of research interest include corrective feedback, sociolinguistics and service-learning. She lives and works in Cairo, Egypt.

Jon Orthman, Reem Arafat and **Dr Nancy Fahnestock** are educators with The Higher Colleges of Technology in Al Ain, at the forefront of using online learning and educational technologies to help students enjoy and succeed in the study of Math.

Julie Lindsay is a global educator, innovator and leader. She has led the way in technology-infused connections and collaborations across six countries including Africa, Asia and the Middle East. Now based back in Australia as a consultant, presenter and workshop leader she is kept busy as Director of Learning Confluence, Director and co-founder of Flat Classroom® and Global Collaboration Consultant for THINK Global School. Julie is completing her EdD with the University of Southern Queensland with a focus on facilitating positive social change through effective pedagogy for collaboration.

Cris Rowan is an impassioned occupational therapist who has first-hand understanding and knowledge of how technology can cause profound changes in a child's development, behaviour and their ability to learn. Cris received her Bachelor of Science in Occupational Therapy in 1989 from the University of British Columbia, as well as a Bachelor of Science in Biology, and is a SIPT certified sensory integration specialist.

Cris is a member in good standing with the BC College of Occupational Therapists, and an approved provider with the American Occupational Therapy Association, the Canadian Association of Occupational Therapists, and Autism Community Training. For the past 15 years, she has specialized in paediatric rehabilitation, working for over a decade in the Sunshine Coast School District in British Columbia. She is also CEO of Zone'in Programs Inc offering products, workshops and training to improve child health and enhance academic performance.

Cris designed *Zone'in, Move'in, Unplug'in* and *Live'in* educational products for elementary children to address the rise in developmental delays, behaviour disorders, and technology overuse. She has performed over 200 Foundation Series Workshops on topics such as sensory integration, attention and learning, fine motor development, printing and the impact of technology on child development for teachers, parents and health professionals throughout North America. Recently she has created *Zone'in Training Programs* to train other paediatric occupational therapists to deliver these integral workshops in their own community.

Simon Hayhoe is currently a faculty member of the Higher Colleges of Technology, UAE, and a Centre Research Associate at the London School of Economics, UK. Previously he was a technology teacher, key-worked students with special educational needs, and devised inclusive courses for school students. In intervening years, he researched educational attainment with the universities of London and Toronto and was a Fellow of the Metropolitan Museum of Art, New York.

Yara Azouqa is from Amman, Jordan, but lives and works in Abu Dhabi. She has been a TESOL teacher and holds an MA in English Language & Literature from Jordan University and a CELTA from Cambridge. She is currently working on an MA in Education from Deakin University and an MS in Education Management and Policy from the Higher Colleges of Technology. (See Pat, Josephine and Greg's chapter)

El-Sadig Yahya Ezza is Associate Professor at Majma'ah University, Saudi Arabia. He has been teaching there since 2009 on secondment from the University of Khartoum, Sudan.

Khaled Almudibry is Assistant Professor at Majmaah University, Saudi Arabia. He has PhD in the field of Computer Assisted Language Learning (CALL) from Durham University.

Kasim Kasuri has been CEO of Beaconhouse since 2005. During this period, along with the steady consolidation of Beaconhouse Pakistan, Kasim has been the driving force behind the international development of Beaconhouse. He is passionate about change in the educational status quo and was closely involved in the establishment of TNS Beaconhouse, a progressive new school in Lahore that challenges conventional thinking about teaching and learning. He has also played a defining role in organizing and curating the organization's "School of Tomorrow" international conferences from 2005 to 2012.

Foreword

Andrew Callaghan

As a teacher and advocate of educational technologies I am delighted to be able to introduce this important book, which challenges many assumptions about teaching and learning in the digital age. It is timely to welcome a book by teachers for all those interested and concerned about the kinds of debates, arguments and ideas which are influencing and changing the nature of teaching and learning in the early decades of the 21st century.

In this volume you will hear voices from the field of education speaking about their experiences in a time of unprecedented technological change and innovation in teaching and learning. These contributors, from around the world and across all sections and levels of the educational sector, share their experiences of working with educational technologies, mobile and digital learning in their day-to-day lives in schools, colleges and universities. The main themes, arguments and reflections found in this volume highlight the dramatic effects and changes technology is having on the human experience generally and in teaching and learning in particular.

Cris Rowan shares her unique understanding as an occupational therapist on how technology can change a child's development and their ability to learn. Yasemin Allsop argues that technology will enhance a child's learning experiences especially if they are given a degree of latitude in designing their own digital games. Julie Lindsay, a staunch advocate of educational technologies, shares her views on the future of teaching and learning through the Flat Classroom project, and Lisa Martin, a veteran educator of 20 years, shares a wonderful story about an online Model United Nations program.

There are important lessons to be learned from Ieda Santos, Dianne Evans, Dawn Seddon, Michelle Estable, Roudaini Houjeir, Nancy Favnestock, Jon Orthman and Reem Arafat, who bring to this collection their unique experiences of working in the tertiary sector during rapid and unprecedented changes in curriculum delivery through the introduction of Lap-Tops, iPads and BOYD (Bring Your Own Device). Their experiences, reflections and research are compulsory reading for teachers and students and other schools and colleges preparing to radically change and adapt their teaching and learning environments to meet the demands and challenges of the digital era.

Reflections and opinions about publishing and teaching and learning in a digital age are shared by Clyde Coreil, Yara Azouqa, Tanya Tercero and Lawrence Burke. Their awareness and insight from a personal and professional perspective offer cautionary tales on embracing the *wow factor* over critical pedagogy when it comes to being a 'true believer' in all things digital and technological.

On the other hand the voices of reasoned research and argument prevail with Simon Hayhoe, Serge Morissette, Pat Dougherty, Josephine Butler, Greg Vrhovnik, El Sadig Yahya Ezza, Khaled Almudibry and Yasmine Salah El Din. Their chapters demonstrate how educational technologies have enhanced and developed their professional practice and they share with us the importance of maintaining an all inclusive student-centered approach to teaching and learning using educational technologies.

Today all professional learning communities agree that there is added value in utilizing technologies to enhance and facilitate student success. This volume seeks from us a critical and informed answer to one of the most important educational questions of the day: how successful will learners be in the digital age?

Andrew Callaghan is Theory of Knowledge Coordinator at
BD Somani International School, Mumbai, India
http://mrctok.blogspot.in/

Introduction

Lawrence Burke

The progress of humanity and civilization is beholden to technology. Some of our most rudimentary creative inventions from taking a piece of stone and shaping it into a cutting device to the creation of the wheel have propelled us into futures which we could never have been imagined or foreseen. It's even harder for us as a species to imagine what the alternatives might have been.

Similarly, the technologies of the 20th and 21st centuries have irrevocably changed the way we perceive ourselves and our place in time and space. For example we can see beyond some of the farthest reaches of the known universe and our spacecraft continue to speed through galaxies into interstellar space. The extraordinary Voyager 1 launched on September 5th 1977 is the farthest man-made object from earth-as far as we know-and continues hurtling through infinity. Back on earth we've created and invented technologies which change lives, educate lives, entertain lives, heal lives, saves lives and destroy lives. Such is the inherent complexity, contradiction and ignorance of the human species that we seem unable to prioritize and harness technology for the good of all humanity all of the time. Yet, technology in itself isn't the problem, because it isn't capable of making moral and ethical decisions for us.

Technologies of any kind do not possess the ability to reflect on their own progress and development. Nor can technology of any design or usefulness acquire human morality or values or make choices based on an ethical understanding of its consequences. They are pieces of machinery that carry out the pre-programmed tasks and actions of human beings. Technology cannot know through empathy, compassion and concern the joys, pains and sufferings of the human condition, but if pre-programmed they may exacerbate or alleviate some of the best and worst conditions of the human experience. However, today one could be forgiven for thinking otherwise. It is forecast by futurists that in the not too distant future we will be subordinated to a world of Transformer like machines ruling over a brave new digitally centric universe.

We are all indigenous to and responsible for the technological changes of the late 20th and early 21st century just as human beings have been indigenous to and responsible for the political, social or technological changes of past eras. Notwithstanding the neo-colonialist labelling of humans as either digital native or digital immigrant, the arguments propounded by some educators and the producers and marketers of technology products, that our brains have changed significantly in the past 40 years due to the emergence of human and digital interactive communicate processes is simply not true.

Schachner correctly argues that "Homo habilis, the first of our genus Homo who appeared 1.9 million years ago, showed an expansion of a language-connected part of the frontal lobe called Broca's area. 500,000 years ago early homo-sapiens had brains slightly smaller", but within the range of today's capabilities and there's been little change in the last 10,000 years (Schachner, 2006).

In the schizophrenic early years of the 21st century, digitally driven social communicative processes blur the lines between a rational world view and a pseudo-rational virtual/augmented reality. The Director of Oxford University's Future of Humanity Institute, Nick Bostrom, believes "we've entered a new kind of technological era with the capacity to threaten our future as never before" (Coughlan, 2013).

Such an insight is pause for reflection given the nexus of power which exists between technology corporations, leading educational institutions and some major educational book publishing houses who are determining the parameters and methodologies of how we should teach and learn in the 21st century (in most instances without consultations with parents, students and teachers). This volume of writings by teachers offers some insight and guidance here. It suggests teachers, students and parents have a pivotal role to play in pursuing a critical appraisal of the usefulness of technologies in an age of digital teaching and learning, as well as offering leadership in affirming a reality primarily based on a rational and informed worldview.

References

Coughlan, S. (2013, April 24). How are humans going to become extinct? Retrieved from *BBC News: Business:* www.bbc.com/news/business-22002530?print=true

Schachner, E. (2006, June 6). How Has the Human Brain Evolved? Retrieved February 14, 2014, from *Scientific America*: www.scientificamerican.com/article/how-has-human-brain-evolved/

Chapter 1

A plugged in, turned on, totally engaged Model United Nations

Lisa Martin

On a recent Saturday afternoon, at 13.00 UTC to be exact, I watched a Model United Nations debate take place that was breathtaking in its diversity. The two co-chairs were from Taiwan and Turkey. Team members hailed from the USA, Australia, Saudi Arabia and Taipei. More amazingly, delegates came from an astounding 19 countries, ranging from Jordan to Nigeria, Gaza to South Korea, and Singapore to Costa Rica. This wasn't a traditional, once a year, face to face big name conference. This was a regular occurrence in a rather remarkable movement called Online Model United Nations, or O-MUN for short.

Right now, hundreds of high school students are creating the most innovative Model UN program in the world. Dependent only on a Blackboard Collaborate online classroom and a vast social media network driven by Facebook, students are laying the groundwork for a truly collaborative network of interested individuals to bring the much loved Model UN academic simulation to an entirely online environment. What started as a monthly gathering of 20 students has grown into five global debates a month; a Facebook community of over 2000 students; a leadership team spanning 20 countries; a middle school program; a university level program (recently profiled on ABC Radio Australia); and a half dozen national programs in places like Turkey, Singapore, France and Palestine.

When I started O-MUN in the fall of 2011, I knew what it could be: a great debate platform; a place where students could hone their debate and chairing skills; and a place to engage in all manner of topics related to international relations. What I didn't know, and what is the focus of this article, is what I would learn as an educator and how that would change my very concept of learning and teaching. But let's start at the beginning, because O-MUN's original birth within a for-profit educational institution is an important lesson to be pondered in our technology driven age.

The origins of O-MUN

Online debates started with rather humble begins in 2009, when as a teacher at an online high school, I started a MUN club. I needed to model for my young delegates what a debate looked and sounded like. We gathered together what we thought were going to be six or seven delegates for a brief ten-minute mock debate. When we opened my online classroom to figure out exactly how this was going to work, something truly amazing happened. Word got out via social media that students were meeting to try out an online debate. Students started logging in from Singapore and Malaysia, and then other places around the world too.

We experimented online on how to copy The Hague International Model United Nation's (THIMUN) rules and procedures in this new environment. And when we thought we could wrap up the session and close the room, another wave of students would find us. That first day, in a little online MUN gone viral scenario, our two hour test turned into 19 hours of near continuous student engagement, with wave after wave of delegates finding us online, helping us develop our earliest online protocols: note passing, how to raise a placard, how to vote and submit amendments. I slept with my computer on next to my bed that night, volume on low, listening to the chatter of those first hours of online discussion. It was this moment, looking back now, that I realize that online Model United Nations was born.

A brief debate in January 2010 was followed by another in February, but this time we developed all the necessary moderating positions to run it correctly. We pulled from THIMUN's top officer team for our chair, moderators and participants, students who had deep debating skills and a real passion for MUN. At every turn the face-to-face version of debate found life in an online equivalent, was found to be engaging and an accurate reproduction of a real debate, and soundly endorsed by the delegates themselves. In a move that almost cost me my job, but unable to contain my excitement by the speed of developments, I shared the lobbying and debate with a teacher in Singapore, who immediately saw the potential of an online program. These were exhilarating days for me personally, feeling as if I had stumbled upon an undeveloped market and use for a program that I had loved and supported for many years.

Like other innovative and successful ideas that emerge in the shadows of corporate America my school, being a for-profit institution, reacted unfavorably. My MUN program was quickly shut down while attorneys at the school were brought in to try and patent and monetize this 'MUN invention'. I was disheartened and disappointed and after many months of haggling about what a future online MUN program might look like, I returned to Abu Dhabi.

After a rocky start at continuing my employment in the UAE I was increasingly uncomfortable with the direction the online program was beginning to take, so I made a hard decision and walked away from my job and my virtual classroom, the great inspiration of my online program. I then pulled out my contract and re-read the non-compete clause, and took seriously the diktat to refrain from competitive endeavors for a year. I waited, until the summer of 2011, to re-launch online Model United Nations, today known as O-MUN.

O-MUN basics: how it works

O-MUN debates occur in an online classroom, using the audio feature only, but around these debates an entire community of delegates, moderators, chairs, student officers and ambassadors has emerged. Students usually find us through a simple Google search. They register through our website, and then can click on a calendar/debate event to register for. Delegates are assigned a country and prompted to join us on Facebook – not a requirement, but helpful. Delegates engage in discussion, ask questions, and get to know their diverse fellow delegates via Facebook and also Mightybell, our topic research tool of choice!

On debate day, a student logs into a virtual conference room to be met by students from around the world. A multi-continent high school moderating team then runs the debate modelled on THIMUN protocol. What is lost (the face to face interaction and expensive overseas trip to an international conference) is made up for in part by the sheer diversity of students, the ability to connect with students who would never be able to travel to a prestigious conference, and of course, our rather lax 'no suits required' dress code.

Students, empowered by the O-MUN platform and connected through social media, have begun to use these powerful tools to create wonderful initiatives, and to draw in a diverse group of global youth. O-MUN's mission is to diversify and democratize the MUN program to any student with internet connection, and the results are impressive. Currently under construction is the first French language version of O-MUN, outreach to students in Gaza, national debating programs in Turkey, France, Jordan, Palestine, Israel, Singapore and Taiwan, expansion into the vast Pacific region (O-MUN Timor Leste, anyone?), and MUN tutorials for middle school students.

O-MUN made its first foray into traditional conferences with their debut at THIMUN 2013, where the seven nation delegation rendezvoused in The Hague, met face-to-face for the first time and proceeded, as a delegation representing OPEC, to leave their mark on a conference whose theme was Energy and Sustainability. The team was trained entirely online and represented an incredible cross section of private and public school students from around the world: Taiwan to Jordan, Israel, the UK, USA, Singapore and Lebanon.

O-MUN's online incarnation of a traditional academic program taught me that most of the great things we do in classrooms or face-to-face can be done online, and that the power of the technology can drive learning, personal fulfillment and community in new and unexpectedly wonderful directions.

Innovation, technology and the role of students and teachers
In the 18 months since O-MUN was founded, I have learned a great deal

about technology and education, and even more about myself personally and my attitudes and limits of my comfort zone in this digitally-driven world. Several large themes emerge in my own journey, and they break down roughly into four large ideas: transparency and openness; the power of engaged communities; teachers as mentors and innovators; and online communities that act as leadership incubators.

Transparency and openness

One thing an online program does is strip you of anonymity; how you portray yourself online becomes the sum total of your identity for those who will never meet you face-to-face. Once I realized how important it was to be accessible online, fully as myself, the more the traditional barriers of privacy and distance began to break down. I had to overcome my 'Friending' fear on Facebook when I realized that students were not flocking to our closed learning management system (LMS) on OrgSync.

Being on Facebook and willing to connect with students there was a significant milestone in my professional life. I now use Facebook like students use Facebook: to explore, snoop around, and get a sense of who people really are. I definitely learned to self-censor myself at times. While I've stayed true to my political and religious beliefs, I have become mindful of how students in other parts of the world would interpret my status updates.

I have become acutely aware of what my friends post, and how the negative cousin or racist distant friend reflects poorly on me. I realized that my collection of diverse acquaintances and friends on Facebook said as much about me as what I actually said. We tell students this all the time: mind the company you keep as your friends are a reflection of you. Online communities take this to an entirely different level, and possibly make us more reflective of our statements and comments. It's what we want students to learn and be mindful of, and as a teacher, I have had to do the same thing. There is great value in talking honestly about these issues, to help students understand that they have to make some mindful decisions about their digital footprint.

The power of community

If you have ever experienced a class environment, either as student or teacher, when things went exactly right, or when a project, driven by collaboration, has gone exceedingly well, you will understand the tremendous feeling of camaraderie that is felt by the group. This same feeling of accomplishment and of esprit de corps that results can also be found in online environments. When I explain to people that O-MUN has been an experiment in crowdsourcing Model United Nations, what I really have suggested is that there is tremendous power and energy within online communities and that meaningful projects and products come out of this kind of group collaboration.

My previous employer was committed to running this MUN online program from behind a veritable firewall of student protection and anonymity. The school was big enough to create its own online community, and to try and give students the feeling of an open and diverse universe of opinion. In reality, it wasn't. The community felt artificial, constrained and limited. Importantly for schools, this boxed in environment is at odds with where most students find a growing part of their identity and their lives.

They share artwork on Deviant Art, play Minecraft together, share their writing on Fan Fiction, make movies to share on YouTube, and spend hours chatting on Skype (making and breaking down conversation groups with rapidity). They are all on Facebook, Tumbler, and possibly cruise about in the Twittersphere. Yet, when they come to school, students are put on lock down. We wonder why they tune out. How many adults would gravitate towards an artificial 'discussion' at their place of work, thrown together in a seemingly arbitrary way and run off a monitored/closed system set up by the IT department, when these same teachers could be discussing something meaningful, important or engaging, if given the flexibility and opportunity to do so in a more expanded and more collaborative and social environment?

This is what a professional learning circle attempts to do, yet we get very nervous when we begin to think of offering students this freedom and flexibility. By relegating artificial communities to school, and dynamic and engaging ones to the rest of our waking hours, we take away powerful mentoring and modelling opportunities within education.

Being able to work and develop a fluid, empowered and engaging online community has indeed been professionally life-changing for me. Imagine starting a global venture with a workforce of 14-16 year-olds, most of whom you will never meet face-to-face. Envision the building a website with a team of students from three continents, or developing quality control standards with juniors and seniors who have never been in the same room. The risks are enormous. You have, as the team's leader, no recourse, no real authority, no power to issue grades or certifications, and yet they come and, magically, amazing things get developed. The end product is a result of those unique individuals at that unique moment, yet the product endures, to be improved upon by the next wave of students. And importantly, when something doesn't work, it just gets scrapped and we try again.

This is messy work and frustrating at times. A website that works at 80% capacity might as well not have been built if you can't get it to do what you want. How do you convey urgency to a team via Facebook chat? How do you rally a core group of leaders in an email? How can we efficiently design a product when we are in three time zones and the product was needed yesterday? How do you pivot politely away from something that is taking too much time with little value added, and move and shepherd the larger group? If you substituted a hospital ward, a team at Google, or an architecture firm working on a project, these 'working through complexities' would be part of a normal day's work.

In education, however, this degree of messiness and false starts is often purposely stripped away. It is inefficient and not easily benchmarked. It falls between measurable outcomes tied to standards. But it is at this deeper level of innovation that students seemed to be most engaged. Students love projects (usually), and this is a project on a global scale. I have told students 'I don't have an idea how to fix this. Can you make it work?' And they do, usually. Sometimes we admit defeat together, but usually enough talent emerges to solve our problem. This is what I call the student-sourcing aspect of our O-MUN platform. This engaged, community-driven kind of learning is one of technologies greatest gifts to teachers and students, and one that must be purposefully nurtured.

Teacher, innovator, collaborator among equals
A student recently messaged me and asked 'What do I call you?' I laughed when I got this message, but it led to some deeper reflection on my role in O-MUN. When the student asked, 'Do I call you Ms Martin? Lisa? Miss?' what he was really asking me to do was to define my role. As a teacher, I should logically be called Ms Martin, but yet, online communities lead

to greater degrees of informality. I often ask for help, rarely have all the solutions, and put most of our current program open to discussion. I have capitulated on topics when a student I trust makes a strong case to do it her way. I almost always say 'Go for it...' when an idea emerges.

This feels very different from a traditional classroom where I would most likely set the tone, the agenda and call most of the shots. In a traditional program, teachers depend on student compliance. In O-MUN, the glue that holds us together is of an entirely different dynamic, based on student initiative and engagement. This makes the program feel light years away from traditional education, even though parts of the program are 'traditional' or more old school.

Leadership incubator

Similar to large face-to-face conferences, the demands placed on students to organize online debates is immense, and for those able to rise to the occasion it provides unparalleled leadership opportunities. The integration of the necessary technology skills, as well as the development of a superior online presence, are each valuable unto themselves. Taken together, however, they provide an extremely unique opportunity to integrate high level academic and leadership skills with technological skills and applications.

Within O-MUN's reach exists the added benefit of global, peer-to-peer collaboration, making O-MUN a unique academic program. Fundamental to our ability to grow has been a student officer structure that puts the emphasis squarely on the development of student leadership. Maybe more impressive than debates is the fact that O-MUN has become a leadership incubator.

The center of power within the O-MUN universe is also hard to pin down, since the leadership team is spread out around the globe and never able to work together in the same time zone. But there are numerous examples of the ways in which students take initiative, and then work together to accomplish a task. This can be something as simple as me reminding my moderators and chairs that we need to fill the two empty positions on a debate roster (which is then taken care of rather magically by students).

In one example that proves the power of technology to connect individuals to O-MUN for an experience they would not have had otherwise, a young woman from northern Somalia contacted me about getting involved in MUN, something that didn't exist in her country. She participated as a delegate, then as a moderator, and finally as an assistant director overseeing the Middle East and Africa. In April 2013 she was selected to present several workshops related to O-MUN at the Qatar Leadership Conference in Doha. Her engagement in the community has been tremendous, allowing her a level of organizational challenges she might not have had otherwise. Most recently, she worked with her highly-motivated team from Nigeria, Tanzania, Zimbabwe, Egypt, UAE, Jordan and Qatar to set a yearly debate schedule, organizational tasks that needed attention on Facebook, and a discussion about goals for Africa and the Middle East for the new school year.

This is a team that has never met face-to-face and probably never will. Together they are forging interesting programs and initiatives in a totally collaborative effort, something that will outlive their own collaborative relationship as the program grows. The esprit de corps is palpable even across the internet and through their shared Google docs. When one young woman in the region commented 'O-MUN has changed my life' I have no doubt about that. Wouldn't it be great if we could construct classrooms around similar initiatives and with comparable levels of buy in?

It's not about the technology, *per se,* but what we allow students to do with it. Catching a glimpse of how this globally connected leadership team works together gives me hope for the potential that technology enables. It is up to educators and administrators to lay the groundwork to make it happen within education programs. Otherwise, students will look away from school for engagement, a wasted opportunity and a dereliction of duty, in my opinion.

Conclusion
I have several reflections from my experience in developing a global, online educational program. The first is perhaps the most obvious. Technology has empowered teachers and students to innovate programs and solutions that meet real academic needs. Traditional barriers in the form of classroom walls to vast geographical distances are increasingly irrelevant, and O- MUN epitomizes the power of connecting the planet's youth.

The second is that tried and true academic programs with access to technology can transform themselves into beautifully reincarnated and dynamic programs, with renewed relevance and dynamism breathed into them. Thirdly, student engagement can thrive if appropriate social media activity and leadership structures can be married to academic activities that are both engaging and relevant. And lastly, it *is* possible to teach an old dog new tricks! This one has surprised me the most. Having discovered a new universe of education innovation driven by students and embraced their peers, some of the joy and passion that carried me through my first years of teaching has returned.

Connecting with those individuals able to contribute and facilitate online debate's growth has been exhilarating, and only pales when compared to the sense of accomplishment I feel when I see O-MUN's online classroom buzzing with discussion such as analysis of the causes of endemic poverty; the role of sustainable development in emerging markets; the complexities of a major international crisis; and so much more.

When I see a delegate from Singapore supporting a student from Nigeria, or a home-schooled student in Tennessee mentoring an experienced European MUN director many years her senior, or an O-MUN-trained assistant director from Egypt assisting Turkish students in setting up a regional debate, I see academic collaboration and engagement at its best. It makes me believe that despite the very significant obstacles teachers face in today's test-driven, budget-constrained environment, it is alright to think and dream big, and to know that students will not only embrace these opportunities, but assist in their development and expansion.

Chapter 2

Considerations on a blended learning project

Patrick Dougherty, Josephine Butler and Greg Vrhovrnik

Introduction

In April 2010 we faced a challenge. Appointed to develop and teach a graduate program in a 17-campus public university system in the United Arab Emirates, we had two cohorts of students who needed to take the same course, one in Abu Dhabi, and the other in Dubai. A normal procedure would have been to hire two teachers, one to teach the course in Abu Dhabi and the other to teach the course in Dubai.

However, time, staffing, and resources were limited. Searching for an answer, we decided to teach both courses simultaneously using technology that was at hand: video conferencing, e-mail, and free access websites. This led, ultimately, to the development of a distributed delivery system for the entire Master of Education program, and the adoption of this delivery template for another graduate program in the university system.

The Master of Education program employs a distributed delivery system utilizing tele-presence to allow students in separate cohorts to join together for a course of studies. A teacher teaches the course from one of six campuses on a rotating basis. Each cohort of students is tied-in to the lecture and presentation via video conference technology. They can hear, see, and participate in all classroom activities in real-time.

This technological aspect is paired with a very human side of instruction in that the teacher visits each cohort, spending one or two five-hour class sessions at each campus. Additionally, each cohort is assisted by a site designated tutor who supports the academic progress of the cohort members via tutoring sessions, Q&A exchanges, and general editorial and presentation rehearsal support.

Hence the distributed delivery system can be called a new school and old school mixed pedagogical paradigm that mixes elements of adult and autonomous learning to provide the following benefits to adult students:

access to a certified graduate program in Education;

a method of connecting with colleagues across the Emirates; and

an exemplar of technology at use in education in a manner that is culturally and socially sensitive and supportive of their academic goals.

The opportunity here is to reflect on the lessons learned in administering and teaching in this system. The authors have developed a list of suggestions for those in positions to establish, renovate, or teach within such a blended learning environment.

Research was conducted in 2011 and 2012 to ascertain student perceptions of the delivery system, and this research informed policy decisions that impact not only the Master of Education program but also provide context for other graduate and undergraduate programs in the university system that were designing their own methodologies to address the issues of student access. This research was presented at four local education conferences and two international conferences.

It was subsequently published as two papers in international, refereed educational journals. The initial research was done when the program had two 'urban' cohorts and only two locations. It was revisited when the program expanded to six locations, and included more rural campuses. The initial research agenda was dedicated to ascertaining the success of the disbursed delivery system via student perceptions of the system and its support for their academic aspirations and goals.

This stage of the research examines the administrative and pedagogical elements involved in creating, maintaining, and working within such a distributed delivery system. The focus is on the administration and teachers who work within this milieu and the purpose is to reflect on the lessons learned in administering and teaching in this system. The reflection was guided by the following question: what structural elements must the developer include in the arrangement to allow for the best use of the distributed delivery system? Reflection on this question has given the authors the opportunity to develop a list of suggestions for those in positions to establish a video conference infused distributed delivery system.

Methodology

Our experience in the program is unique in that we taught and tutored all of the initial courses delivered using the disbursed delivery system. We were, therefore, closely involved not only in the development and evolution of the course delivery structure but also had first-hand experience in taking the possibilities and limitations of the structure in developing a viable learning environment for the students studying for their Masters of Education in the context of the United Arab Emirates.

Used here are our reflections, and notes from two in-depth interviews as well as notes from interviews with three additional faculty members who taught in the program. These observations are supported by a survey of the tutors who worked in the program, data from the two published research studies, and a report developed by a graduate student who was given access the Master of Education program to conduct focus groups, student and teacher interviews, and observations of Master of Education classes as part of his final research project for his Master of Arts in Teaching English to Speakers of Other Languages.

The distributed delivery structure

Twenty-one courses as part of a Master of Education program were taught simultaneously from up to six college locations within a public university system in the United Arab Emirates: Abu Dhabi, Dubai, Ras Al Khamiah, Ruwais, Al Ain, and Fujairah. The classes were linked electronically via a video conferencing system that allowed presentations, lectures, discussions, and videos to be shared electronically in real-time. The teacher was physically present at each site on a rotating basis, and was supported by location-designated tutors, with one tutor for each location.

The tutors remained with their designated cohort on a permanent basis. In addition to the tutor, most locations had technical support staff in attendance during class sessions. The physical environment for all classes, and at all sites, was in conference room facilities or, in the case of one campus, a purpose built video conference supported classroom. This format of instruction can be defined as 'blended learning'.

Hijazi *et al* (2006) defined a blended course as one that unites distance learning, or face-to-screen interaction, with face-to-face instruction, the idea being that students being instructed in blended, or hybrid, systems will experience the best of both types of instructional delivery approaches. According to Dziuban, Hartman and Moskal (2004) blended learning is an instructional approach that unites the socialization of the traditional classroom environment with the possibilities and active learning aspects of the on-line educational medium.

The delivery system in this case study utilizes video-conferencing technology as a method of uniting disparate cohorts of students. It provides a dispersed student population the opportunity to interact both together and with the material, and it can be a forceful tool in the blended classroom (Twigg 2001). Bates and Picard (2005) asserted that, though dispersed geographically, discussion via tele-presence could be carried out quite successfully if the teacher was flexible in his or her pedagogical approach, and this call to flexibility was echoed by Young (2002), who advised the teacher to present material in a variety of formats to help increase student engagement.

Each class met four times, on alternating weekends or once per work-week, with separate time to meet with the tutors. Each class meeting was five hours in length. The calendar length of each course was approximately 15 weeks including research time. Students were expected to write article critiques, research papers, and conduct team presentations on education related topics.

Initially the system, which was first used in the second term of the 2010-2011 academic year, had only two sites, Abu Dhabi and Dubai. In the first term of the 2011-2012 academic year the system was expanded to include two additional sites, and in the 2012-2013 academic year two more sites were added, as well as a weekday program at two sites. Figure 1, below, shows the campus locations from which, and at which, the courses were taught.

As can be seen from the map, when a course was being delivered, the teacher and the students were in contact with colleagues across the breadth and width of the United Arab Emirates. We spoke of the experience, "You have a snapshot of the entire country in front of you when you teach, with all corners represented."

A student remarked (Dougherty, Butler, and Vrhovnik, 2013):

> We are only five here, but imagine, with this chance we can discuss things with 20 or more students in other groups. I think that interaction and collaboration are part of overall knowledge; that adds to your knowledge... So, I think that this has been a great part of this program, and the fact that we can be in one place although we are in different places. This idea for me, this is the first time that I've lived this experience, and I can see how the world is coming together through technology. (p3)

In Figure 2 below, the reader can see a screen shot of a typical class. To the left is the PowerPoint display and to the right are the six visual cells where each cohort can see each other and themselves. The large cell shows the teacher. He can zoom in and out as needed to show either himself only or all the students at the location where he is teaching. The system is set up whereby the site where a person is speaking highlights, enlarges, and moves into the premier position on the screen. All discussion, PowerPoint displays, and video are heard and shown in real-time.

Begun as a solution to a course delivery problem, we noted that our ability to simultaneously offer courses at multiple sites was providing access to students who might otherwise not be able to avail themselves of graduate studies. Access was an issue for some of the students for two main reasons: Ministry of Education regulations that discouraged on-line, or distance, education; and social/cultural circumstances.

One of the ironies with online learning in the UAE is that its Ministry of Higher Education and Scientific Research (MoHESR) does not recognize on-line graduate degrees as being valid for career or job advancement for government employees or teachers in government schools (MoHESR, 2013). Nonetheless, of approximately 75 students who have been or are in the Master of Education program, 88% are Emirati.

Most Emirati professionals work for the government, and almost all of the Emirati students attending the Master of Education program worked in public, government funded schools; hence, this precluded them from taking on-line graduate degrees as they would not be recognized by their employer as valid for the purpose of career advancement.

Of the 75 students, 84% were women. Religious, cultural and social traditions affect students in work or education and, for a woman, this can translate to limitations of geographic mobility and the ability to travel (Al Khateeb, 2001). A distributed delivery system not only provides access to educational opportunities for students in more remote locations, it also allows students to meet and learn as a group. Stewart, Harlow and DeBacco (2011) point to the importance of student–student and student–teacher interaction for satisfaction in such a learning environment, and such interaction can be synchronous (video-conferencing or chat) or asynchronous (email or discussion, blogs, wikis *etc*).

This is applicable to the delivery system under investigation here as it involves video-conferencing, email, and the use of university websites, as well as regular face-to-face sessions with teachers, classmates and tutors. In the specific case of this program, one subject (Dougherty, Butler, and Vrhovnik, 2013) explained that there were no other programs in that part of the United Arab Emirates that met the students' needs and accommodated their social and time constraints. Indeed, as related by one of the teachers, several students explained that they would not have been able to attend a course of studies unless it was offered via the disbursed delivery system, enabling them to attend classes at their local college site (Vrhovnik, 2012).

As a student from one of the smaller northern emirates stated when asked if she would be able to travel to another city to study for a graduate degree: "I have tried for three years to join a Master's program, but I couldn't, it just wasn't possible because it's not here in RAK [Ras al Khamaih]; so, I had no chance until [this] program was available…" (Dougherty, Butler, and Vrhovnik, 2013, pp 4-5).

Another subject in the same focus group agreed that it was important that the classes were held near to their homes because it would be difficult for them to travel long distances to attend. This element of convenience was further emphasized in another focus group discussion, where one respondent (Dougherty, Butler, and Vrhovnik, 2013, p5) explained that, "…the opportunity to complete our Master's is very limited, especially in education, and, because of the distance to the main cities, if we would have to travel to Abu Dhabi or Sharjah, I doubt that we could do that, but this gives us the opportunity to complete our ME [Master of Education] degree locally..."

Lessons learned

Our reflection was guided by a central question: what structural elements must the developer include in the arrangement to allow for the best use of the distributed delivery system? The structure for the distributed delivery system under review here had these elements, excluding the basic necessity of a secure and effective video conferencing system:

A professor who traveled to each cohort site in turn.

A tutor assigned to each cohort for the duration of each course.

Technical support staff to help with the video conference system and other course related tech issues.

Cohorts of students ranging in size from three students to 15.

A website or social learning platform as the repository of course announcements and information, handouts, video and presentation links, and a place for student input and questions.

One of the teachers offered a detailed reflection on her experience with the disbursed delivery system during the course of her interview. Let us review each in relation to the data from earlier studies and the results of teacher and tutor interviews and surveys.

A professor who traveled to each cohort site in turn

Regarding the professor and his or her movement to different locations, the findings from earlier studies indicated a general acceptance of the efficacy of the structure and fairness of the division of the professor's time. Students interviewed felt it was important for the lecturer to alternate his physical presence between the campuses. Occasionally having the professor physically with them gave the teacher and students a 'better understanding of one another' (Dougherty, Butler and Hyde 2011, p. 552).

One student stated that he felt more confident in answering questions when the teacher was physically with his cohort (Dougherty, Butler, and

Vrhovnik 2013). This can also be vital culturally, as one subject indicated that in Emirati society it was important to meet face-to-face to establish a sense of communion and commonality (Dougherty, Butler, and Vrhovnik, 2013). This need to make personal contact was considered in other focus groups, and a subject explained that, in the UAE, it was important for Emiratis to know who they were speaking to and to understand his or her background (Dougherty, Butler, and Vrhovnik, 2013).

Further, the students felt that they were more engaged and asked more questions when the lecturer was physically present rather than when his input was viewed via video-conference. Students also noted that they were quieter and interacted less when the lecturer was at the other location (Dougherty, Butler, and Hyde, 2011). Another student felt it was easier for her to follow the lesson when the teacher was physically present (Dougherty, Butler, and Vrhovnik, 2013). This is consistent with the literature on blended learning. Garnham and Kaleta (2002) pointed to studies showing that students learn more and engage more actively with the teacher in blended courses than in traditional courses. Figure 3 is an example of teacher presence in the disbursed delivery system.

From the teachers, we had this observation among several remarks concerning the need to meet with students in person at their college sites:

> I felt that it was important when I actually went to [a college site] to give the session, that I actually took time to meet each of the students individually, to have some time to talk one-on-one, to get a sense of who they were, and what they were doing, and wanted to get from their studies… It became apparent to me that meeting the individual students was going to be very important, this type of personal contact and a sense of building a community… And it relates to Lave and Wenger's *Communities of Practice* and I'm a great believer in establishing that personal contact at some point. And I think this is especially true when you are in the Emirates where the personal relationship is very important…

This sentiment, that a personal visit and a personal connection were essential was echoed in each of the five teacher interviews. As explained by another teacher, "What is vitally important is that you do get around to each of the M E groups and physically make a connection to develop a relationship." It was deemed of great importance that the teacher be able to visit each cohort of students in person for a class or a face-to-face tutorial.

One additional method made to defeat the challenge of distance, and extending the need for personal connection and presence to all the members of the course from all the cohorts, was to gather the students together twice a year for a Master of Education Graduate Student Symposium. It was

> important for developing a *Community of Scholars* which is vital to our program... This involves getting all the cohorts together so they can meet and relate to everybody, to connect the voice and screen presence with the actual, living, breathing, person ' (Dougherty, personal communication, 2012, May 20).

These observations regarding the importance of visiting each site were supported by all the teacher interviewees.

A tutor assigned to each cohort for the duration of each course

Each course had four class meetings that lasted five hours, giving a total of 20 hours of class time. Additionally, tutors were required to provide 20 supplementary hours of tutorial support to their assigned cohort. Site-based tutors were considered essential to the system by the administrator who established the program's structure. As he explained:

> Each site has a [university] tutor who is permanently stationed with the cohort who acts as a facilitator and assistant for the students, so they are never without a support network (Dougherty, personal communication, 2012, May 19).

The tutor, according to the administrator

> ...has no evaluative capacity as far as the students' course work is concerned, they are simply facilitators... Their task is to support the group; the professor does all the grading (Dougherty, personal communication, 2012, May 19).

When asked in the on-line tutor survey to describe the support given by the tutor during class time, one respondent explained that (Tutor Survey, 2013)

> I mainly operate as a facilitator. I mean usually when things are going OK I have minimum interference. When there are topics to discuss, I try to pose stimulating questions; when they are brief in response I try to ask more questions to expand [the students'] horizons, and when

they are viewing things I try to ask some different kinds of questions to keep them thinking about different scenarios. (Para 4)

Responding to a survey question asking how the tutor divided up his or her 20 hours of out-of-class tutoring time another respondent gave this description:

For this course it included a small group meeting twice, one to one meetings with some of the students, email and document exchange. Some of the students email me their drafts; I look at them and make my comments. Some prefer to come over and talk with me regarding the feedback. (Tutor Survey, 2013, para 1)

The importance of the tutors to the students was confirmed in earlier research findings. Many felt the tutor's presence at all the sessions was necessary, in particular as the lecturer alternated between sites. Some students commented how they found the tutor useful as a resource for clarification or to give an opinion and for general support. One student commented that knowing the tutor was there made her feel more secure.

Responses from the students highlighted the importance of the tutors, especially at the beginning of the Master of Education program. Some students had not studied recently and required intensive support with English, time management, and study skills, including referencing (Dougherty, Butler, and Hyde, 2011). Another respondent commented on the fact that if she had a question and the teacher was at another site, she felt comfortable asking the tutor for assistance and this sense of ease was also articulated by other students (Dougherty, Butler, and Vrhovnik, 2013). From the teachers, the importance of the tutors was emphasized. As we remarked, 'The tutors have impressed me, they have all been very professional, and I think the students are getting good support service from them (Dougherty, personal communication, 2012, May 20).'

Technical support staff to help with the video conference system

Gill, *et al*, (2005) recommended the assignment of dedicated technical assistants to any program utilizing video-conferencing in instruction. The importance of this key element of Gill's was reinforced by those who had instructed in the distributed delivery system and those who were instructed. As one teacher remarked, "Congratulations to the IT support in the colleges, because we couldn't have done it without their help, who made it as trouble free as possible."

The program administrator required that each campus site either provide a technical assistant or agree to have the technical staff train the tutor in opening and monitoring the system on class days. Of the six cohort sites, only one opted to train the tutor rather than provide a technician. In the process of running the program, this was effective, and the tutors at the site were able to handle any technical challenges that arose during the course of class time. Even the students mentioned the assistance was appreciated; as one stated, she chose the program over a purely on-line format because she did not have such technicians at home to help her when there were computer problems (Dougherty, Butler, Vrhovnik, 2013).

Cohorts of students ranging in size from three students to 15

The importance of belonging to a cohort was also emphasized by the students at all stages of the research. One respondent felt that the cohort members provided her with emotional support and another mentioned that, when she felt like quitting the program due to a mix of family and work obligations, it was her cohort that supported her and encouraged her to continue.

Another student felt that providing the chance to belong to a cohort was one of the strengths of the program because she could work with her fellow students and gain and give support as needed. This was seconded by another member of the same focus group (Dougherty, Butler, and Vrhovnik, 2013). As the transcription below illustrates, belonging to a cohort was considered to be very important by the students in the program (Dougherty, Butler, and Vrhovnik 2013, p. 4):

Student 1: For me, having all the girls here and we are discussing things together also with the other groups makes our learning much more rich, and we add our experience to the discussion. Like for example, if we were sitting by ourselves at home, and we wanted to ask a question or to negotiate with someone to get the information we want, then we can't do that by ourselves. We need our peers to negotiate with.

Student 2: It would be very boring for us to sit at home with our computer all alone. And sometimes with the connection, the internet goes down, and what can we do?

Student 3: That's really the reason I didn't study at [an online university], first our connection is bad, and what can I do if I have questions, there's no one to help me. I don't have my friends or the group. Here, if I'm lost, or have a question, then someone will help me.

Student 2: Actually, having people to help and support us makes a difference.

Student 4: Yes, it's the group support that helps us.

Student 1: And sometimes at the end of class when [the teacher] asks us to meet and summarize the lesson, many times I've understood the topic in a different way than someone else, and we all have a different view, and that helps us to understand the lesson better as we all reflect when we share together.

That the cohorts developed a sense of group identity was confirmed by all the teachers. As one teacher explained in detail:

Yes. This is visible in three ways. First, students ask questions to other students across the screen so there is a sense that it is one class. Secondly, if I am asking the students which group should respond first, they will reference their location as a group, *eg* "Al Ain to answer" or "Let's go to Abu Dhabi". Thirdly, if we are discussing a point, input will come from different locations so the discussion is across locations. So the group sense comes through a combination of me as a teacher coordinating input across the group and students initiating questions/ comments across the group.

Belonging to a cohort, meeting them regularly in classes and tutorials gave the students a sense of community and was, as indicated by their own responses, of importance. This is in line with research on individuals learning more effectively via supportive social interaction and achieving new levels of capability (Vygotsky, 1978). As Wenger, *et al* (2002) indicated, learning can be improved where the pedagogy and structure allow for socially-supported learning interactions. An example of this external to the UAE system under review would be Campbell and Uys's (2007) description of how Charles Sturt University, a multi-campus institution of higher education in Australia, utilizes information and communication technology (ICT) to enrich contact for isolated members of student clusters.

Another example comes from the United States. The University of Tennessee's (UT) Physician's Executive Master of Business Administration program includes classroom instruction with a video-conferencing connection to off-site locations and self-paced on-line learning (Physician's Executive MBA Program, UT, 2012).

A website as the repository of course announcements and information, handouts, video and presentation links, and a place for student input and questions

In order to facilitate group interaction, we initially used only e-mail communication with the students. This was effective, but wanting in that students frequently changed their email addresses, failed to use their university provided email address, or the course emails got lost among the many others that the students received.

Though email communication was always continued, we felt that an internet site that could serve as a communication hub and repository for course materials and documents was necessary. After some consultation with other educators, we selected to use Edmodo™ as a course site. The reasons for selecting Edmodo™ were basic: (1) it was free; (2) it was secure and inaccessible to casual third parties (which is always important but in the context of the social environment of the United Arab Emirates with mostly female students in the program, was of paramount importance); and (3) the teacher could open the link for the students on command and had complete control of access. Figure 4 shows a typical Edmodo™ course site.

Another benefit, as elucidated by one teacher, was that having such a site allowed students to see questions asked by other students and the answers delivered by the teacher, a tutor, or fellow students. This provided some respite for a teacher in that he or she could answer or deal with a question once rather than receive numerous identical questions from students via email. The need to provide such a site, easily accessible to the students, yet secure and providing a private digital setting for course and student interaction and the provision of course materials, follows Al Harthi's (2005) instructions on teaching environments best suited for the culture of the United Arab Emirates and the Middle East in general:

> ...instructional design must be organized and clearly articulated through upfront and detailed descriptions of course processes, activities, and expectations ... for greater stability and learning support (p 1).

This also allowed students to feel, digitally as well as physically, part of a learning community and have access to that learning community on a continual basis for information, reflection, and support.

This aligned with Fullan's (2001) view of the importance of the establishment of such 'mechanisms for learning in the daily-ness of organizational life' (p 14). As he explains, individuals are best able to make significant transitions in thinking, behaving, and learning, by having complex, deep, and continuous access to ideas, arguments, information, and interactions with others moving within the educational milieu. A website that allows for this was a significant contributor to the operation of the delivery system.

Conclusion

The research question around which our inquiry swirled was simple: what structural elements must the developer include in the arrangement to allow for the best use of the distributed delivery system?

From the confluence of such considerations, of pedagogical best practice, learning styles in the social and cultural context of the United Arab Emirates, and budgetary considerations, we identified the importance, and significant interplay, of the five key components of the distributed delivery system:

A professor.
A tutor assigned to each cohort.
The provision of technical support staff.
Forming students into cohorts.
The use of a website for each course.

Each component was proven necessary via student, tutor, and teacher feedback and a perusal of the relevant literature on teaching and learning in such blended learning environments, video conferencing, and cultural considerations within the context of the United Arab Emirates. There interplay is given graphic formation in Figure 5.

Figure 5: the interplay of the five key components of the distributed delivery system.

Each of the five components proved its own importance via the data obtained in the course of the research. Though predicated on the existence of an effective video conference system to support the structure, other forms of technology could be substituted as developed as long as the new technology can provide real-time communication between all sites in the system. The five components would still be necessary to include in the development or evolution of a distributed delivery system using the new technology.

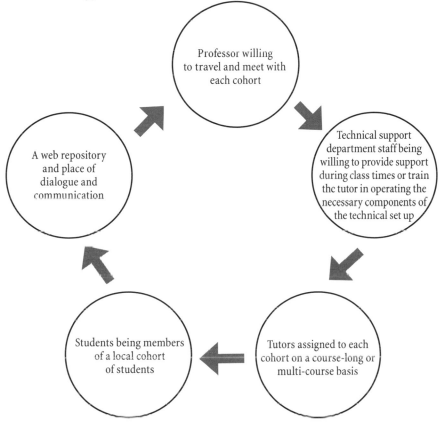

It was intended that this enquiry and the answers it afforded should be of benefit to individuals or groups given the remit of developing a distributed delivery system. As is often the case, this research project led the researchers to other research questions, to be dealt with in future case studies. A paramount question rests on our interest in how the pedagogical paradigm shifts when a teacher is required to teach in such a distributed delivery system. Does the teacher need to change his or her methodology? What is the best pedagogical practice for teaching within the framework of such a system?

References

Al-Harthi, A.S. (2005). Distance Higher Education Experiences of Arab Gulf Students in the US: A Cultural Perspective. *The International Review of Research in Open and Distance Learning,* 6(3), 1 – 8. Retrieved August 28, 2013, from www.irrodl.org/index.php/irrodl/article/viewArticle/263.

Al Khateeb, H. (2001). Gender Differences in Mathematics Achievement among High School Students in the United Arab Emirates, 1991–2000. *School Science and Mathematics* 101: 5–9. doi: 10.1111/j.1949-8594.2001.tb18184.x.

Bates, A., and Picard, J. (2005). *Technology, E-learning and Distance Education.* 2nd edition. New York: Routledge.

Campbell, M., and Uys, P. (2007). Identifying success factors of ICT in developing a learning community. *Campus-Wide Information Systems, 24* (1), 17 – 26.

Dougherty, P., Butler, J., and Hyde, S. (2011). A Hybrid Instructional Model for Post Graduate Education: A Case Study from the United Arab Emirates. *International Journal for Cross-Disciplinary Subjects in Education* 2(4), pp. 549–54.

Dougherty, P., Butler, J., and Vrhovnik, G. (2013) A hybrid instructional delivery system in UAE graduate education. *International Journal of Learning in Higher Education* 19(4).

Dziuban, C., Hartman, J. and Moskal, P. (2004). Blended Learning. *EDUCAUSE* 7(3). Retrieved August 3, 2013, from www.educause.edu/library/resources/blended-learning

Fullan, M. (2001). Leading in a culture of change. San Francisco: Jossey-Bass. Retrieved July 28, 2013, from citeseerx.ist.psu.edu/viewdoc/download?doi=10.1.1.117.9888&rep=rep1&type=pdf

Garnham, C., and Robert Kaleta, R. (2002). Introduction to Hybrid Courses. *Teaching with Technology Today.* University of Wisconsin-Milwaukee. 8.6. Retrieved July 20, 2013, from www.uwsa.edu/ttt/articles/garnham. htm

Gill, D., Parker, C., & Richardson, J. (2005). Twelve tips for teaching using videoconferencing. *Medical Teacher, 27* (7), 573 – 577.

Hijazi, Samuel, Maureen Crowley, M. Leigh Smith, and Charles Schafer. 2006. Maximizing Learning by Teaching Blended Courses. Proceedings of the 2006 ASCUE Conference, Myrtle Beach, South Carolina. Retrieved July 22, 2013, from faculty.ksu.edu.sa/mhabdelgawad/My%20documents/blnded%20learning.pdf

Lonely Planet. n.d. United Arab Emirates [map]. Retrieved August 10, 2013 from www.lonelyplanet.com/maps/middle-east/united-arab-emirates/

Ministry of Higher Education and Scientific Research, United Arab Emirates. (2013) Retrieved July 31, 2013, from http://MOHESR.gove.ae

Physician Executive MBA Program – University of Tennessee. (2012, January 1). *Physician executive MBA program – University of Tennessee.* Retrieved July 28, 2013, from www.pemba.utk.edu/

Stewart, Anissa, Danielle Harlow, and Kim DeBacco. 2011. Students' Experience of Synchronous Learning in Distributed Environments. *Distance Education* 32(3): 357–81.

Tutor Survey. (2013, January 20) On-line Master of Education tutor survey. Retrieved August 15, 2013, from www.quia.com/sv/601825.html

Twigg, C. (2001). *Innovations in online learning: Moving beyond no significant difference.*

Troy, NY: Center for Academic Transformation, Rensselaer Polytechnic Institute.

Vrhovnik, G. (2012). *Perceptions of a hybrid-delivery based graduate program in the U. A. E. – A case study.* Unpublished thesis. Institute of Education, University of London.

Vygotsky, L. S. & Cole, M. (1978). Mind in society: The development of higher psychological processes. Cambridge, MA: Harvard University Press.

Wenger, E.; McDermott, R.; Snyde, W. (2002). Cultivating Communities of Practice. Boston: Harvard Business School Press. Retrieved August 10, 2013 from www.cihm.leeds.ac.uk/new/wp-content/uploads/2011/08/Cultivating-Communities-of-Practice-Etienne-Wenger-for-COP-NW3-P2.pdf

Young, J. (2002). Hybrid teaching seeks to end divide between traditional and online instruction. *The Chronicle of Higher Education.* Retrieved July 23, 2013, from chronicle.com/free/ v48/I28/ 28a03301.htm

Chapter 3

Discussion boards as an extension of student learning

Serge Morissette

Introduction

Very little research has been done on the use of discussion boards with students in a formal learning environment. Buckingham (2006) argues that today's students are inquisitive, digitally savvy, critical, explorative, manipulative, and nonconforming – challenging and questioning established authorities. Ajayi (2009) adds that a new understanding of our students should start from an appreciation that technologies such as cell phones, television, computers, videos, iPods, personal data assistant (*ie* iPhone, BlackBerry, Samsung) *etc* play a major role in their everyday social interactions.

Johnson (2006) observes that the asynchronous discussion board is collaborative and interactive and thus opens new opportunities for students. Using online resources expands the opportunities for students to reflect upon their thinking and experience the discourse with other students and the teacher. The BBVista Discussion Board is a website that gives students access to a place where they can read, post, and respond to messages. The discussion board is threaded which means different topics can be separated from each other. Threaded discussions also allow the participants to read and respond to specific posts.

This chapter shares findings on communications through a discussion board by students serving as classroom assistants in local schools in Al Ain, United Arab Emirates, and communicating in a second language (English). Although research has focused on numerous benefits and limitations of asynchronous communication, Andresen (2009) argues that two components in the literature emerged as being particularly important for a successful asynchronous discussion forum: the role of the teacher and achieving deeper/higher learning. I will be sharing both topics.

The role of the teacher and understanding the differences between the medium and the classroom

Andresen (2009) argues that some obstacles, specific to an asynchronous online discussion and its learning process, must be overcome. Asynchronous discussions usually separate the teacher and the learner (as well as most learners) from each other in space and in time. This means that a discussion participant cannot be 'cut off', and there is a transcript of the discussion for study purposes after the discussion takes place.

In four years of using the discussion board as a communication tool, we found these arguments to be very important considerations. We realized that the 'classroom time' was extended to whenever the student wished to participate. To the student, this was a plus because

She was not limited by the short discussion time allowed by the teacher in the classroom.

She could reflect on what she wanted to say.

She had the time to relate what she was going to say to what happened or to what she did in the school on that day.

She had the time to reflect on what her colleagues had said.

She could respond without the fear of being cut-off by the teacher or by another student.

She could offer thoughtful help or advice to her colleagues.

She could express her own opinion and take the time to think about it.

She could choose her own topic to write about.

She could write about something that was meaningful to her and not just to the teacher.

Although little research has involved the advantages to the teacher, we were easily able to conclude that the teacher could also benefit from

Being able to see most of the students express themselves instead of the same few.

Discovering a very different dynamism in student discourse given that writers and speakers use different learning styles.

Recognizing much more reflective thinking.

Noting more conversations about the application of knowledge, skills and attitudes to real life situations.

Observing a significant increase in supportive and collaborative discourse.

Having the time to respond to each student in a reflective way.

On the other hand, each one of these positive results could also become a pitfall (non-participation, negativity, bullying, control, evasion, duration (time), pressure...) unless rules and principles are established early before the exchanges start and then managed efficiently throughout the duration of the exercise.

Understanding the culture of the students

Zhu (2012) notes that cultural context has to be considered when applying new technology. I teach the students of Al Ain Women's College who are all Emirati females. They are preparing for a role as a classroom assistant in one of the national schools. Emirati culture is conservative compared to western cultures. Religion and culture are very closely related in Emirati daily life. Women wear an *abaya* (robe) and a *hijab* (scarf) and will often don a *niquab* (face veil) in public. Family, faith, respect, collectivism and collaborative learning are important values for Emiratis.

Although they do not socialize very much with people of different cultures, Emirati women are very respectful of other people and have very strong family values. Socializing within the extended family circle and close friends is taught very early on and they excel at one-on-one or group conversations; these skills are further developed when they start attending schools with other females.

The UAE is a rich country and its leaders have insured that the wealth of the country is shared with its citizens. The advent of personal data assistants such as iPhones, Blackberries and other mobile technologies in a society that can afford them has permitted these young ladies to stay in contact with each other and their families even as their daily routines and responsibilities have increasingly separated them from a shared physical environment.

In the case of Emirati classroom assistants placed in different local schools as apprentices, some in small groups, some on their own, asynchronous communication via the discussion board often becomes a lifeline wherein they can put into practice their culturally shared collaborative skills and reach out to communicate and support each other both personally and professionally.

Establishing rules and training

Anderson (2004) argues that the teacher needs to structure online discussions to configure with classroom content (and experience in the schools). In preparing for my students for their school placement in semester three (three weeks) and in semester four (four weeks) I had to teach them how to use the discussion board as a communicative tool. The training was more extensive in the semester three since this was the first time many students used the BBVista Discussion Board.

Each week of their school placement they had a series of topics posted on the discussion board. Every day, before midnight, the students would have to post at least one message under a topic of their choice and they would also need to respond to one of their colleagues. Because the students had until midnight to post their messages, they were allowed to provide their supportive comments and advice the following day.

These two postings were the minimum requirements for a passing grade. If the students wished to get higher marks they would need to increase the number and/or the quality of their postings. Students were told that they would be assessed according to the number of postings made, the support they provided to their colleagues, their depth of reflection and their writing fluency. Given the difficulties of writing reflective thoughts in a second language, the teachers informed the students that they would not check the grammar and spelling but they would mark the fluency and precision of the writing as a means of expression in order to encourage the students to write.

Rules of netiquette were then discussed and agreed to. The teacher then trained the students on how to access the BBVista discussion board. By the second and third week of the apprenticeship students were very much on task and many students' reflections demonstrated how they were taking ownership of their own progress.

Designing the discussion board

Biggs (1999) suggested that active teaching methods that involve learning through active experimentation and reflective thinking encourage a high-level of student participation in the learning process. This implies that the topics of discussion have to be related to what the students have learned at the college and what they are doing in the schools as apprentices. Many researchers believe that the design of the discussion board should allow different forms of interaction, for example student–teacher, student-content and student-student (Anderson, 2004).

Each year, our two cohorts of 20 to 23 students operated their own discussion board because we wanted to expedite the initial process of establishing relationships. Each week, the teachers posted eight to 12 topics. This allowed the students flexibility to choose one or more topic a day and it also enabled small groups of students to exchange around a specific topic reflectively. The teachers ensured that the theme of the topics was general enough so that the students could come back and write a second or third message during the week on the same topic.

The topic 'I need some advice' helped to develop some very professional student-to-student interaction with students providing sound advice and often relating the issues to their own experience in the classroom. The topic 'Things I did today' was an easier topic for those who had trouble expressing their ideas or who simply preferred to do so. The topic 'My reflection for today' enabled students to reflect on their day at school.

As we progressed into the fourth semester, the questions became more program specific in order to ensure that the students were able to transfer the theoretical content of the courses into the reality of the classroom.

Group size

Research on the ideal size of a group for an online discussion varies and is dependent to a large extent on outcomes established by the teachers. The teachers decided early on that, due to the relationships that were created in class and that existed previously, they should not try to mix them or use only one discussion board for both groups. The objective was to extend the feeling of community that existed in the classroom to the discussion board and improve on it.

Given that the students were commenting on their experiences at their school when responding, the experience was very successful with exchanges of two, three and sometimes four students on topics such as a common experience they had during the day, a specific problem in dealing with a child, a teaching strategy or how they felt about being responsible for children.

We found that each cohort developed a sense of community because of the lifeline support, advice and encouragement they provided to each other while being partly isolated. This also forced them to be more reflective in their responses in order to be of real assistance to their colleagues. Teachers noted that some new relationships were created which they could not have foreseen when some students went out of their way to support a colleague they had not worked with before.

Time management

Teacher and students are separated by time and space. They are not in the same room and they most often communicate at different times. Because of this, students have more time to reflect on what they have done and what they have read. The research is very relevant as to how the discussion board is to be used and how the time and space factors can affect learning but the medium still has to be managed well by the teachers to ensure that all students benefit from it.

The students were in schools until 12.00 to 14.00. Some of them had work handed to them by the teachers to do at home for the next day and they also had their college projects to manage. Because the temperature in the

United Arab Emirates can be very hot in the afternoon, people are most active in the evening. Students had until midnight to post messages every day. On Thursday (the weekend in the UAE is on Friday and Saturday), they did not have to post right away: they had until Saturday midnight. Because some students waited until close to midnight to post messages and other students went to bed earlier, responses to other students were allowed on the following day.

Teacher participation

Andresen (2009) states that the research on this dimension of the asynchronous discussion forum is quite clear for the teachers: back off. Swan and Shih (2005) find that the perceived presence of a teacher is more important than the perceived presence of peers in student satisfaction. However, a teacher that contributes significantly to a discussion tends to decrease the length of discussions. The question of when, how and how often to participate is one that the teachers struggled with for quite a while.

As research indicates, the teachers need to provide feedback (sometimes immediate). They had to focus the discussion, encourage participation, encourage reflective thinking and ensure that proper and helpful responses and advice was given by other students. On the other hand, if they answered someone directly, it would stop the conversation because they were considered the experts. Students wanted the teachers to read their messages and responses and they also wanted their feedback.

The teachers finally initiated the following process. If, while reading the students' messages, they found that a student needed immediate feedback (problem with the teacher, attendance, abuse, bullying), they would offer an immediate response. Otherwise, they waited until all the messages were written and they responded the following day. To encourage participation and reflective thinking, they identified stars of the day; they rated and summarized the messages and responses and they provided feedback to each and every student in a positive way.

Providing feedback

Balaji (2010) states that students learn faster and more effectively when they are provided with the feedback of their current performance and what might be needed in order to improve. The provision of feedback from the teacher and from other students proved to be the resource that had the largest influence on the creation of a close-knit learning community.

As stated previously, teachers faced the dilemma of either providing immediate feedback and being regarded as 'the experts' and thus influencing the level of the discussion, or waiting until after the discussion was completed to make their comments. In some cases, the nature and level of the issue required the immediate feedback of the teachers and that had to be accepted.

Generally however, the teachers waited until the next day to provide feedback on the student postings. In the case of student responses to each other, the students were trained beforehand on the use of positive and professional feedback in order to advise or to support their colleagues in the managing of their roles and responsibilities as classroom assistants.

In particular, the teachers knew, from classroom discussions of students in the previous years, that classroom management and the discipline of children were the areas where students felt most uncertain. They therefore included the topic 'I need some advice' in the discussion on a daily basis. This proved to be a topic of sincere and profound feedback for both recipients and advisors.

Facilitating

Rohfeld and Hiemstra (1995, p 91) describe the online teacher's role as the responsibility of keeping discussions on track, contribute special knowledge and insights, weaving together various discussion threads and course components, and maintaining group harmony. The facilitation of the discussion board was a work in progress for the teachers.

To encourage participation, they designated stars of the day in their daily posting 'My comments for today'. They would comment on the support and the reflective thinking of individual postings to encourage depth of thought and meaningful responses. There was a concerted effort to provide positive advice and encouragement to the students. In order to ensure them that they had read all their reflections, the teachers summarized and rated every posting.

Leadership

Given the differences in the characteristics of the asynchronous discussion board, it was interesting to note a shift in the roles of the students.

Leadership of the discussion usually passed from the strong, confident and socially adept characters of the regular classroom to the strong, quiet and reflective students. Other students were often very quick to recognize sound reflective thinking and would often rally around a discussion started by those individuals.

Applying the topics of discussion to the outcomes of the curriculum

Andresen (2009) contends that when discussion questions or topics were specific and related to a concept or idea within the course, the discussions were more successful in generating complex interaction between learners. The importance of the transfer of the concepts, skills and attitudes taught in the college classroom to the real life application while the classroom assistants were on apprenticeship was deemed to be a priority by the teachers.

In this case, it was not only the outcomes of one course that were addressed but the general outcomes of the Classroom Assistants Program. This was a barometer used not only to encourage discussion on practical subjects but also to assess the relevance and usefulness of the materials and outcomes of the courses taught. The two adages 'If it's not useful in real-life applications, then it shouldn't be taught[and [If the student cannot apply the concepts, skills and attitudes taught in call to real life situations, then they should not be encouraged to pursue this career[were cornerstones of the apprenticeship experience.

Management of the teacher's time

Mazzolini and Maddison (2003) state that the role of the teacher, and thus the time spent on task, depends on what he or she wishes to accomplish. Given that we wanted to use the asynchronous discussion board to monitor student reflective thinking and personal growth as professionals, it quickly became apparent to us that the teacher had to be someone who already knew the students and what they could do before the apprenticeship. We found it very difficult to give the task of teacher to someone other than the teacher of these students.

Although the teachers had to read the students' messages often after normal school hours, it must also be taken into consideration that the students were away all week and the teachers did not have to teach during the apprenticeship. Depending on the participation and the depth of thinking of the students the teacher had to spend between two and four hours per day in order to do a proper job of facilitating and monitoring the exchanges. Time constraints became more of a factor when the teacher had to go to the schools to evaluate the students at work.

In some years, the responses of the teachers had to be written a few days after the postings of the students due to the increase in student output. Although it was still encouraging for the students to know that the teachers were reading the postings, the immediacy of the feedback was lost in time. Time is definitely a challenge that has to be addressed as the skills of the teachers improve and the participation of the students increases. We found that there is a definite relationship between the participation and the reflective content on the one hand and the time that has to be allocated to facilitate, provide feedback and monitor the students' progress on the other hand.

A sense of community

Balaji (2010) found that the interactions in the online forum promote a sense of community or social connectivity between the learners and the teachers. We found this to be true in each and every year of the program. The discussion board created a lifeline to the classroom assistants who were able to communicate and support each other although separated by time and space. They could communicate, collaborate and seek advice from their colleagues even when they were in another school across the city and when they went online at different times of the day. This helped to reduce their isolation and their uncertainty towards their daily responsibilities.

The teachers found that, when the participants returned to the college after their apprenticeship, they had to be given a certain amount of free time to share their online experiences in a face-to-face setting especially with the colleagues they had undertaken exchanges with through the discussion board. The teachers also noticed a marked improvement in the sense of community inside the college classroom once the participants were back and this could be linked directly to the experience they had lived together online on the discussion board.

Collaboration

Johnson (2006) observed that the discussion board is collaborative and interactive and thus opens new opportunities to learn how to teach in innovative ways. In our experience with classroom assistants we found this to be very true in different areas. The sharing of positive classroom and behaviour management strategies was especially noticeable during the apprenticeship, in part because students are insecure when having to manage the behaviour of 20 or more children during their apprenticeship.

The inclusion of the 'I need your advice' topic enabled students to collaborate and share personal and observed strategies. They were also able to help each other to create a bank of behaviour strategies that they constantly relied on and added to in order to support each other. The same can be said of teaching and learning strategies which they shared through the 'Teaching strategies that really work' topic.

Finally, the collaborative actions of students were very noticeable in their postings on the progress of the two projects they had to implement while on apprenticeship: the creation and reporting of a display to support the teacher; and the application and reporting of behaviour modification strategies to support a child in the classroom.

Reflective and critical thinking

Schellens and Valcke (2006) found that discussion forums attained a greater proportion of higher phases of knowledge creation because the vast majority of communication in the asynchronous environment was task-oriented. They also found that groups with more discussion resulted in higher level of knowledge construction. The creation of a sense of community and the application of the discussions to real life enabled the teachers to identify some very basic personality traits of the students.

In this case, we will have to broaden the meaning of 'reflective thinking' to mean 'the reflective application of ideas and concepts to real life'. Many personalities of Gardner's Multiple Intelligences Theory (1983) were easily identifiable. There were students who reflected deeply on a topic such as how to approach a child with special needs or how to deal with behaviour modification; others focused their attention on helping their colleagues find a solution to a problem; others addressed the practicality of a teaching strategy; others focused on the display they were creating. Some would write multiple messages while others were satisfied with a few but many found a way to dig into themselves and express what they observed, what they saw, what they felt, what they learned and what they want to do with it.

Writing

Doering (2003) concluded that participants develop important skills in writing of different genres and communication through multimedia. As mentioned previously, writing was not corrected but was assessed on communicativeness. One of the teachers, Hiebert (2012), conducted a survey asking about whether or not they improved in their reading, writing and vocabulary: 60% of participants said they thought ADB helped their writing improve a lot, 30% said it improved very much and 10% said it improved a little. When asked about vocabulary, 20% said they used new words every time they wrote, 70% said they used new words most times, and 10% said they used new words rarely.

Hiebert also noted that more solid research was needed to establish the quality of student growth in terms of writing and vocabulary. Specifically, investigation is needed into the area of structural levels and syntax sophistication. It would appear that by not correcting students' grammar and syntax, it encouraged them to write more and it improved their vocabulary and fluency but the teachers did not notice any improvement in the spelling and grammar.

Assessment

Most researchers agree that real learning occurs while the students are actively engaged in the exchanges on the discussion board and thus the facilitation techniques of the teachers and the feedback they provide are essential to the process of learning. Andresen (2009) agrees, however, that many learners need an incentive to participate and will only do so if there is a summative assessment.

Johnson (2007) contends that since students learn differently, assessment criteria should therefore be built around the learning process that is the construction of knowledge instead of the actual knowledge. For this exercise, the teachers decided that the following four areas were the most important factors affecting the construction of knowledge: participation; support or collaboration; writing; and reflective thinking. A rubric was drawn up to enable this outlining the values: reflective thinking 40%; participation 20%; writing 20%; support and collaboration 20%

Dennen (2005) noted that courses with a higher quantity of discussion also displayed a higher quality of discussion. Participation is also a good indicator of student satisfaction with the process. Teachers used a variety of techniques to encourage the participation of students. The most successful techniques turned out to be:

Providing next day assessment and feedback on the quality of each posting.

Rating the participation of everyone in class and determining the stars of the day.

Ensuring that the feedback and comments contained a note of positive reinforcement explaining to the students how to improve their posts.

Given that English was their second language, commenting on the fluency of the writing rather than on the grammar and spelling.

The results were rather astounding. These techniques were refined as the process evolved. The participation of the students went from 591 and 766 messages and responses posted by the two cohorts in the first year of the program to 7162 and 3633 postings by the two cohorts of the third year of the program during a four-week apprenticeship.

The length of the postings varied from five word messages of support to 15 to 20 lines of reflective thinking and transfers of knowledge. The sheer number of postings rendered it impossible for the teachers to provide immediate feedback and students had to be given two days free of postings while the teachers caught up to the backlog.

In 2010, Denise Murray, a verifier for the Scottish Qualifications Authority (SQA) Accreditation Unit noted the following about her meeting with students of the program: 'They found the use of Blackboard Vista allowed them to ask for support out of college hours from both their tutor and each other. They were using the programme to think deeply about their classroom practice and seek answers to questions about behaviour management *etc.*' (Murray, 2010)

The students were surveyed on a yearly basis on their satisfaction with the BBVista Discussion Board exchange during their apprenticeship. Positive comment included:

I love the support I received from my colleagues, I liked the support of the teachers, I improved my reading, writing and vocabulary, I especially liked the fact that the teacher was reading all of my messages, I did not feel alone, I could see what my colleagues were doing and thinking, I learned how to apply what we were taught in school, I felt supported, I learned to be a problem solver by helping others, I learned many useful strategies for teaching, learning and classroom management *etc.*

Other comment included:

I did not participate as much as I would have liked to, it is very useful but it is also very demanding of our time, I could not always participate because I had to take care of my children, I had to do some work for the teacher, the Internet was not working, BBVista was not working, I was tired after a day at work, I was sick for a few days so I could not participate *etc.*

Conclusion

In conclusion, we can certainly say that the four-year experience on the use of the discussion board during the course with classroom assistants supports most of the findings of previous research on the use of discussion boards. It would seem, however, that additional research still needs to be undertaken in a few areas associate with it.

Although a lot of research has been done on the benefits of the discussion board for the students, what are the benefits for the teachers?

We need to research and address the question of time required of the teachers who must manage the discussion.

Although most research agrees that the discussion board provides an extension of the school day, we must address the questions of how much time should be required of the students? What about their other responsibilities at the school and at home?

Can a teacher who has not taught the student in class do a credible job at managing the discussions?

How can we get adult English-as-a-second-language students to write more in order to demonstrate reflective thinking and yet help them to improve their grammar and spelling?

References

Ajayi, L. (2009). An Exploration of Pre-Service Teachers' Perceptions of Learning to Teach while Using Asynchronous Discussion Board. *Educational Technology & Society, 12* (2), 86–100.

Anderson, T. (2004). Towards a theory of online learning. In T. Anderson, & F. Elloumi (Eds.), *Theory and practice of online learning* (pp. 33-60) Athabasca University Press.

Andresen, M. A. (2009). Asynchronous discussion forums: success factors, outcomes, assessments, and limitations. *Educational Technology & Society, 12* (1), 249–257.

Balaji, M. S. & Chakrabarti, D. Student Interactions in Online Discussion Forum: Empirical Research from 'Media Richness Theory' Perspective *Journal of Interactive Online Learning* Volume 9, Number 1, Spring 2010. ISSN: 1541-4914 Retrieved September 28, 2013 from www.ncolr.org/jiol

Biggs, J. (1999). Teaching for Quality Learning at University, Buckingham: *The Society for Research into Higher Education and Open University Press.*

Buckingham, D. (2006). Is there a Digital Generation? In Buckingham, D. & Willett, R. (Eds.), *Digital generations: Children, young people, and new media* (pp. 1–13), Mahwah, New Jersey: Lawrence Erlbaum.

Dale, B.(2009). External Verification Report – SVQ. *Scottish Qualifications Authority (SQA,* October 2009.

Doering, A., Johnson, M., & Dexter, S. (2003). Using asynchronous discussion to support pre-service teachers' practicum experiences. *TechTrends, 47* (1), 52–55.

Gardner, H. (1983). Frames of Mind – The Theory of Multiple Intelligences. *Basic Books* New York, NY 10016-8810. 1983.

Hiebert, S. (2012). Building a Professional Learning Community. *Paper presented at the Middle East – North Africa Writing Centre Alliance (MENAWCA).* Doha, Qatar. November 2012.

Johnson, H. (2007). *Dialogue and the construction of knowledge in E-learning: Exploring students' perceptions of their learning while using blackboard asynchronous discussion board,* Retrieved January 21, 2009 from www.eurodl.org/materials/contrib/2007/Henry_Johnson.htm

Johnson, G. M. (2006). Synchronous and asynchronous text-based CMC in educational contexts: A review of recent research. *TechTrends, 50* (4), 46–53.

Mazzolini, M. & Maddison, S. (2003). Sage, guide or ghost? The effect of teacher intervention on student participation in online discussion forums. *Computers & Education,* 40(3), 237 – 253.

Rohfeld, R. W., & Hiemstra, R. (1995). Moderating discussions in the electronic classroom. *Computer Mediated Communication and the Online Classroom: Distance Learning, 3,* 91-104.

Schellens, T. & Valcke, M. (2006). Fostering knowledge construction in university students through asynchronous discussion groups. *Computers & Education,* 46(4), 349 – 370.

Swan, K. & Shih, L.F. (2005). On the nature and development of social presence in online course discussions. *Journal of Asynchronous Learning Networks*, 9(3), Paper 8.

TeacherStream, LLC (2009). Mastering Online Discussion Board Facilitation. *TeacherSteream LLC, 2010.*

Zhu, C. (2012). Student Satisfaction, Performance, and Knowledge Construction in Online Collaborative Learning. *Educational Technology & Society, 15* (1), 127–136.

Chapter 3

Down the rabbit hole: the challenges of blended learning in an adult language program

Tanya Tercero

Is blended learning the best of both worlds in language education? Quite possibly according to Grgurović's article in her case study, 'Blended learning in an ESL class: A case study', (2011). She shows how a technology-enhanced blended course can meet the learning needs of all the students in a course.

One teaching platform does not fulfill all the needs of all students all the time, and blended learning offers opportunities to enhance language teaching, as well as encourage more independent language learning on the part of the learners. Of course, as with any practice in teaching and learning, there are both advantages and challenges in designing, implementing, supporting and evaluating the effectiveness of blended learning; the advantages and challenges will vary depending on different variables, including the context, content, location, and even the demographics and culture of the teachers, learners and institutions.

In this chapter I compare some aspects of technology-enhanced blended learning in two contexts in which I have taught: teaching ESL in an adult education program in the US; and teaching ESL (not EFL) at a women's college in the United Arab Emirates (UAE). Having taught ESL in a US adult education program for seven years and in an English foundations program in the UAE for three years, I have experienced many of the advantages and challenges to blended learning in each context based on my own use of blended learning.

I also discuss how the use of ubiquitous mobile devices, such as mobile phones and iPads/tablets, can supplement the use of, or even replace, computer-based instruction (CBI) in blended learning in these contexts.

In the context of a US adult education ESL program, a blended learning ESL course can be extremely beneficial to the adult immigrants who enroll in these free, non-credit courses which are usually held in the mornings or evenings two to four times a week for a minimum of two hours per class session. Many, if not all, of these ESL learners are working part-time or full-time or are looking for work if they are not primary care givers, since they are self-supporting and often providing for families in their home countries. They are dealing with the stress of learning a new language in a new city and culture.

For them, learning English is very important for access to jobs and educational opportunities because they left their home countries primarily out of the necessity to find work. Often these students are very tired when they come to class, sometimes by bus, before or after working long days, but they are quite motivated to learn English.

When I was teaching ESL for an adult education program, one class period per week was held in the computer lab while the rest were face-to-face. The face-to-face component always included group activities and class discussions, and the class itself provided a social component for the students. I had been part of a pilot study for USAlearns.org, a free online ESL program for adult immigrant learners, and I continued using it in my courses. The program teaches basic reading, writing and life skills, such as finding a job, and teachers can create an online 'class' to track registered students.

Students seemed to be highly engaged during our lab time. They enjoyed using or learning to use the computer (another life skill), and the program reinforced what students learned in class which, as Grgurovic cites Stracke (2007), is vital to the students as they want to see the connection between what they do in class and what they do in CBI.

If students had computers at home, they reported using the program on their own. This also supports an important attribute of successful blended learning, 'that students are autonomous and will take responsibility for their own learning,' as Grgurovic cites Neumeier (2005). Student engagement, autonomous learning, and the reinforcement of both ESL and life skills taught in the class are clearly some of the advantages of technology-enhanced blended learning in adult education, but the potential is even greater if we consider using mobile phones in adult education ESL courses.

Integrating mobile phones in blended learning courses for adult ESL education programs would benefit the students who, despite differing economic circumstances, usually have smartphones with internet connectivity. For the students who are working in jobs with late or long hours (sometimes immigrants are asked to work 12-hour shifts), or for those who might have to stay home one or two days per week because they don't have alternate child care, mobile learning could feasibly make up a large percentage (perhaps as much as 50%) of a learner's ESL course, and learners could practice listening, speaking, reading and writing at a more convenient time for them.

As seen in Mohammed Tamimi's presentation of his Dissertation Proposal Defense on 'Teaching culture in foreign language: learner's affect surrounding the use of blended learning in Arabic as a case study (2013)', it is possible to create interactive language lessons using common and/or innovative online resources, such as Facebook, Eyejot, Byki and YouTube, and these online resources typically have a mobile option. Therefore the question is why not provide these students with accessible and effective language learning opportunities via mobile learning or CBI? What are some of the challenges in this context?

Some of the biggest challenges of providing technology-enhanced blended language learning in adult education include requirements and financial limitations of adult education programs, the status and demographics of adult education ESL teachers, and the demographics of adult immigrant learners. First of all, the largest adult education programs in the US are, for the most part, federally and state funded. The programs are obliged to meet the requirements of these governments in order to maintain funding; one major requirement is physical attendance of students in the classrooms. Students must sign-in for class, and the attendance records are maintained and subject to review when programs are audited for compliance. Obviously students cannot sign-in if they are learning outside the classroom or computer lab.

Another institutional challenge is the lack of money to purchase software programs, such as Rosetta Stone or ebooks from publishers which require expensive licenses for use in CBI. What about those online resources mentioned above? Well, most of the adult education ESL teachers do not have full-time positions and, if they do, they are in the classroom for about 30 hours per week, so they have little time to learn how to use the resources themselves, let alone develop lesson plans to support learning outside their classrooms.

The part-time teachers are paid a small hourly wage only for time spent in the classroom, and they receive no benefits, so the time that would be required for them to develop and implement either CBI or mobile language learning lessons would not be financially compensated. In addition, because the teaching positions are primarily part-time, the teachers are often older, perhaps retired, and they often balk at the idea of using technology in the classroom. It can also be very physically and mentally demanding to be in a computer lab with a lot of students who may need help with both the technology and the material.

Finally, the adult immigrant students may be a challenge themselves. The younger adults, digital natives, are not so challenging; but the older ones, who may be digital immigrants, can be. Many older immigrants come from an educational culture where the teacher is the source of knowledge, and these older students expect to be taught in a traditional classroom setting, one that may, or may not, be challenged by an older or even a younger, inexperienced teacher.

In comparison, blended language learning in the context of an ESL foundations program at a women's college in the UAE offers its own advantages and challenges. In this context, the students are from a collective culture which facilitates collaboration among students. In comparison to adult immigrant ESL learners in the US, these students are relatively wealthy and have both smartphones and iPads/tablets. They are provided with higher education at no cost. They are not highly motivated to learn English, as many do not need to find jobs, or as women, their male relatives will not permit them to work outside the home.

As such, the women often attend school to socialize and experience a bit of freedom outside the home. All the students complete secondary education and their expectations for of the classroom experience at college include didactic learning with little effort on their part. Students attend foundations classes for about 20 hours per week, although there is little consequence for not attending classes, so often some of them attended sporadically.

Students must achieve an IELTS score of the day (the minimum requirement may change from semester to semester) in order to leave the foundations program and apply to a bachelor's program, but few students have the ambition to do the work required to obtain a degree even though an educated Emirati workforce is the initiative of the government in order for the country to be more self-sufficient and less dependent on a foreign workforce.

Some of the advantages of blended learning in this context include greatly facilitating the learning curve of the teachers, meeting the 'edutainment' requirements of the Emirati students/engaging them as digital natives, focusing on improving their weak reading skills, as well as test-taking skills in order for them to be better able to answer questions on the IELTS exam.

Because the college has a lot of money, all the students and teachers have iPads with technology-ready classrooms and an IT staff to support them; there are numerous computer labs installed with ebooks created by publishers who come directly to the college to survey the teachers about what features they would like to see in these etextbooks. Teams of iPad-teaching enthusiasts share favorite language apps in weekly meetings or ishare files.

I used apps such as Listening Master, SoundNote, Keynote, and iMovie to supplement my face-to-face time in the classroom with my students. I would demonstrate the app (they had few problems learning the technology), model an activity and then send them off to produce something on their own. They either emailed me their project or returned to the classroom where we reviewed it together.

They were actively engaged using English, and I was left alone with some precious quiet moments to gather my thoughts (the Emirati students are extremely social and very loud). Another advantage of blended learning was getting them to read using the iPad in the classroom and CBI in the weekly computer lab sessions. Reading is a weak skill for them, and they frequently claimed that they hate reading, but they did not complain when reading via technology for a solid hour. Blake *et al.* (2008) cite Warschauer, claiming that 'DL courses help develop strong literacy skills because so much of this learning environment is text-based'. Well, in this case it is not DL but BL, but one could infer the same effect.

Finally, CBI complemented class IELTS practice as students used test preparation software to give them more simulated practice that they could do at their own pace, and they were more invested in this particular activity because they value the actual IELTS score as a symbol of achievement more than being able to produce language. The advantages of technology-enhanced blended learning are quite evident in this context.

The challenges in this context occurred in the face-to-face mode. My Emirati students rather ironically were not shy to shout out, "I am boring!" when an activity did not meet their requirement for it to be 'fun'. It takes a lot of energy and planning to develop 'fun' learning activities for 20 class hours per week. If one of your activities fails to impress, it can be de-motivating for the teacher since she may have spent two hours designing that 15-minute activity.

Students' expectations of their teacher in the classroom was another challenge, as they expected to be taught and given direct answers to questions that required even minimal critical thinking skills on their part. They were not used to giving explanations or justifying their responses either. It seems that these skills could not be easily taught via CBI.

As for mobile devices, sometimes students were off-task and using their iPads to play games or use Instagram and were frequently chatting with their friends on their BlackBerries, and they visibly resented the teacher for either not allowing phones at their desks or taking them away after asking them to be put away more than once. The challenges were very frustrating for everyone involved.

As one can see, the advantages and challenges of blended learning vary depending on the context of the learning environment, but blended learning definitely increases the engagement of the students. More case studies like Grgurovic's, though, are needed to determine the effectiveness of CBI and mobile learning on student outcomes. Similar frameworks are also needed to be able to make comparisons across contexts.

Bibliography

Grgurovic, M. (2011). Blended learning in an ESL class: A case study. *CALICO Journal*, 29(1), 100-117.

Blake, R., Wilson, N., Cetto, M., & Pardo-Ballester C. (2008). Measuring oral proficiency in distance learning, face-to-face, and blended classrooms. *Language Learning & Technology*, 12(3), p.114-127.

Tamimi, M. (2013). *Teaching culture in foreign language: Learners' affect surrounding the use of blended learning in Arabic as a case study.* (Dissertation Proposal Defense). University of Arizona, Tucson.

Chapter 4

Heretical views from a digitally centric universe

Lawrence Burke

There's no doubt that the iPad and its multiple applications, along with other mobile devices and online learning will bring additional resources and opportunities to learn into the labyrinth of today's educative processes. Yet the global educational sector is conflicted. On the one hand it argues for building educational institutions which nurture a unique community of learners, while on the other hand it embraces technologies some of which have the most devastating and alienating effects on communities and undermines the very concept of nurture and a duty of care towards all learners in schools Colleges and Universities throughout the world.

I am in a unique position as an educator, because every academic year the institution which currently employs me also employs a different learning platform and learning devices each academic year. Such is the quintessential nature of change in education today. We are able to use the very latest in educational technology, as do the students in our courses. For example, we use BYOD, BbbVista, BBlearn, Quom interactive boards, iPads and their multiple applications, AppleMacs, all the Microsoft suites on the latest platforms, as well as our own mobile devices should something untoward go wrong in the high tech classroom-as it inevitably does. And, as a back up in case of a power cut or battery outage we keep a stock of pencils and note pads and a few white board markers-technological remnants of a bygone era; however these are seldom used.

With our digital and technological innovations we can paint, draw, write, publish and print our own text books, create our own diagrams for analysis and even use virtual reality to create those quintessential educative moments where our students can understand a concept or idea in real time. We can share information, collaborate with tasks, set secure online examinations, give instant feedback, chat, discuss, meet and record ourselves, and all of this can occur at the same time, across classrooms, communities, cities, countries and the globe. And this is just the start. Furthermore, for those who may struggle with adjusting to assimilate their corporeal selves into the ubiquitous digital world of constant change and upgrade we have at our disposal Puentedura's adjustment and integration model-SAMR-a deterministic behavior modification model marketed as a supportive sociological and psychological tool for the technology challenged.

In addition to my hands on approach in the 21st century digital classroom I was recently involved with a major publishing house in trialing their various interactive educational materials as they embrace educational technology in its various formats. Yet, notwithstanding all of the above my schooling up to and including my post graduate training and research has taught me that a critical understanding of the kinds of technology we use in today's classroom and why we use it, is the foundation on which today's teaching and learning must be predicated. With this caveat in mind it is quite extraordinary and exciting to anticipate and debate where technology in the educational sector is leading us today.

Critical Engagement with Change

The assimilation of education into the information technology industry has been likened to the way whole cultures, societies and countries were assimilated into the major industrial and technological changes of the 18th, 19th and early 20th centuries. Such major transformations in the past have also shaped education and defined the course of its social history up until today. The printing press, the lead pencil, vinyl records, television and VHS tapes are samples of past innovations which were once prophesied as detrimental to teaching and learning. Most of us have read the funny quotes from the past about 16th century students not preparing their bark properly to calculate problems and how those 20th century pencils and ballpoint pens would be the ruin of education and so on. There are even some educators who use these examples as indicators of obstructions by those who call for a critical and informed debate on digital learning. While some may perceive us as obstructive, in reality we simply are calling for informed and collaborative debate on the uses of technology and digital learning in education.

We pose critical questions about the rapid assimilation of our schools, colleges and universities into the virtual world of technology and mobile learning. We are concerned when this is done without sufficient research having been carried out as to the effects of digitalized learning on the mental and physical well being of our student populations. We want to know whether or not they improve their innate ability to learn. For this kind of reputable critical enquiry we often find ourselves bullied through name calling; we are labeled 'luddites, 'sticklers in the mud", "resisters", " troublemakers" and 'inflexible'. Luddites is the most common term used, and is somewhat of a misnomer because it isn't that well understood. As Postman (1992) points out the Luddite movement was a protest movement, similar to the 'Occupy Wall Street Movement" which indignantly resented the new pay cuts, child labor and the abolition of laws and customs that had once protected skill workers and artisans. One could pose the question has anything really changed in the 21st century?

As educators critical enquiry is our avocation. We have a professional and ethical responsibility to keep ourselves informed and up to date on what is happening in our profession. For example, most of us read vociferously about new developments, new trends, the latest research and innovations because we value and appreciate the vital and responsible role teaching and learning has in creating good citizens and a civilized society. We are committed teachers who are passionate about education and the direction the profession is heading. And it is our well founded conviction that a critical review of technology and its profound and life changing affects and effects on learners today is necessary and essential if we are to provide the very best educational opportunities and experiences for future generations of children and young people.

There is a constantly repeated refrain from the Apple and Ed. Tech. converts, or as one of my colleagues likes to call them 'the Ed. Tech Cult', that the iPad is the "perfect learning companion". In 2011 Abilene Christian University produced a paper entitled *iPad or iFad*, in which the writers produced a rigorous defense of using Ed. Tech through this device as an instructional tool in the paperless classroom; yet they provided no evidence of improved learning outcomes through academic success. Pepperdine University in the USA is currently one of a small number of tertiary institutions to have undertaken a longitudinal case study on the use of the iPad as an instructional and learning device in an attempt to establish the validity of claims made by Apple Inc. that their device is the future for education. They framed their study around two key questions:

1. Does the iPad have the potential to enhance students' performance on course learning objectives?

2. Can we develop a formula for success?

The results which Pepperdine have posted online to date do not show any statistical evidence that using the iPad has "enhanced student performance on course learning objectives", and the results from their questions and surveys do not indicate they have yet "developed a formulae for success" in using this device. It is my opinion that there is an urgent need for more informed, critical debate on whether or not the iPad in particular or Ed. Tech in general is enabling learners to succeed whereas without the aid of these tools they would fail.

Mayer (1993) has argued since the early 90s, that there seems little point in infusing the debate with opinions about those who support or do not support the use of online learning and Ed. Tech. in teaching pedagogy. People being people take time to adjust to the new and untried. It is a matter of respecting this and ensuing that these differences of opinion do not over shadow clear critical thinking when considering what is best for today's and future generations of learners.

Engaging with the Research

From an historical view point of view the educational sector, when it has had the means to do so, has always embraced new technologies for better or worse. We have taken to what works well and what contributes to the genuine development of sound pedagogical processes in teaching and learning. It has never been a simplistic argument about those who embrace the new or those who resist the new and untried. Such a black and white perception of digital learning and what is occurring in education is profoundly naïve simply because there is a huge difference between embracing technology in all its guises as an instructional interface, and having informed, discerned knowledge and understanding about how how such devices affects pedagogical processes; and more importantly how they impact on the psycho-cognitive processes of learners.

Some of the researched literature on the effects of online learning and Ed. Tech tools on children and students is heavily biased towards the organizations that fund the research. For example one key study by the Milken Exchange –a subsidiary of the powerful and influential Milken Family Foundation (Transforming Education through Technology, 1999) claimed that 11% gains made to elementary school learners through mathematics and vocabulary development were directly attributable to technology usage. Yet, if these findings were tested more rigorously through applying a chi square test it may show that there are no significant differences between students who learn online and through Ed. Tech tools, and those who learn offline without an Ed. Tech. interface. The differences claimed in the Milken Exchange study could have been due to many other variables in the teaching and learning processes. I have found similar results in my own research (Burke, 2010, 2011) which suggests that there are too many variables at play to be able to find a control group that will give more than a 50% mean difference between students' achievements and the different kinds of teaching and learning methodologies and processes.

Clarke (1983) argued that there were absolutely no accrued learning benefits through using media of any kind in teaching and learning pedagogy. His famous quip that a new Green Grocer vehicle won't change the dietary habits of a nation is an interesting analogy for today. Yet, we've move beyond such a perfunctory view of Ed. Tech. tools and online learning to one where we are essentially concerned with the impact and affect on the cognitive processes of learners. This is where the debate must center and focus for educators. We need to eschew the technophoria and hype, along with the awe and glamour of new devices, new applications and software, as well as the talk show type debates about online vs. offline learning, and seek a clear critical understanding of how we learn and the cognitive processes most deeply affected through Ed. Tech. tools and online learning.

A number of educators are engaging in this debate; Mayer & Moreno's (1998, 2001, and 2002), well founded research and arguments for controlled and discerned use of Ed. Tech tools are where the debates should be centered today. However it is unfortunate that this may not come about because the IT lobby with its billions of advertising dollars and some major educational publishing houses with their quasi-research projects-all biased towards their own outcomes hinder a clear, critical public debate. This approach was evident in the ITL research group's recent report on innovative teaching and learning (2011) 95% of the report condemns schools and other learning institutions for not using the latest products and gadgetry, there is no informed, clear critical research on how their products perform or affect learners cognitively or psychologically, or of how their products define the methodological and pedagogical processes in a constructive way. It is one thing to argue for every child having an iPad to reduce heavy back packs with lots of books, and quite another to pursue the argument that digital learning will increase knowledge gains for learners.

Traditional classroom style learning with its essential socialization and communicative processes along with the lecture theater are also targets of the corporate IT sector and some educators too. The CEO of AISH (Academy for International School Heads) Bambi Betts recently argued that it is 'game over' for education as we know it today through the flooding of the educational sector with MOOCs (Massive Open Online Courses) and other forms of digital learning. Her carefully chosen description of these courses as 'disruptive innovations" in mainstream education highlights the willfulness of forceful change being imposed on teachers, students, parents and some administrators who question the ethics, efficacy and legitimacy of digital learning, online learning and MOOCs. The assumption that formal learning is an option which can take place anywhere and at any time is false and based on erroneous understandings about how we learn, why we learn, what we need to learn, and how we measure and evaluate successful teaching and learning. An avatar lecturer or a video clip of a lesson hardly qualifies as innovate in terms of teaching and learning, but may well be disruptive to genuine critical enquiry, the acquisition of knowledge, and becoming a life long learner.

Teaching and learning is a highly sociable process. It is built on a fundamental axiom of quality interactive and inter-personal social communicative processes. Moreover, schooling and tertiary studies is a highly controlled social process as well as an intellectual one. We require those who graduate from our high schools and universities to be civil to others and to have good manners and treat people respectfully. Working in the isolated vacuum of virtual realities where "I am my screen" and "I do not have to compete to share my thoughts and ideas" does not contribute to positive social learning outcomes at all. I'm all for 'rethinking education' and embracing technology; but it should be an intrinsic part of any performance management plan which has as its core principle how students learn, not what they like using and doing best.

Where are we heading ethically?

Bearing this in mind it should be clear that any relationship between, internet usage and learning through a computer or mobile device is elementary. While there may be differentiation in the assignments or tasks undertaken (personal as opposed to specialized) the media interface is identical. For example, researching for a project or reading through an online Publisher's book-like interface, or playing a video game, or updating Facebook, or social networking, or using a movie making application, or a language or mathematics based application for school or college courses all involve similar cognitive processes which utilize our working memory, reasoning and creative brain functions. They also involve similar interactive relationships between a human being and a machine, no matter what type of branding and packaging of the machine be it an iPad, a Samsung galaxy, a Microsoft or Lenovo tablet, or any other of the myriad hand-held mobile devices on the market today. So to distinguish between an internet addiction and an addiction to a mobile device is useful only insofar as it delineates the *purpose*, not the interface used for that *purpose*. Spending 6-8 hours online at school or college or playing games or chatting or surfing the net watching YouTube clips or using a computer or mobile device to study or complete research for an assignment all carry the same psychological and physical health risks.

We know very little about the long term psychological and physical effects contemporary technology has on people in general and youth in particular except that some of the early studies are indicating that fundamental changes in social behavior and mental and physical health after extended periods of time using technology are deleterious to human physical well-being, human social relationships and the human character.

For example, there's evidence to suggest people behave more rudely and aggressively online. Psychologists call this the *disinhibition effect*- a sophisticated euphemism for bad-mannered, belligerent, antagonistic and outright cruel and rude anti-social behavior. It is argued people feel less inhibited when not seen and feel they can express themselves more freely and without feeling vulnerable to criticism. But the results of this kind of reasoning put into practice can have devastating and tragic consequences. Recently, a 13-year-old girl hanged herself after being bullied at school for months by a group of her peers who tormented her with names and threats of violence. Seventh grader Rachel Ehmke killed herself after what her parents said were months of abuse at her Kasson, Minnesota middle school. Several days before she took her life, an anonymous text message was sent out to other students at the school calling her a 'slut' who needed to be forced out of the school. (Thompson, 2012).

In another tragic case, a young Indian student committed suicide by hanging herself after two boys posted obscene comments about her on Facebook (Jalandhar, 2012). But probably the most cruel and sadistic example of online anonymity and the *disinhibition effect* is the tragic and untimely death of 13 year old Megan Meier. Megan began receiving nasty messages from a boy a few weeks after she met him, via her MySpace account. After many messages of kindness and support she received one telling her the 'world would be a better place without you'. Megan believed she had been rejected by the boy and committed suicide in her home. However, the boy never existed. He was an online character created by Lori Drew, a 47 year old married woman and a mother herself, who lived four houses down the street.

But it is not only social networking and the improper use of mobile devices which are having such a deleterious effect on our social relationships and our innate capacity for civility, compassion and kindness. The formal use of technology in education is undermining teaching and learning processes and the quest for knowledge. I mark hundreds of essays written by high school seniors every year for an international examining body, and I've noticed an exponential increase in the copying and pasting of information from websites-especially Wikipedia- without any real understanding of content. Moreover, I've also noted a reduced capacity for critical thinking and in-depth analysis from graduating high school seniors across the world.

Whereas teachers were once the bridge between the curriculum and the student, facilitating the teaching and learning processes, now technology is usurping that role, and the once strong, stable pillars of human reasoning, experience, empathy and understanding are being replaced by bridges of aluminum, fiberglass and fairy dust courtesy of Apple Inc., Samsung and Microsoft et.al. In most instances BYOD found across schools and tertiary institutions are basically edutainment platforms for audio-visual media, books, periodicals, movies, music, games, apps and web content. Yet they are being peddled and publicized by a marketing team of corporate moguls, book publishers and educators as a prerequisite for learning in the modern age. They are embraced equally with passion and determination by some teachers and administrators caught up in the youthful but naive claim that teaching and learning methodology and content is outdated and needs to be relevant (to what?), and realistic (whatever that means) and catch up to the 21st century.

Some international schools are even engaging in the marketing and advertising of children as young as five years old as digital natives; in a bid to win a greater share of the increasing lucrative IT funded educational sector. Children and young people, regardless of their age are no less human and no more digitally enhanced than their forbears. But they are vulnerable to ideological manipulation by those who would argue otherwise.

Science, Ethics and Digital Learning

For the most part we can fully appreciate and understand the gains to humanity through the development of technologies which assist and aid us in understanding and improving the human condition. Yet, on occasion events occurs which cause us to pause and reflect on where we are heading. Such a moment occurred for me after reading a BBC news report about a company which markets educational kits for children on learning neurosciences. It has developed a very small electronic device which is glued to the back of a cockroach. The hapless creature is then able to be physically manipulated and controlled through a downloadable app on a mobile phone. The digital user is able to control the movement of the unfortunate creature. Interestingly on the same page of this news story the BBC ran an advertisement on a program detailing the legacy of the Nazi medical experiments inclusive of a picture of Hitler- ironic or not, I thought the coincidence appropriate.

The company argues that through allowing children to dismember other creatures, place electronic devices into them and then control their movements they are giving them a 5-10 year head start on those in graduate schools studying neuroscience. They further argue that they are aware of the shortcomings of the kinds of experiments their bizarre equipment enables kids to perform on other creatures, but claim that they are justified due to the inaccessibility of neuroscience in our current elementary, middle and high school curricula. It is by all accounts a disingenuous and dishonest argument.

Many of us learned a lot at primary school about neuroscience without being asked to torture or dismember another creature. We may recall wonderful teachers who would take us for walks and lets us smell the earth, flowers, sea, and explain why we had such a painful reaction to standing on a broken shell, or nail or piece of glass-it was all quite wonderful, intriguing and followed up with diagrams and drawings of humans and other creatures on how the brain and central nervous system of sentient beings worked. We learned of the effects that dangerous creatures could have on our health and well being. It was an interactive, highly sociable communicative process which instilled in us a life long love of science and a mutual respect for all living creatures-even those we didn't like-the cockroach, spider and ants to name a few. We learned their role in the wonderful complex eco-system called life along with the importance of a human being's necessary moral relationship with other creatures.

It is the lack of awareness of the ethical concerns shown by the company towards our moral and ethical relationship with other creatures which should worry parents, educators and children alike. The thinking which underpins the digital concept of mobile learning by this company is based upon the myopic and disdainful arguments of early Western thinkers who claimed that humans lack any kind of contractual and ethical relationship with other creatures because they are not moral agents and they lack feelings, therefore if we do not perform experiments on them we are failing science. Such ideas have been used over the centuries to push some creatures to the edge of extinction through hunting and killing for their body parts. The same irrational arguments of Rousseau, Robert Boyle and Voltaire on race and the natural world were often used to enslave children, women and men of differing religions, politics, beliefs or color. According to the philosophy which underpins the work of this particular neuroscience start-up company, Rousseau's outrageous claim that "woman is especially made for man's delight" (Wexler, 1976) would be acceptable today! We have after all inherited the imperfect irrationality of Rousseau and his ilk on our relationships with other creatures.

There are much more acceptable moral and ethical ways to teach neuroscience to children in a digital age rather than having them turn defenseless and helpless creatures into electronic toys that may be controlled by a mobile phone application. Just as causing unnecessary pain and suffering to one another is unacceptable, it is unacceptable to cause pain and suffering to other creatures. The study of neural circuitry is important in medical science and has been studied at the appropriate age and level for many years with wonderful success. To argue that allowing children to capture, dismember and insert electrodes into the head and body of another creature will 'create the next generation of neural engineers, scientists and physicians' is disingenuous and dishonest. The kinds of experiments designed to harm other creatures and marketed by the company under the guise of digitally effective human scientific endeavors runs counter to an acceptable ethical and moral worldview we ought to be imparting to our children. Humans and other creatures have an equal interest in maintaining an eco-system –even in the digital age– which ensures the survival of all species. Other creatures matter a lot. It is this key idea which children need to understand and learn to live with more, to counter the emerging abuses associated with mobile learning in the digital age.

In addition to the nightmare scenario of apps which control other creatures at our pleasure there's also serious ethical issues emerging in how technology is being utilized in warfare and a country's national security policy. The use of drones in foreign countries, by the United States of America under presidency of a man who was nominated and won the Nobel Peace Prize in 2009 is an indication of things to come, notwithstanding its many contradictions. At the time of writing an merging international crisis is once again developing in the Crimea, yet this time cyber attacks by Russia on Ukraine's infrastructure are a central strategy in the propaganda war in attempts to break the morale of the Ukrainian people.

Time for Reflection

Notwithstanding the success of assistive and adaptive technologies for those with learning differences, there's no conclusive research and evidence which suggests that digital and mobile learning, (e-learning, m-learning, BYOD and the many other acronyms which are emerging in the field), online education such as distributed hybrid delivery systems, MOOCs, online language learning courses etc. is going to enhance and transform the learning success of school, college and university students. What we do know through research is that the kinds of experiences the iPad, laptop , mobile device or desk top computers or any other piece of educational technology offers is limited to the innate ability of the user to use these tools and the same time learn. In other words, we could convert every curriculum into an online course, and distribute a mobile learning device or lap-top or computer to every pre-school, school or college age student in the entire world, yet this will not make an iota of difference to whether they learn or not. Why? Well leaving aside intrinsic motivation, country, culture, social class and equal educational opportunities, the same cognitive processes are involved in learning whether the instructional tool is a person or a machine. Working memory, the key cognitive bridge between knowledge acquired and knowledge transformed through building on what's retained, functions under whatever environmental conditions it encounters in the teaching and learning process. However, the caveat is this; cognitive overload a psychological and intellectual state which occurs when too much material of an auditory, visual- spatial or narrative nature is presented, undermines and prevents the uptake of key information and knowledge sequences in the teaching and learning process. And presently the educational technology currently used in schools and colleges without impunity are designed to increase rather than decrease the likelihood of cognitive overload. Tools and applications which encourage multi-tasking (a very dubious concept in itself) in learning, do not always act as facilitators of learning; they simply provide seductive distractions to what is required to be taught, learnt and remembered. Human beings on the other hand, are better placed to avoid this pit-fall, as they understand and have empathy with the learning process-two key human qualities not yet mimicked through any technology available anywhere in the world.

The long-term effects of technology use on physical health are only beginning to be understood. Changes in the physiology of the brain have been detected through long-term online interaction; for example microstructure abnormalities in adolescents with internet addiction disorder suggests that poor goal directed behaviors along with impaired working memory are the direct result of prolonged long-term exposure to a computer or mobile learning device. (Yuan, et al., 2011) While the destructive and negative effects spawned through technology induced social behavior are now self-evident. The international mental health encyclopedia known as the 'Diagnostic and Statistical Manual of Mental Disorders' (DSM-IV) will include Internet-use disorder as a condition "recommended for further study" in its forthcoming May 2013 edition.

As educators, regardless of personal opinions and vested interests, we would be well advised to take heed of this, and to monitor the implementation of educational technology and the effects it has on the impressionable, vulnerable minds and bodies of those in our pre-schools, schools, colleges and universities. It is one thing to be swept up in the hype and technophoria of the current era and quite another to be held accountable for the long term psychological and corporeal effects and ethical consequences that mobile and computer based learning is having on the physical and mental well-being of present and future generations of learners.

References

Burke, L & McLaren, P, Spelling Achievement & Ability in ESL Tertiary Learners, *Empowering Learners through Educational Technology*, TESOL Arabia, 2011.

Burke, L, Multi-Tasking, Working Memory & Brain Functionality, *Empowering Learners through Educational Technology*, TESOL Arabia, 2011

Clark, R. E. (1983). Reconsidering research on learning from media. *Review of Educational Research*, 43(4), 445-459.

ITL Research: Innovative Teaching & Learning, www.itlresearch.com/images/stories/reports/ITL%20Research%202011%20Findings%20and%20Implications%20-%20Final.pdf

Jalandhar. (2012, August 16th). *Student hangs herself over obscene Facebook comments*. Retrieved October 13th, 2012, from Deccan Herald: http://www.deccanherald.com/

Mayer, R. E.; R. Moreno (1998). "A Cognitive Theory of Multimedia Learning: Implications for Design Principles". www.unm.edu/~moreno/PDFS/chi.pdf.

Moreno, R., & Mayer, R. (1999). "Cognitive principles of multimedia learning: The role of modality and contiguity". *Journal of Educational Psychology* 91: 358–368.

Mayer, R. E. (2001). *Multimedia learning.* New York: Cambridge University Press.

Moreno, R. & Mayer, R. E. (2002). Verbal redundancy in multimedia learning: When reading helps listening. *Journal of Educational Psychology*, 94, 156-163.

Mayer, R. E. (2002). Cognitive theory and the design of multimedia instruction: An example of the two-way street between cognition and instruction. In D. F. Halpern & M. D. Hakel (Eds.), *Applying the science of learning to university teaching and beyond* (pp. 55-72). San Francisco: Jossey-Bass.

Milken Exchange Study on Ed. Tech. Meta-analysis (1999) www.mff.org/pubs/ME161.pdf

Postman, N, *Technopoly: The Surrender of Culture to Technology*, Vintage Books, 1992, New York

Thompson, P. (2012, October 13th). *Girl, 13, hangs herself after months of torment at hands of girls who scrawled 'slut' on her school locker and warned her to leave.* Retrieved October 13th, 2012, from Mail Online: www.dailymail.co.uk/home/index.html

Wexler, V. (1976). Made for Man's Delight Rousseau as AntiFeminist. *The American Historical Review*, Vol.81.No.2, 266-279.

Yuan, K., Qin, W., Wang, G., Zeng, F., Zhao, L., Yang, X., et al. (2011). Microstructure Abnormalities in Adolescents with Internet Addiction Disorder. PLOS , 1-21.

Chapter 5

iPad therefore iLearn? Part 1

Michelle Rogers-Estable and Roudaina Houjeir

Introduction

In April 2012 the United Arab Emirates' (UAE) federally-managed education system implemented iPads across nationally-supported basic literacy programs. The goal was to imbed multimedia technology that would aid students in ESL and math content acquisition. The federal system comprises three different university systems that serve more than 41,000 students (Cavanaugh, Hargis, Munns & Kamali, 2013). The use of iPads in education is gaining recognition around the globe and the effective application of this new technology into any curriculum requires a modification of teaching and learning practices and approaches. In support of this aim a series of professional development programs were offered to teachers across the tertiary sector in the UAE in support of technology-enhanced learning using iPads in the classroom.

The iPad professional development programs encouraged engagement of teachers and students through high quality mobile learning design and delivery, including: iPads as cognitive tool boxes; applying student-centered teaching and learning practices; peer-to-peer collaboration of best practices; and inclusion of internal and external stakeholders in the design and delivery process (Cavanaugh, 2013). A series of conferences and workshops across the tertiary sector encouraged teachers to share best practices and methods with each other.

As of September 2013 a significant number of teachers in the UAE have been using modified and augmented curricular practices with iPads in the classroom for two full semesters. This chapter reports on some perceived effective practices using iPad applications in education.

Background

It is argued that a clear definition of mobile learning is elusive (El-Hussein and Cronje, 2010) and difficult to clarify since mobile learning is an evolving field with expanding terms (Rossing, Miller, Cecil, & Stamper, 2012). El-Hussein and Cronje (2010) have defined mobile learning as

> any type of learning that takes place in learning environments and spaces that take account of the mobility of technology, mobility of learners, and mobility of learning (p 20).

Traxler (2005) defined mobile learning as

> any educational provision where the sole or dominant technologies are handheld or palmtop devices (p 262)

which included all portable devices and a Bring Your Own Device (BYOD) approach. A definition for eLearning is

> the use of electronic media and devices through networks and interactive telecommunication system to connect learners, resources, and teachers (Association of Educational Communications and Technology).

Rossing *et al* define mobile learning as

> the efficient and effective use of wireless and digital devices and technologies to enhance learners' individual outcomes during participation in learning activities.

These four definitions all hit upon essential characteristics important to iPad use as a medium in the classroom: anytime learning, anywhere learning, any-device learning, access to networks, and finally connections between learners, teachers, and learning materials. For the purpose of this chapter, we connect these definitions, and define mobile learning as learning that is constructed anywhere, anytime, and any-device learning is learning available through networks and interactive telecommunication systems to enhance connections between students, learning resources, and teachers.

Current mobile learning developers and designers point to the development of teaching and learning practices in conjunction with the integration of mobile technologies into educational programs (Traxler, 2007). Mobile learning (mLearning) offers educational groups the opportunity to connect and learn outside the walls of the traditional classroom (Alexander, 2006), and facilitates opportunities for students to approach education from a variety of different learning styles (Rossing et al., 2012).

Some of the research suggests that enhanced engagement is central to positive student learning outcomes (Prince, 2004). Through enhanced engagement, students can benefit from learning that is more hands on and collaborative, and this may contribute to improving their critical thinking skills (Cavanaugh, 2013; Crawford & Vahey, 2002; Crawford & Vahey, 2002; van 't Hooft, Brown-Martin, & Swan, 2008).

Mobile learning may include distance learning activities that students do in their own time, or as blended learning activities where mobile technologies and lessons are incorporated into regular face-to-face courses. This latter situational use of mobile technologies has been introduced at The Higher Colleges of Technology in the UAE with a degree of success.

In the UAE's new iPad integrated learning environments, the teacher uses the iPad as a teaching aid to create more interactive and engaging face-to-face learning materials and activities for students (Cavanaugh, Hargis, Munns, & Kamali, 2012). This chapter shares some of the iPad teaching and learning approaches across several campuses within the Higher Colleges of Technology in an effort to describe successful best practices that other teachers may in turn adopt it into their own practice.

Each example used literacy skills which have been formulated from Bloom's Understanding, and Gardner's Multiple Intelligences as follows:

Basic literacy: An individual's ability to read, write, speak in English, compute and solve problems at levels of proficiency necessary to function on the job, in the family of the individual, and in society.

Critical literacy: An individual's ability to critically think through logical thinking and reasoning.

Digital literacy: An individual's and ability to use computers and related technology efficiently, with a range of skills covering levels from elementary use to programming and advanced problem solving.

Environmental literacy: An individual's basic understanding of ecological principles and the ways society affects, or responds to, environmental conditions.

Media literacy: An individual's ability to question, analyze, interpret, evaluate, and create media messages.

Global literacy: An individual's ability to understand and appreciate the similarities and differences in the customs, values, and beliefs of one's own culture the cultures of others.

Creative literacy: An individual's ability to communicate imaginatively in any medium.

Health literacy: An individual's capacity to obtain, process, and understand basic health information and services needed to make appropriate health decisions

Approach

We wanted to examine the current attitudes and best practices in integration of iPad apps and activities into curriculum planning. We reviewed and reported on the data from online volunteer-based questionnaires concerning uses of iPads with students. The online survey was sent to current practicing teachers within the Higher Colleges of Technology Foundations program, which is comprised of math and English studies for first year students.

In response to the open-ended questions on two things teachers liked and disliked about using iPads in the classroom the following points were highlighted:

Table 1. Reported Likes and Dislikes of Using iPads in Education.

Likes	Dislikes
• No need for paper and pen.	• Secured testing is difficult.
• Students don't forget it (unlike textbooks and laptops).	• Many iPads on Wifi at same time can slow down connections.
• Integration of camera and other tools offer multiple creative options and more fluid instructional presentations.	• Students are not developing hand-writing skills.
• Great pair and group work tool.	• Can be difficult to monitor and control if students are sticking to task.
• Easy to use.	• iPad Pens do not allow precise writing.
• Fast to use.	• Students may not like to switch iPads for group work due to privacy concerns.
• Quick switching between different apps in same lesson.	• Technical glitches and app or tool malfunctions delay lectures.
• Adaptability – many app and tool options for any lesson need.	• Students with poor typing skills have more difficulty.
• Excellent for writing, recording, and sharing class notes.	• Can be distracting. (Games were mentioned repeatedly).
• 'In vogue' media use keeps student attention.	• Battery life is too short, and difficult to get replaced.
• Allows different students to work at different paces.	• The cost of some apps limits their use.
• Quick access to Internet resources.	• Screen too small for some tasks
• Well-designed eTexts are interactive, with many on one device.	• Word processing options inferior to MS Word.
• Students are motivated to use it.	• Difficult to see and correct students' work (to take submissions of assignments).
• Supports learning-by-doing.	• eBooks inadequate replacement for normal textbooks.
• Portable – for both students and the teacher.	• Set up of iPad and associated tools and resources can be cumbersome.
• Teacher can walk around among students while presenting.	• Lack of file manager.
• Offers students opportunity to learn more on their own time.	• Technical issues with the Apple TV interferes with instructional presentations and class time.

We have selected the following iPad activities to share in this chapter:

Name of Method:	*Vocabulary Expansion Through Audio Recording*
Teacher:	Tandy Bailey
Apps / Tools used:	Garage Band, SoundCloud, and Qrafter (QR codes)
Difficulty of Use:	
Subject:	English / ESL
Level:	2
21st Century Literacies:	Basic Literacy, Digital Literacy, Creative Literacy
Bloom's Understandings:	Remembering, Understanding, Applying, Creating
Gardner's Multiple Intelligences:	Linguistic, Bodily-Kinesthetic, Interpersonal, Intrapersonal
T&L Methods Used:	Peer-to-peer learning, review-n-redo learning
Activity Time:	Three hours
Short Description:	The teacher had students record a description of their best friend using key vocabulary with Garage Band, and then they sent that clip to SoundCloud where the teacher made a QR code from the recordings and posted them around the room. Then students used the Qrafter app to scan the code and then listen to their friends' descriptions. They had a checklist of the vocabulary to listen for and tick off.
Lesson Plan:	Following is a brief lesson plan: 1. Students are divided into teams of two. 2. Students write about their team member using target vocabulary centered on appearance, interests and personality. 3. Students submit this draft to the teacher who quickly corrects errors and returns the paper to the students. 4. Students re-write the description. 5. Students then audio record their description using Garage Band. 6. Students upload the sound file into Sound Cloud, using the teacher's login information. 7. On a PC, the teacher converts the sound files in Sound Cloud (Click on EDIT to get URL) into QR Codes by pasting the URL into www.qrstuff.com/ 8. The teacher prints the QR codes for each recording onto paper. 9. The teacher makes a table of the target vocabulary for students. 10. The teacher places the QR Codes around the room. 11. Students scan the QR Codes with the app Qrafter, listen to the sound files (this requires headphones), and tick the vocabulary they hear. 12. Follow up with a spelling quiz.

Other Notes:	This method gives students the chance to use the vocabulary in speaking and next in listening. They had to focus on what was being said. They reported that it was fun and interesting and that it helped them learn the target vocabulary.
Resources:	More QR Code ideas: www.schrockguide.net/qr-codes-in-the-classroom.html fispsipads.wordpress.com/

Name of Method:	*Visual Teaching of Modal Grammar*
Author:	Robert Dobie
Apps / Tools used:	Built-in Camera, Pages
Difficulty of Use:	2
Subject:	ESL
Level:	2
21st Century Literacies:	Basic Literacy, Critical Literacy, Digital Literacy, Creative Literacy
Bloom's Understandings:	Applying, Analyzing, Creating
Gardner's Multiple Intelligences:	Spatial, Linguistic, Bodily-Kinesthetic
T&L Methods Used:	Peer-to-peer learning
Activity Time:	1 Hour
Short Description:	Teaching grammar: Modal: may / might. Students work for 20 minutes both inside and outside the classroom. They take 'close-up' pictures of objects (they must know the word of the objects). Pictures are later shown to classmates (in small groups) who have to guess what the objects are (*eg* 'I think it might be a ...'). Points are awarded for correct guesses and a winner is chosen.
Lesson Plan:	This iPad Lesson is practice with modals of probability (must, might, could, may, can't) and vocabulary building. 1. Write the following short dialog on the white board: • What do you think this is? • I think it must/might/could/may/can't be a 2. The teacher provides students with a vocabulary list of common objects, for example: • tree • flower • stone • insect • sidewalk • car • wheel • book • desk • chair • fire extinguisher • door • wall • *etc.* 3. The teacher models the activity by mirroring two or three of his/her own photos that she/he took before class. • Some of the objects in the photos should be on the list of objects above.

<table>
<tr><td></td><td>

4. Have the students try to guess what the objects are by using the short dialog above.
   - To make the activity more difficult, begin by zooming in on each photo – by pinching out – and then gradually expanding the photo.
   - Tip: the photos should have been taken relatively close-up, so that each object is not easily identifiable. Also, for the purpose of class demonstration, each of the teacher's photos should have been copied and pasted into the Pages app (mirrored photos in the camera roll do not zoom in or out; it is necessary to use another app for this).
5. Allow the students ten or 15 minutes to roam about the classroom, the hallway, parking lot, *etc* (mirror a count-down timer to help enforce a strict time limit, or the teacher may lose some students!).
6. Students should take several close-up shots of objects that are on the list, and even some that are not on the list.
7. After the students return to class, have them sit down in small groups and practice the activity/dialog with their own photos.
8. Wrap-up with one student standing and practicing (with one or two photos) with the whole class.
9. Answer any vocabulary-related questions that students may have.
10. Create and send out the list of new words (both from the original list and that came up during the lesson).

</td></tr>
</table>

Other Notes:	This activity enhances learners' interest and motivation in studying grammar.
Resources:	The inspiration for this activity came from children's activity books and television programs where children try to guess the objects from close-up photos.

Name of Method:	*Marking Writing with Explain Everything*
Author:	David Edwards FMC - English Faculty
Apps / Tools used:	Pages, DropBox, Screen capture/photos, Explain Everything (or other video app; Ask3, Educreations, etc.)
Difficulty of Use:	Easy
Subject:	English / ESL
Level:	Level 2 and 3 or Pre-University Bridge Program (CEFR A2 – B2)
21st Century Literacies:	Critical Literacy, Digital Literacy, Media Literacy, Global Literacy, Creative Literacy
Bloom's Understandings:	Remembering, Understanding, Applying, Analyzing, Evaluating, Creating
Gardner's Multiple Intelligences:	Spatial Intelligence, Linguistic Intelligence, Logical-Mathematical Intelligence, Bodily-Kinesthetic Intelligence, Interpersonal Intelligence, Intrapersonal Intelligence

T&L Methods Used:	Individual
Activity Time:	Five minutes per 100-120 words.
Short Description:	Teacher using app Explain Everything to provide feedback for student's writing. He had the students submit a piece of writing in Pages or Notes, and then he took a screenshot of it. He imported it into Explain Everything and recorded himself speaking while marking their writing. He has already taught them a few simple proofreading symbols, which he reinforces in the video markup. This provided them with a shareable knowledge object that they can pause, rewind or watch again.`` This gave the students something of value, rather than a paper covered in indecipherable marks that they may not visit again.
Lesson Plan:	Following is a brief lesson plan: 1. Students submit a piece of writing on pages or notes. 2. The teacher marks Student Writing with Explain Everything to provide feedback for the students. 3. The teacher, 'Why hand back students' graded writing covered in indecipherable and mute proofreading symbols when they can easily turn it into a dynamic shareable knowledge object (SKO)?' 4. The teacher asks students to submit writing they've created with Notes or Pages (or other) to a DropBox folder they share with the teacher. 5. The teacher takes a screenshot of it. 6. The teacher imports that photo into an app that provides screen recording. 7 The teacher looks at student work to get an overall feel for the submission; turn on the record button and think aloud while you're making your suggestions. 8. The teacher record himself speaking while marking their writing. 9. The teacher teaches students a few simple proofreading characters and lets them see and hear why these inscriptions are appearing on their text. 10. The teacher provides students with a shareable knowledge object that they can pause, rewind or watch again. 11. Students embed videos in their Creative Book Builder or Ever Note to enhance their learning journals.
Other Notes:	This method gives students a marked increase in the accuracy of their writing. They didn't make the same mistakes as often. This method is still relatively novel, and the teacher hasn't been tracking results in any action research way as yet.
Resources:	Table of stylus-friendly writing symbols here: webster.commnet.edu/writing/symbols.htm)

Name of Method:	*Vocabulary Expansion Through Shake 'n Make*
Author:	Baha Eddin Abu Khait English teacher
Apps / Tools used:	Shake 'n Make
Difficulty of Use (1-5, 5 being very difficult):	1
Subject:	ESL
Level:	All Levels
21st Century Literacies:	Basic Literacy, Critical Literacy, Digital Literacy
Bloom's Understandings:	Remembering, Creating
Gardner's Multiple Intelligences:	Linguistic Intelligence, Bodily-Kinesthetic Intelligence .
T&L Methods Used:	Peer-to-peer learning, groups and individually.
Activity Time:	5-10 minutes
Short Description:	Students shake their iPads and then two letters pop up in two bubbles. They had to type a word that started with the first letter and ended with the second one. The exercise can be practiced in pairs and groups as a class contest.
Lesson Plan:	Following is a brief lesson plan: The teacher divides students into groups of four or five. Students shake their iPads. Then two letters pop up in two bubbles. Students have to type a word that starts with the first letter and ends with the second one. The winning team is the one with the highest score The teacher adjusts the difficulty (easy/medium/hard) according to the class level. No need to set time limit as the game has its own timer. The game can also be played individually.
Other Notes:	This exercise is very motivating and adds lots of energy to vocabulary lessons. It helps learners with building up their lexical repertoire, memorizing new words and practicing spelling.
Resources:	Shake 'n Make, Opposites

Name of Method:	*Project Management through iPad Integration*
Author:	Aaron Matte
Apps / Tools used:	Bb Learn, YouTube, Nearpod, Explain Everything, Notes Anytime, Box, Keynote, and iMovie.

Difficulty of Use:	3
Subject:	ESL
Level:	2
21st Century Literacies:	Critical Literacy, Digital Literacy, Media Literacy, Creative Literacy
Bloom's Understandings:	Remembering, Understanding, Applying, Analyzing, Evaluating, Creating
Gardner's Multiple Intelligences:	Linguistic, Logical-Mathematical
T&L Methods Used:	Flipped classroom, mobile / blended learning, project-based learning, leadership-based learning.
Activity Time:	One week
Short Description:	The iPad was used to support a blended, flipped classroom delivery of a mini-project. The Make Life a Better Place Project was a short project concerning improvement of a local space. Students used the iPad as both a consumption and production tool, and to access reading resources and core activities supporting the project, and instructional video lectures. As a production tool they communicated ideas and opinions by creating multimedia presentations for the project. Finally, they used the iPad as a mobile fieldwork tool for recording, taking pictures and videos for the project.
Lesson Plan:	This lesson plan is one part of a week-long blended-learning project using the iPad as a mobile learning device. **Pre-project Steps** 1. At the start, students access a short tutorial video about the grammar target, then complete a short guess and check activity in real-time with the video. 2. Next, students confirm their understanding in a short online Q&A concept check with immediate feedback. 3. Then students take a quiz. **Project Steps** 1. Students choose a place on campus or their local community and describe it through a multi-media production and presentation about it. Apps used by students for this have included (but are not limited to): Explain Everything, iMovie, KeyNote. 2. Students analyze, determine, and organize their recommended changes the place should have in order to improve it. 3. Students combine their action plan, notes, and videos and images into a multimedia presentation they give to the class.
Other Notes:	The iPad and its use makes the students more active and engaged learners. It 'reformats' their understanding of their role in their learning, and I've done my best to develop and design tasks that leverage these new expectations. Students can work at their own pace; they are encouraged to skip scaffolding tasks and accelerate, as they like. Alternatively, students can take their time, review instructional material, and complete tasks more than once until they get it right, free from in-class distractions.

Name of Method:	*Exploiting Language Skills through Creating an Online Magazine*
Author:	Emily Saavedra
Apps / Tools used:	SOUNDNOTE, ZITE
Difficulty of Use:	1
Subject:	English/ESL
Level:	Foudations, Level 4
21st Century Literacies:	Basic Literacy, Critical Literacy, Digital Literacy, Media Literacy and Global Literacy
Bloom's Understandings:	Remembering, Understanding, Applying, Analyzing, Evaluating, Creating
Gardner's Multiple Intelligences:	Linguistic Intelligence, Interpersonal Intelligence
T&L Methods Used:	Peer-to-Peer learning, Group Based Learning, Flipped Classroom
Activity Time:	Two hours
Short Description:	This method gives students the chance to set up their own personalized online magazine using ZITE. First students choose topics of interest and are asked to select an article that they enjoyed or found interesting. They then record a brief summary or commentary on the article using SOUNDNOTE, and share their recordings with each other.
Lesson Plan:	Following is a brief lesson plan: **Part I** 1. Teacher walks students through setting up their own personalized magazine using ZITE (or a similar app). 2. Teacher asks students to select a minimum of 5 topics of personal interest to start with and students set up their magazine. 3. Teacher reviews skimming and scanning techniques, and then student scan for topics of interest. 4. The teacher allocates 20 minutes for individual silent reading time of the topics. 5. Teacher asks students to be able to choose 2 articles of interest at the end of this time and there is a class discussion about the topics they chose. **Part II** 6. The teacher demonstrates the use of the recording function in SoundNote. 7. The teacher asks students to choose one article. 8. Students open SoundNote and type the title of the article in (or they can copy and paste). 9. Students record a brief description, ± 2 mins, of what they remember from the article and their personal opinion about it (they should be discouraged from writing a script to read from). Students should focus on fluency and content. 10. Students may record, listen and re-record if necessary until they are happy with their recording.

	Part III
	11. Students choose a partner they trust and physically exchange iPads.
	12. The partner should listen to the recording, pausing when necessary, and try to type what they hear.
	13. The partner can use the pen function to annotate, any areas for improvement, discussion, questions, fluency, syntax, text construction, and connectors.
	14. iPads are returned followed by pair discussions of articles, annotations, and conversation practice.
Other Notes:	Students complete this lesson in two separate parts/lessons (part one first followed by parts two and three combined), combined into a double class, or flipped (part two done at home). Students choose their own content and so are more likely to engage with it. Students often choose topics that I might have traditionally shied away from and I find they experiment more with a variety of topics. This means when we come back together as a group to report on each others choices they are very animated in what they can teach each other. Referring to the questions below regarding 21st Century digital literacy skills I think most, if not all, can be relevant depending on the commentaries made and the topics chosen.
Resources:	Zite: itunes.apple.com/ae/app/zite/id419752338?mt=8 SoundNote: itunes.apple.com/ae/app/soundnote/id364789577?mt=8

Name of Method:	*Writing Improvement Through Knowledge Objects*
Author:	Alaa Selim
Apps / Tools used:	Live-paper App
Difficulty of Use:	2
Subject:	Math
Level:	Any Level starting from Foundation to Calculus
21st Century Literacies:	Basic Literacy, Critical Literacy, Digital Literacy, Media Literacy and Creative Literacy
Bloom's Understandings:	Remembering, Understanding, Applying, Analyzing, Evaluating, Creating
Gardner's Multiple Intelligences:	Spatial Intelligence, Linguistic Intelligence, Logical-Mathematical Intelligence, Interpersonal Intelligence, Intrapersonal Intelligence.
T&L Methods Used:	Peer-to-Peer learning, Group Based Learning, Flipped Classroom, Learning-by-doing, Challenge-Based Learning.
Activity Time:	Any Class Time period.
Short Description:	Teacher was able to utilize an app. called Live-paper full as a smart board (full use to all tools of a smart board) and had used it during all lectures (writing-recording-link to internet and many other useful features).

Lesson Plan:	Following is a brief lesson plan: 15. Teacher uses Live-paper App. as a smart board for writing class notes, recording, and linking to internet, and for sending notes and recorded lectures to students. 16. Students receive by email a soft-copy and a recorded lecture for the lesson so they can review the content at home and at their own pace. 17. Students save all class lectures for future studies and test review. 18. Students can use the app to complete class projects (using all the app. features cut/paste/recording/taking pictures).
Other Notes:	This method gives students the chance to have the lectures and the notes with them at home for further studies. It was like having their Teacher with them at home (recorded lectures and notes). They were able to save all class notes throughout the semester and this helped them in preparing for exams. They were also able to complete their learning-by-doing project through the use of Live-paper full.
Resources:	www.geogebra.org

Name of Method:	*Writing Improvement Through Interactive iPad DLOs*
Teacher:	John Vogels
Apps / Tools:	Authoring tool SoftChalk, Blackboard learn mobile app for the iPad, iMovie, Pages
Difficulty (Scale of 1-5):	3
Subject:	English / ESL
Level (1-4):	2, 3
21st Century Digital Literacies:	Basic Literacy
Bloom's Understandings:	Remembering, Understanding, Applying, Analyzing
Gardner's Multiple Intelligences:	Linguistic
T&L Methods Used:	Peer-to-peer learning, group-based learning, review-n-redo learning
Activity Time:	Varies
Short Description:	Using an authoring tool that makes mobile-ready digital learning objects (DLOs) and lesson, such as Softchalk that was used in this case, the teacher created an online writing and grammar course accessed through BBLearn on the iPads. The DLO gave instant feedback to students as well as being available anytime, anywhere, for students to practice. Students receive feedback and rewrites through Pages.

Lesson Plan:	Following is a brief lesson plan: 1. Teacher creates a digital learning object (DLO) with SoftChalk for a course in Blackboard. It is a lesson on the given topic. 2. Teacher then leads a face-to-face discussion with the students on the topic, including review of questions presented to the class. 3. Student access the DLO in Blackboard on their iPads, via the Bb Learn mobile app, and study the activity and content on their own. As students are working individually or collectively on the SoftChalk DLO, The teacher gives one on one feedback to individuals on previous writing assignments. 4. Students then submit their work in Softchalk that gives the teacher information such as time spent on lesson, a score for short answer and multiple choice questions and also the writing assignment for the unit to the teacher. 5. The teacher reviews and edits the work in Pages, and emails it back to the students to redo using a supplied checklist of items to revise. In order to develop the students self-editing skills. 6. Students then use iMovies to create a video about their writing and add the movie along with their rewritten assignment to their Writing Portfolio that they have created in CBB – Creative Book Builder.
Other Notes:	Introduces new materials and allows for students to interact and learn with peers and receive individual feed back.
Resources:	SoftChalk is one of many authoring tools one can use to make interactive Digital Learning Objects. Others are WImba Create, StudyMate, and Raptivity. However, SoftChalk and Raptivity create HTML5 DLOs that are iPad/mobile ready.

Discussion

Among the benefits of iPads to education, many of the teachers pointed out that flexibility in tool choice was a key factor. That is, if one tool didn't quite do what they needed, or had some technical glitches, there were plenty of other similar tools they could choose to replace it. Sampled teachers also liked that the iPad offered many educational needs in one, small, portable device, including access not only to all the tools, but access to files, taking notes, sharing notes and lectures, and reading eBooks. Several teachers listed the portability of the iPad as a key benefit, in that students were more likely to remember to bring it to class, and that the teacher could use AirPlay and thus walk around the room with it during their presentation, which allowed them to keep students on task and away from distractors such as video games.

The drawbacks to iPads listed by currently practicing teachers included pedagogy, infrastructure and technical support, and distractions.

Problems with access to Wifi or other technical problems were barriers to smooth implementation of the iPad in the classroom. The setup of iPads and apps caused delays in teaching time. The lack of a file manager, or an easy means of submitting, grading, and returning student work, was another drawback. Finally, the smaller screen-size and cost of some apps limited some types of activities.

Teachers who responded to this survey used a variety of different types of tools. The iPad apps Explain Everything and Popplet were both mentioned as being excellent tools for remedial English activities. Every activity save two used at least two or more apps or tool in conjunction, switching between them at various points during the learning activity. Most methods include using a series of tools, software and apps in collaboration with each other, and iPads do offer a unique ability to access a variety of user tools, and further offer flexibility in the tools.

Overall, teachers in this survey reported satisfaction with the iPad, and felt that students were more engaged in learning. However, this type of sampling method has the drawback of bias, as it was volunteer-based, and the teachers willing to submit the survey may also be those who perceive disproportionately higher levels of value with the iPad.

Future directions for similar research would be to collect methods from teachers and combine them into a book on curricular approaches that can be used to support teacher training. This study focused on math and English activities; however, it would benefit the community to capture effective practices across different domains since faculty teaching different subjects areas will apply methods using different curricular approaches, and will use different tools.

It is also important to study further the types of teaching and learning practices being implemented, such as looking with greater detail into how peer-to-peer, collaborative, project, and flipped learning are taking place. Collecting these kinds of snapshots into current teaching and learning practices would offer further insight into digital learning practices.

References

Alexander, B. (2004). Going nomadic: Mobile learning in higher education. *Educause Review, 39*(5), 6.

Cavanaugh, C. (2013). An engaged and engaging learning ecosystem: Early findings from a large-scale college iPad program. iNACOL Ed Tech blog. Retrieved from researchinreview.inacol.org/2013/10/02/cathy-cavanaugh-an-engaged-and-engaging-mobile-learning-ecosystem-for-k-12-online-and-blended-learning/

Cavanaugh, C., Hargis, J., Kamali, T., and Soto, M. (March 2013). An engaged and engaging mobile learning ecosystem: Early findings from a large scale college iPad program. Presented at the BCS International IT Conference, 31 March–1 April, Fairmont Hotel, Abu Dhabi, UAE

Cavanaugh, C., Hargis, J., Munns, S., & Kamali, T. (2012). iCelebrate Teaching and Learning: Sharing the iPad Experience. *Journal of Teaching and Learning with Technology, 1*(2), 1-12.

Crawford, V., & Vahey, P. (2002). Innovating the Use of Handheld Technology in K-12 Teaching and Learning: Results from the Palm Education Pioneers Program. Presented at the American Educational Research Association Annual Conference. New Orleans, April 1-5, 2002.

Diemer, T. T., Fernandez, E. & Streepey, J. W. (2012). Student perceptions of classroom engagement and learning using iPads. *Journal of Teaching and Learning with Technology*, 1(2), 13-25.

El-Hussein, M. O. M., & Cronje, J. C. (2010). Defining Mobile Learning in the Higher Education Landscape. *Educational Technology & Society, 13* (3), 12–21

Fowler, F. J., Jr. (2009). *Survey research methods* (4th ed.; L. Brickman & D. J. Rog, Eds.). Thousand Oaks, CA: Sage.

Gay, L. R., Mills, G. E., & Airasian, P. (2006). *Educational research: Competencies for analysis and applications.* Upper Saddle River, NJ: Pearson Prentice Hall.

Lodico, M. G., Spaulding, D. T., & Voegtle, K. H. (2010). *Methods in educational research: From theory to practice.* San Francisco, CA: Jossey-Bass.

McConnell, B., & McConnell, S. (2011, June 26-29). Mobile Devices in a Project-Based Physics Classroom: Developing NETS-S in Students. Paper presented at the International Society for Technology in Education (ISTE) conference, Pennsylvania, PA.

Prince, M. (2004). Does active learning work? A review of the research. *Journal of Engineering Education, 93*(3), 223-231.

Rice, A. (2011, October 18). Colleges take varied approaches to iPad experiments, with mixed results. *The Chronicle of Higher Education.* Retrieved from chronicle.com/blogs/wiredcampus/colleges-take-varied-approaches-to-ipad-experiments-with-mixed-results/33749

Rossing, J. P., Miller, W. M., Cecil A. K., & Stamper, S. E. (2012). iLearning: The future of higher education? Student perceptions on learning with mobile tablets. *Journal of the Scholarship of Teaching and Learning, 12*(2), 1-26.

Traxler, J (2005). Defining mobile learning. IADIS International Conference Mobile Learning. Retrieved from www.academia.edu/2810810/Defining_mobile_learning

Traxler, J. (2007). Defining, discussing, and evaluating mobile learning: The moving finger writes and having writ. The International Review on Open and Distance Learning, 8, 1-13. Retrieved from www.irrodl.org/index.php/irrodl/article/view/346/875

Trochim, W. M. K. (2006). *Nonprobability sampling.* Retrieved from www. socialresearchmethods.net/kb/sampnon.php

van 't Hooft, M., Brown Martin, G., & Swan, K. (2008). Anytime, anywhere learning using mobile devices. In L. Tomei (Ed.), *The encyclopedia of instructional technology curriculum integration* (pp. 37-42). Hershey, PA: Idea Group References. Retrieved from www.rcet.org/research/publications/Tomei37_Anywhere_2008.pdf

Chapter 6

iPad therefore iLearn?
Part 2

Dianne Evans

Introduction

Apple Inc has had notable success in iPad sales, reaching 170 million in October 2013 (Hughes, 2013). The sales figures in education to date are 4.5 million sold to US educational institutions and 8 million sold worldwide (Jordan, 2013). What is the story behind the mass introduction of iPads in the United Arab Emirates (UAE), indeed some could argue enforced introduction for some teachers and students, to use iPads as tools for learning in 2012?

The context of this chapter is the experience of the introduction of iPads, the largest adoption undertaken up to December 2012 according to Robby & Gitsaki (2013), into a community college environment offering higher education programmes in the framework of traditional semester-based courses with the requirement for traditional assessment strategies. Senior managers of the institution displayed a remarkable determination that the iPads would revolutionise the learning experience, using positive terminology with teachers such as 'iCelebrate' to influence perceptions of change.

It is planned to provide an initial review of the use of iPads in education, establish the pedagogical issues with e-learning and explore the claims made by interested parties regarding the benefits of using iPads. The questions I will address in this chapter are:

iPads in education: planned strategic development or effective marketing?

What are the strengths and weaknesses of learning online?

How will the iPad affect pedagogy and vice versa?

What are the benefits and drawbacks of iPads for the teacher?

the Apple marketing education strategy

Apple Inc is well-known for vigorous and innovative marketing of their products. A division totally devoted to education was launched in 1979. The senior vice president for world-wide marketing at Apple Inc, Phil Schiller, said that 'Education is deep in our DNA, and it has been from the very beginning.' (Hong, 2013). In 2012 he announced that 'more than 1.5 million iPads are in use in educational programs and that the App Store currently has over 20,000 education related apps' (Brian, 2012).

Other than an effective way to sell products, particularly to young people, was there an Apple vision to transform education? Isaacson (2012) reported Rupert Murdoch's recollection of Steve Jobs' dismissal of the notion of education being transformed by technology. However, Jobs did agree that 'the paper textbook business would be blown away by digital learning materials'.

Isaacson reported that Jobs had the objective of transforming the $8 billion a year textbook business by 'digital destruction'. He was concerned about the weight of student backpacks and planned to work with publishers such as Pearson to offer the textbooks free of charge on iPads. Such a collaboration would be a huge advantage for iPad sales in education, although the deal does not appear to be in the favour of the publishing companies.

General problems of online learning

The last decade has seen a radical development in technology which has been adopted in education. However, as noted by Alonso et al (2005), there is a lack of equivalent pedagogical development or curriculum design. Over the years, we have continued to add on technological resources to a traditional educational structure that is becoming something like Frankenstein's monster. There is pressure from educational theorists and management to stay up-to-date, but educators are rarely given the time to fully develop ideas and, more importantly, radically overhaul the curriculum to fully incorporate new learning and assessment vehicles to take advantage of technology.

My recent experience of being involved in curriculum design is an excellent example of disjoined thinking. As a teaching team we had been told by senior managers that all teachers and students would have to use iPads in the upcoming academic year – a radical development which was celebrated by educational leaders.

Conversely, in the same year a curriculum development team was told to use textbooks and professional websites to develop learning objectives and lecture content. The team-leader of my group did not mention iPads or how they could change the way that the curriculum could be delivered. The system curriculum managers who checked our work did not discuss the impact of the iPad to urge us to 'think differently'. It was a lost opportunity to completely reconfigure how the courses should be delivered and it was left to the individual teachers to manage, adapt and transform traditional material on what should be an interactive device. It is a clear example of traditional curriculum design viewed separately to the new tools on offer, with no attempt to integrate the facilities available on the iPad.

Alonso *et al* discussed how 'the internet has radically changed the teaching paradigm' and note that:

> There is a serious dysfunction between the profusion of technological features that are put forward and the shortage or non-existence of teaching principles for e-learning. (p 218)

Some early adopters of the iPad as an educational tool have enthused about using the device to facilitate independent learning and collaboration, packaged as constructivism. A warning bell sounded at reading such comments. How many subjects can have multiple interpretations? While it may promote engagement to give learners a topic and tell them to find information using the iPad, what are the issues about time management and accuracy? How do we know that learning is taking place? What is the role of the teacher in this activity?

Alonso *et al* advocate that 'the best teaching policy is to provide the subject-related conceptual models and substructures' to avoid misinterpretation of data by learners. These errors can then be passed on if learners are encouraged to collaborate and share their ideas, reinforcing incomplete or inaccurate knowledge. Constructivism – the methodology of expecting learners to discover a topic independently – is not effective for every topic and, if used all the time, can provoke a backlash from the learners.

In 2007 I had a class of teenagers rebelling at my constructivist approach, shouting "teach us – tell us!". Some iPad enthusiasts have reported that learners felt stressed at using unfamiliar technology which relies on the internet, and insecure about the validity of their search for information. Constructivist learning activities need constant feedback and guidance and that is the role of the teacher in the design of the learning as well as facilitating learner activities.

Alonso *et al* propose an e-learning instructional model for using learning management systems which has been summarised below:

Stage 1: analysis of what needs to be taught leading to clear learning objectives, a definition of knowledge and skills to be acquired and a breakdown of appropriate tasks to fulfil identified outcomes. A useful adjustment to their first stage in a true e-learning environment would be to analyse what has to be *learned*, rather than what has to be *taught*. Yet again an example of bolting on technology to traditional ideas. What's needed is 'upside down thinking', to quote Charles Handy (1989).

Stage 2: design of how learning will take place. Alonso *et al* recommend the use of 'a structured presentation of the information using an information diagram or road map'. This stage is missing in my experience. There is a danger that because we use the term 'e-learning' that we assume learning does take place. I believe that we should refer to 'e-delivery' and that we should always check what learning has taken place.

Stage 3: development of the learning process and identification of appropriate tools and resources.

Stage 4: implementation of identified structures and resources.

Stage 5: execution of the learning process with monitoring of problems encountered and testing acquisition of knowledge.

Stage 6: evaluation of the effectiveness of e-learning tools, using statistical data generated from learner logs available on VLEs where possible.

Educators tend to concentrate on stages 1, 3 and 4, with limited monitoring of problems in stage 5. Stages 2 and 6 are often neglected, mainly because of time constraints and pressure of work.

iPads and pedagogy

Manuguerra & Petocz (2011) state that mobile learning (m-learning) is the next development after e-learning and 'have the potential to fundamentally change the ways that learning and teaching are carried out, greatly favouring constructivist and collaborative approaches to learning, and flexible and adaptive approaches to teaching'. They described their experience of using iPads to teach mathematics subjects in an Australian university, concluding that the iPad improves student engagement in the following ways:

Presentations can include multi-media, facilitate annotations on live media and can be recorded for further review.

Points of theory can be videoed and accessed by students when needed, which makes the students feel 'safer'.

The iPad provides a tool for integration of technologies delivering content.

Distance learning students can access recordings of complete lectures.

Another advantage of iPads identified by the authors is the facility to have assignments uploaded and marked in pdf format, which they claim gains approval with young people who are environmentally aware. They made use of pdf-based apps which allow for annotations and audio feedback on students' files. The students obtain rich and, apparently, timely feedback and the teacher maintains an archive of assessments. They have not stated how much time was taken to provide such feedback or commented on the storage issues for so many pdf files as well as other uploading problems with the iPad.

Manuguerra & Petocz are technology enthusiasts; they belong to the minority group of early adopters and change champions who gain personal pleasure from 'playing' with the latest device and will work hard to beat a path through the unknown wilderness. The rest of us make tentative inroads to adapt our approach to teaching by using their ideas. However, because of their enthusiasm, Manuguerra & Petocz may see only what is positive; they are not objective critics. Let's examine Manuguerra & Petocz's sales pitch for iPads more deeply:

> Multimedia presentations: have been available for a decade using standard presentation software and are easily accessed by students on shared drives and VLEs.

> Videos of points of theory can be made available via a private account on YouTube, or Vimeo and many other platforms. A decade ago educational managers were becoming very excited about the prospect of using recorded lectures online and sacking expensive teachers.

> Another issue with recording lectures is that there are teachers who would not be comfortable being recorded; indeed some people may not be suitable.

> Finally, is it an advantage for learners to feel safe while watching a lecture? What are the dangers of learners being relaxed, or even missing lectures because they know they can access a recording at a later time?

> Integration and access by distance learning has been possible for several years through normal email and VLEs. The iPad did not make educational resources more accessible of itself, but provided a tool with attractive affordances which entices people to use it.

According to Wakefield & Smith (2012), mobile technology has become embedded in society, referred to as 'ubiquitous technology' by Haythornthwaite & Andrews (2011) and Apple Inc (2008). Recently I asked a retired friend why she needed a smart phone. She replied that she was accustomed to receiving her emails any time and anywhere and did not want to lose this facility. She is actively considering purchasing an iPad, as well as a tablet android telephone, for the convenience of being able to access the internet from her sofa or read online books on a journey.

There is, of course, the cool factor and Apple's clever marketing, using education as a key vehicle, pushing society's 'must have' button. Wakefield & Smith insist that educational resources will become digital and interactive as a result of the continuing development of mobile devices. However, they comment on the lack of reported research into strategies for educators to use technology.

There is a plethora of articles and blogs, identifying apps and describing examples of what is considered good practice. These piecemeal stories are written with breathless, self-congratulatory excitement, but often focus on the process of introducing the device into a specific learning situation rather than examining a total strategy or evaluating actual subject learning. While it is essential for practitioners to share their experiences and their experiments, what is missing is the collation and analysis of best practice based on formal evaluation.

The pedagogical value of using iPads in education, referred to as iPadogogy according to the New Media Consortium, has yet to be fully researched and examined. Enthusiastic iPad educators try to 'sell' the idea of the serious benefits of using iPads by showing what fits with existing theories, for example Bloom's taxonomy (Appendix 1). This gives experienced, and possibly wary, teachers something familiar to understand – a pathway to follow to use the iPad.

However, there must be a danger of premature pigeon-holing of methodology, instead of starting from scratch. Simon (1999) quoted Lev Vygotsky's view of pedagogy which 'must be oriented not towards the yesterday of development but towards its tomorrow'. Educators will agree that the iPad brings new opportunities and challenges that have not yet been fully exploited. Vygotsky's view can be said to be a warning to most educators, including myself.

I am steeped in the past because I have learned what worked and what I believed did not work – *at that time*. I am expecting learners to learn the way that I did, in spite of being a 'curious player' with technology and open to its use in the classroom. How many of us know what skills and knowledge will be needed in 2030? How many of us stay in the past because it is comfortable and familiar?

Perhaps trying to convince educators to use the iPad as a substitute for other traditional teaching methods, instead of exploring new methodologies that meet the needs of the future, may be doing everyone a disservice? Currently, there is a preoccupation with the 'coolness' of the iPad and, perhaps more importantly, the plethora of apps that have become available and increase daily. Reading the various articles about using iPads in education, there is more attention paid to the process of using the device than to evaluating educational effectiveness.

What is being done to investigate the development of pedagogy to meet future needs? Individual countries are carrying out research into the knowledge, skills and abilities needed by employers in the future, but what is being done to consolidate key findings? In today's global marketplace it would benefit everyone if research was done collaboratively. After all, Apple Inc sells to the world. The US government (Partnership for 21st Century Skills 2008) has reported that:

> Advanced economies .... require more educated workers with the ability to respond flexibly to complex problems, communicate effectively, manage information, work in teams and produce new knowledge (p 8).

New pedagogical models are being developed such as the SAMR model (Appendix 2) developed by Ruben Puentedura cited in Chell & Dowling (2013). Puentedura's explanation of the model is light on theory, as he uses a visual presentation. It is not recognisable as a pedagogical framework, but is more of a marketing concept which can be seen in Appendix 2. Puentedura has analysed the stages of how technology is used in learning, beginning with substitution and ending with 'the creation of previously inconceivable'; therefore unknown to anyone.

Similarly, a revered guru of iPadogogy is Alan November (2009), who purports that 'informating is a more powerful way of thinking about technology than automating' which will eventually lead to empowered learners. Like Puentedura, November's pedagogical framework lacks rigour and appears to be of more use in selling the idea of using technology than offering a revision of pedagogical design. Nevertheless, Cavanaugh *et al* (2013) propose the adoption of the SAMR model as a way of mapping existing practice to explore the transformative paradigm.

Technology and constructivism can be used to encourage learners to develop problem-solving, communication, information management and team working skills. Pachler, Bachmair & Cook (2010) advocate a 'comprehensive theoretical and conceptual framework' to make sense of innovative technology. This view is shared by Duhaney (2000), who concludes that educational technology 'should not just be as an appendage' but should be used in conjunction with clear learning objectives. With no frame of reference, the majority of educators will flounder in a sea of information, inevitably grabbing ideas and practice from the adventurous minority.

Few people have the time or inclination to break ground to fully deconstruct the potential of iPadagogy. It is the minority, as Steve Jobs might have called them, the 'crazy ones' who will spend many hours playing with new technology and who are prepared to be pioneers. However, the techno-pioneers need to be supported by an exploration of the nature of learning.

Haythornthwaite and Andrews (2011) posit that how learning occurs when using technology is different than when using traditional methods. Learning theory appears to have been neglected in our excitement to try the next new gadget. There may be a polarising effect where the pioneers travel further in hyperspace and the traditionalists are left behind, trenchantly clinging to known practice. Apple Inc has already recognised what needs to happen in education to maximise the benefits of using technology illustrated in Figure 1.

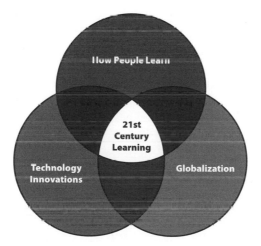

Figure 1: Apple Inc identified three major influences on 21st century learning. (2008)

Gunawardena *et al* (2000) regard the use of technology in learning as applied constructivism. Researchers have categorised the use of the iPad as constructivist. They examined the issues of evaluating student satisfaction when using technology in a learning environment. They referred to the trend of constructivism and stated that this pedagogy made evaluation difficult as each learner has 'a unique perspective from the learning experience'.

This unique experience has been encouraged by educational leaders as it is believed that the individual discovery method will be more engaging and so enhance learning. However, even in a traditional classroom environment, learners will have their individual experiences, depending on their ability in the subject, their interest, their background, even what happened at lunch time that day. The main difference, of course, is that learners are not actively engaged in uncovering the information they need. This in itself can be problematic when some learners will understand quicker than others about the subject and have better research skills.

Gunawardena *et al* examined learning from two perspectives: (1) content/ subject theory and (2) using an electronic device and the influence to the individual's learning process. This is an area to be developed further in this review: are educators spending as much or more time on the actual process of learning as the content the learner needs to know?

Wakefield & Smith (2012) reported research carried out in universities, which found that students using an annotation app 'scored 25% higher on questions involving transferring learning... 75% agreeing that the iPad enhanced their learning'. These findings are questionable. What do learners mean when they state that their learning was enhanced? The introduction of a new tool or resource is likely to increase the interest of learners, just as when computers were first introduced en masse, and Google was considered an appropriate resource for academic research. Both of these facilities are now commonplace and we no longer consider that they enhance learning.

We always seem to be searching for the next high, rather than finding a meaningful strategy that supports and encourages effective learning. Online delivery was supposed to subsume traditional delivery. People could learn at any time and anywhere and would not need a teacher. This proposal foundered quickly, as most experienced educators knew it would. The next trend which salvaged reputations and exploited technology was the notion of blended learning. Thus, there has always been a tentative acceptance of technology in education. We know it should be a sensational tool that will ensure success for all learners, but we're not wholly convinced that we should submerge ourselves completely.

I suggest this suspicion may be caused by the following:

The lack of understanding of educational technology by senior education managers.

The expense of buying and maintaining equipment and software.

The time needed to develop educational methodology using the equipment and software.

The need for educators and learners to learn to use equipment and software quickly.

The diversity and compatibility issues of different devices.

The diversity and compatibility issues of educators and IT support staff.

The differing skills and aptitude of educators and learners when using technology.

The inertia of educational publishers in adapting resources to make the most of the potential of technology, *ie* interactive rather than just a book on a computer.

The dynamic nature of technology, with regular updates and new developments.

The unreliability of technology when there is so much reliance on uncontrolled environments, particularly the internet.

Wakefield & Smith reported the use of iPads in a student-centred situation wherein learners would critically evaluate information on the internet and use appropriately. This is not a new learning strategy and there is no specific for iPads to carry out online research. Apart from the fact that iPads are lighter and easier to carry, netbooks and laptops are also capable of facilitating the described activity.

The professor in the case study did not explain how to use the iPad as he wanted students to find out for themselves. This is an excellent problem-solving activity if it met a specific learning objective relevant to the course of study. However, it may also be a time-consuming distraction from the real learning goals because the professor had no idea how to use the iPad.

Educators and learners are all starting from the same point of ignorance.

Wakefield & Smith made one observation that highlights a possible danger of the mobility of the iPad, and now the iPad Mini and android tablet telephones. They noted that students in the classroom were confident in giving answers when they could use their iPad, but were noticeably reticent when asked to give answers without the device. Wakefield & Smith do not project possible issues for education and ultimately society and employment if this reliance on a technological crutch becomes widespread.

Simon (1999) argues that technology, even in pre-iPad days, needs a new pedagogical model with clearly defined 'goals, structure and adult guidance'. He warns that if we 'play' with learning via computers, and now iPads, that individual learning could stagnate at the lower levels of cognitive development because there are insufficient activities to reach higher cognitive levels. Murray & Olcese (2011) discuss the need for pedagogical change to respond to the opportunities afforded by mobile technology. They conclude that there is a need for a better understanding of modern learning.

Who should be the architects of the evolving iPadagogy? Evans (2001) concluded an investigation into how an existing course would benefit from incorporating technology by stating that:

> subject teachers are not the most appropriate people to make the change from tradition to technology effectively. Lack of time, software expertise and fear of failure leads to the risk of old methodology transferred to new technology. It is likely to be more effective to have the subject teacher work with an instructional designer and web designer to ensure that the learners' needs are the first priority and that the online materials will be well-designed and, as far as possible, foolproof. (p 24)

Cavanaugh *et al* (2013) discuss the concept of iPadagogy and future plans to develop eLearning objects to 'support Challenge-based Learning and Inquiry-based Learning'. From a teacher's perspective, I would be much more receptive to pedagogical developments if there was more substance and fewer acronyms. Online learning objects can be very effective, but take years of development and cannot meet the needs of every aspect of education.

They state that 'iPadagogy builds from the foundation of general educational technology', which implies that there was a solid foundation built on sound pedagogical practice in the first place. There is a danger that it is assumed there is rigorous pedagogical design in the use of iPads by using the term iPadagogy, just as there can be an assumption that learning takes place because of the term 'e-learning'. Both assumptions must be challenged or the Monster, this education beast comprised of sewn-on technological tools in the hope that learning will be more effective without revisiting pedagogical design, will continue to grow.

iPads and the teachers who have to use them

Tolisano (2012) investigated how iPad success in education is measured. Success cannot be measured until it is clear what has to be achieved, which is why it is so important to establish the pedagogy. Keane *et al* (2012) carried out research that revealed that success is dependent on the enthusiasm of the teacher and not the device, and that the most important aspect of using iPads in education was to have a 'dedicated curriculum program'.

Three years after the launch of the iPad, a minority of teachers are comfortable with using iPads. In some situations, the learners, who will have been using iPads for personal use, will be much more familiar and knowledgeable about using the iPad in the classroom than the teacher who may have been told to use the device the week before classes began. What impact will this have on the other learners and the confidence of the teacher?

Will it improve the learning situation to have some learners who are already advanced, some who are willing and want to learn how to use the device and some who are nervous, in addition to a teacher who is very confident with traditional delivery, but has very little or no idea of the potential of the iPad? How does the need to learn to use the device impact on the time allotted to learn the content?

The iPad has enabled almost total online and technological methodology because of the ease of use, complete portability and the range of apps available, many of which for free. How much research has been completed to evaluate the effect on learning? Many teachers have yet to embrace the existing technologies of computers and virtual learning environments. They will need training and mentoring to manage the use of the iPad as a conduit for lesson planning and delivery.

Robby & Gitsaki (2013) surveyed teachers who were forced to use iPads for the first time and discovered that they were not overwhelmed with the iPad. They accepted that the device allowed them to repurpose existing materials and develop additional digital materials. However, the iPad did not facilitate improved communication, homework distribution or sharing of materials. The majority of teachers did not feel that their teaching had improved or that the iPad enabled greater learner focus.

The best outcome in the first semester was the use of activities not usually possible from a textbook. Their view of the benefits to learners was ambivalent as they considered there was no improvement in motivation and perseverance. More than two-thirds of respondents disagreed that concentration on activities was enhanced. The best outcome for learners was improved collaboration with peers.

A snapshot of views was obtained for this review with the aid of Survey Monkey during the last month of the academic year. There was a 95% response rate to ten questions about the experience of using iPads for the first year. All respondents were English teachers, some of whom were compelled to use the device in the classroom under threat of termination of employment.

How was the training and development provided to help you use the iPad?

Answered: 15 Skipped: 4

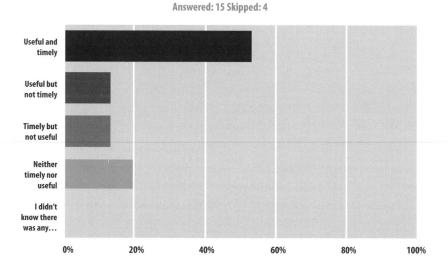

Figure 2: Reaction to training and development provided by HCT.

Just over half of the teachers considered the training was useful and timely. A fifth of teachers responded that the training was neither useful or timely. Further research to compare experiences in other educational institutions would be needed to establish if this is acceptable. What is interesting is that a fifth of respondents gave up trying to use the iPad (see Figure 5), but it is not known if it is the same people. Clearly good initial training and support are key to the success of any implementation of change.

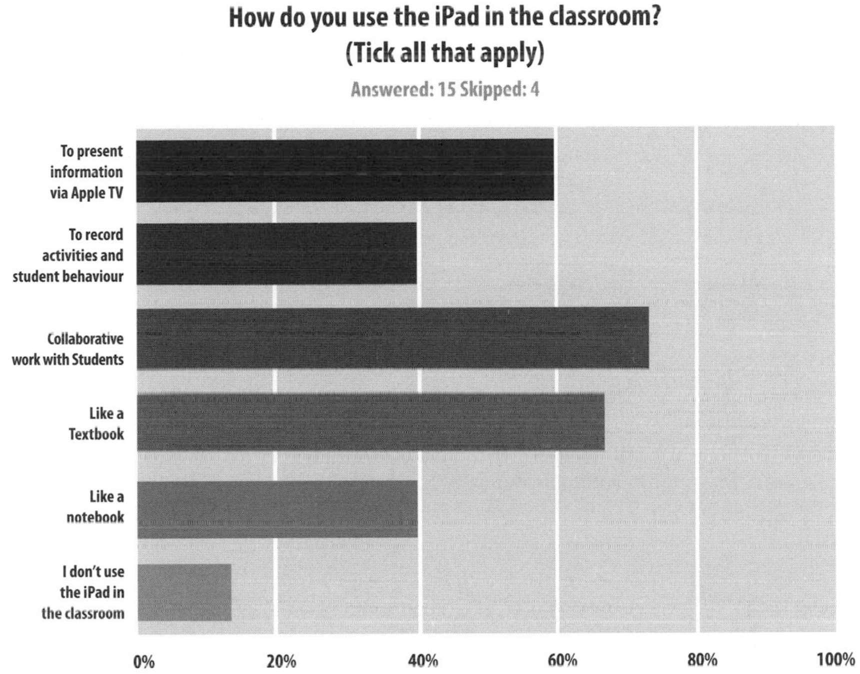

How do you use the iPad in the classroom?
(Tick all that apply)
Answered: 15 Skipped: 4

Answer Choices	Responses	
To present Information via Apple TV	60%	9
To record activities and student behaviour	40%	6
Collaborative work with students	73.33%	11
Like a textbook	66.67%	10
Like a notebook	40%	6
I don't use the iPad in the classroom	13.33%	2

Figure 3: How the iPad was used in the classroom.

The main use of the iPad was to allow students to work collaboratively. Sixty-seven per cent used the iPad like a textbook, but it is not clear from the response if the online books were static or interactive. Evans (2001) concluded that if technology is used in the same way as paper-based materials it will not enhance the learning experience and may actually be more difficult for learners to access. Sixty per cent of teachers used the iPad as a presentation tool in conjunction with the Apple TVs provided.

One of the complications of using iPads is the requirement for teachers and learners to buy apps. At the time of research, the college IT support function could not pre-load apps. Teachers were required to set up an account with the Apple Store, use their own credit cards and then claim back the cost of apps that were approved for use by college management.

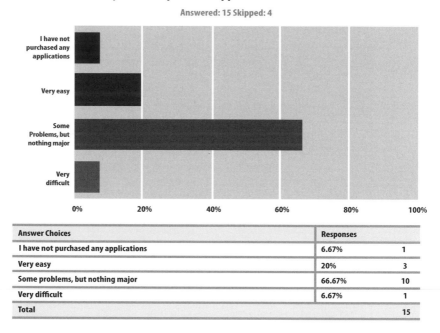

How easy was it to purchase applications for educational use?

Answered: 15 Skipped: 4

Answer Choices	Responses	
I have not purchased any applications	6.67%	1
Very easy	20%	3
Some problems, but nothing major	66.67%	10
Very difficult	6.67%	1
Total		15

Figure 4: Ease of purchase of apps for educational use.

Finally, the survey asked teachers to describe their overall experience of using the iPad as an educational tool. Sixty-four per cent felt that the experience had been positive. Follow up interviews are needed to expand on what the respondents considered was positive. This attitude reflects the philosophy of the teaching profession in the face of constant change. Most teachers will try to make change work to ensure their students have a good experience of learning.

As can be seen in Figure 5, almost a fifth of teachers found the experience of using iPads so difficult that they gave up. Further research into the reactions of teachers in other educational institutions is needed to establish whether this level of attrition is acceptable. It should be noted that 8 of the 19 respondents skipped this question.

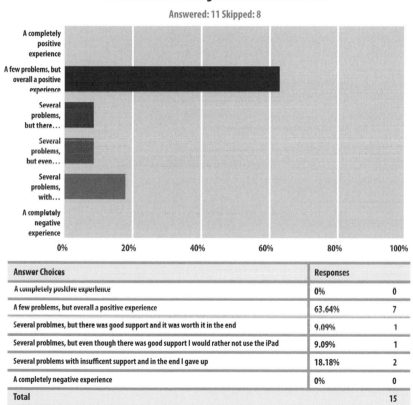

How would you describe your experience of the transition to using iPads in the classroom?

Answered: 11 Skipped: 8

Answer Choices	Responses	
A completely positive experience	0%	0
A few problems, but overall a positive experience	63.64%	7
Several problems, but there was good support and it was worth it in the end	9.09%	1
Several problems, but even though there was good support I would rather not use the iPad	9.09%	1
Several problems with insufficent support and in the end I gave up	18.18%	2
A completely negative experience	0%	0
Total		15

Figure 5: Description of experience of transition to iPads.

As always with the introduction of new technology, there are enthusiastic pioneers who have no hesitation in accepting the iPad and take pleasure in exploring what can be done with the device. The 'techno-geeks' thrive on the new experience and learn quickly. This is not true of the majority of teachers, most of whom are willing to try new ideas with support, but there will be a small group of teachers who do not see the point and who believe that this is just another fad.

One issue when introducing new technology is the ease of use. How much time will it take for users to be competent in operating the device? Isaacson reported that Jobs was affected by a story written by Michael Noer. While using his iPad Noer was staying in a rural area of Bogota in Colombia. A poor six year-old boy was curious about the device, so Noer handed it to him. He instinctively began to swipe the screen, launched apps and began to play a game. 'Steve Jobs has designed a powerful computer that an illiterate six-year-old can use without instruction,' wrote Noer.

The question remains: is this just a 'cool tool' or is there something more that can be gained by teachers and learners when they use iPads? Isaacson quoted Lev Grossman of *Time* who stated that while computers had developed to generate creativity from users

> The iPad shifts the emphasis from creating content to merely absorbing and manipulating it. It mutes you, turns you back into a passive consumer of other people's masterpieces.

The question returns – are iPads about the process of using the device or about learning effectively? Murray & Olcese (2011) discuss the need for pedagogical change to respond to the opportunities afforded by mobile technology. They conclude that there is a need for a better understanding of modern learning.

Conclusion

Steve Jobs talked about heavy books and corrupt government, as he envisioned a future where all textbooks would be available for free on the iPad. There is no mention that the iPad will transform education and ensure learning success. It is just a tool that is more practical and convenient than carrying a laptop plus textbooks.

At the HCT Education without Borders 2013 conference, a student from Dubai Women's College gave a presentation summarising her research into students' views of the introduction of iPads. The top advantage identified by students was that it was much easier to carry. It seemed such a trivial answer for a device which has received so much attention, but could it be the main advantage of the iPad? It is a tool with almost everything that a learner and teacher needs in a device almost the size of an A4 sheet of paper.

Is the iPad more about convenience than pedagogy? The iPad is multi-functional and expensive to replace, so learners are more likely to keep them with them at all times ready to make notes as events occur. The iPad's affordances make them an attractive tool for users, which may be its main advantage.

The range of apps, although varying in quality and cost, are another crucial benefit, but they require extensive evaluation and an easy purchasing mechanism. What is clear from the review is that the success of the iPad in education rests with the individual teachers. The iPad may have the power to transform education, but only with the co-operation of the main users. Educational managers must ensure that the introduction of the iPad is strategically planned using instructional designers in collaboration with practitioners.

The iPad is a tool. Its affordances have potential for improved teacher and learner interface and engagement. To date, educators have found the main advantage is improved collaboration between learners, although this interaction has drawbacks. The iPad itself will not provide improved learning without the effective conduit of the teacher and the support of the educational institution. The teachers cannot implement enhanced learning, using behaviourist and constructivist models, until the pedagogical design has been overhauled. Look back at Figure 1 showing the three major influences on education in the 21st century, according to Apple Inc. How people learn is a major factor in the educational technology revolution, but it is an area neglected by many educational decision-makers.

One day the iPad will be as dull as a netbook is today. Will the way we learn have changed?

Bibliography

Alonso, F, López, G, Manrique, D & Viñes, J (2005) An instructional model for web-based e-learning education with a blended learning process approach. *British Journal of Educational Technology, 36(2),* 217-235.

Apple Inc. (2008) Apple Classrooms of Tomorrow—Today: Learning in the 21st Century.

Brian, M (2012) Apple: 1.5 million iPads are used in educational programs, with over 20,000 education apps. Retrieved 18 September, 2013 fromthenextweb.com/apple/2012/01/19/apple-1-5-million-ipads-in-use-in-educational-programs-offering-over-20000-education-apps/

Cavanaugh, C, Hargis, J, Munns, S & Kamali, T (2012) iCelebrate Teaching and Learning: Sharing the iPad Experience. *Journal of Teaching and Learning with Technology, 1(2),* 1-12.

Chell, G & Dowling, S (2013) Substitution to Redefinition: The challenges of using technology. Retrieved 21 October 2013 from shct.hct.ac.ae/events/edtechpd2013/articles/Chell-Dowling.pdf

Christensen, C, Horn, M and Johnson, C (2010) *Rethinking Student Motivation: Why understanding the 'job' is crucial for improving education.* Innosight Institute.

Duhaney, Dr D (2000) Technology and the educational process: transforming classroom activities. *International Journal of Instructional Media,* 27(1).

Evans, D (2001) *Managing the process of introducing online delivery into the Office Technology programme of the Higher Colleges of Technology.* Unit 2 assignment in part fulfilment of the MBA in Educational Management for the University of Leicester, UK.

Gunawardena, C N, Lowe, C and Carabajal, K (2000) *Evaluating Online Learning: Models and Methods.* Society for Information Technology & Teacher Education International Conference: Proceedings of SITE 2000 (11th, San Diego, California, February). Volumes 1-3.

Handy, C (1989) *The Age of Unreason.* Boston, Mass.: Harvard Business School Press.

Haythornthwaite, C and Andrews, R (2011) *E-learning: Theory and Practice.* London, UK. Sage Publications Ltd.

Hong, K (2013) *Apple pushes hard for education market with iOS 7 improvements.* Retrieved 20 September, 2013 from thenextweb.com/apple/2013/06/26/apple-pushe-hard-for-education-with-ios-7-improvements/

Hughes, N (2013) *Apple has sold 170M iPads to date, implying sales near 15M in Sept. quarter.* Retrieved 24 October 2013 from appleinsider.com/articles/13/10/23/apple-has-sold-170m-ipads-to-date-implying-sales-near-15m-in-sept-quarter

Isaacson, William (2012) *Steve Jobs.* Simon & Schuster.

Jordan, P (2013) *iPad in Education: 8 Million iPads Sold to Educational Institutions.* Retrieved 24 October 2013 from ipadinsight.com/ipad-in-education-2/ipad-in-education-8-million-ipads-sold-to-educational-institutions/

Keane, T, Lang, C & Pilgrim, C (2012) *ACEC2012- PEDAGOGY! IPADOLOGY! NETBOOKOLOGY! LEARNING WITH MOBILE DEVICES.* ACEC2012: ITs Time Conference, Perth, Australia. Retrieved 10 July, 2013 from acec2012.acce.edu.au/sites/acec2012.acce.edu.au/files/proposal/80/ACEC2012-ipad%20paper%209%20June%20Final.pdf

Manuguerra, M & Petocz, P (2011) Promoting student engagement by integrating new technology into tertiary education: the role of the iPad. *Asian Social Science,* 7(11).

Murray, O & Olcese, N (2011) Teaching and Learning with iPads, Ready or Not? *TechTrends,* 55(6).

November, A (2009) *Empowering students with technology.* 2nd Edition. Corwin.

Pachler, N, Bachmair, B & Cook, J (2010) *Mobile learning: Structures, agency, practices.* New York, NY: Springer Science + Business Media.

Puentedura, Dr R (2012) Retrieved 21 October 2013 from www.hippasus.com/rrpweblog/archives/2012/08/23/SAMR_BackgroundExemplars.pdf

Robby, Dr M and Gitsaki, Dr C (2013) *iPad Project Implementation: Interim Report* Higher Colleges of Technology, UAE.

Simon, B (1999) Why no Pedagogy in England?' in J Leach and B Moon (Eds.) *Learners and Pedagogy* London, Paul.

Tolisano, S (2012) *iPad App Evaluation for the Classroom.* Retrieved from langwitches.org/blog/wp-content/uploads/2012/06/iPadAppEvaluation.pdf

Wakefield, J & Smith, D (2012) From Socrates to Satellites: iPad Learning in an Undergraduate Course. *Creative Education, 3(5),* 643-648.

Blogs

ewb.hct.ac.ae/ewb2013/student-presenters/marwa-almeeza/ [accessed 24 September 2013]

www.hippasus.com/rrpweblog/ SAMR Model by Ruben Puentedura [accessed 15 July 2013]

langwitches.org/blog/2012/08/23/what-do-you-want-to-create-today/ [accessed 28 July 2013]

www.nmc.org/publications/2013-future-education-summit-communique [accessed 24 September 2013]

www.slideshare.net/fullscreen/langwitches/i-have-ipads-in-the-classroom-now-what/1 [accessed 12 September 2013]

Appendix 1

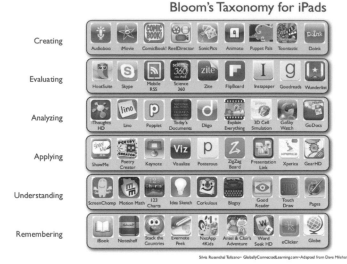

Source: Silvia Rosenthal Tolisano, www.GloballyConnectedLearning.com

Appendix 2

The SAMR model for pedagogical transformation using iPads designed by Dr Ruben Puentedura

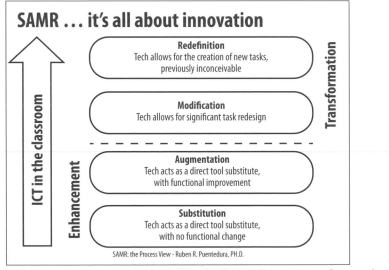

Source: padagogy.net/wp-content/uploads/2013/05/SAMRdiagram.jpeg [accessed 24 October 2013]

Chapter 7

Key challenges in BYOD teaching and learning

Ieda M Santos

Introduction

More and more students are arriving at university campuses equipped with personal mobile devices. They may be carrying with them Smart phones, tablets, e readers or netbooks of all brands and models. In many cases, a single student may own more than one device.

Mobile devices have become a central part of students' lives, for accessing the internet, making use of the communication services, media and applications (Lundin, Lymer, Holmquist, Brown & Rost, 2010; Melton & Kendall, 2012). The number of personal mobile devices will not only increase in university contexts (Fang, 2009) but will also be increasingly used to complement learning activities.

Widespread ownership of mobile devices among students creates opportunities for educators to explore these devices for education (Stoerger, 2013). The use of personal technology in Higher Education (HE) has, in fact, begun with the adoption of laptops in the late 1980s (diFilipo 2013). However, the ways mobile devices can be used now are different in that they allow access to information and communication tools anytime anywhere not previously envisioned (Cherwell Software, 2012).

Stoerger (2013) stated that:

> These [mobile] devices can be used to connect the internet, take pictures, and record videos, as well as send and receive information... Students with a mobile device have the ability to access information at their fingertips, which enables them to learn while standing in line at the store, taking a break at work, or waiting for the bus. The educational opportunities are endless. (p473)

The ubiquitous mobile devices allow HE institutions to adopt 'bring your own device' (BYOD) programmes (Kobus, Rietveld, & van Ommeren, 2013). More specifically, students' own mobile technology is used to support teaching activities in and outside the classroom. However, a BYOD programme presents both benefits and challenges to institutions. It has been seen an attractive option because of the perceived reduced costs as it takes advantage of the already available technology that students own (Traxler, 2005; UNESCO, 2013).

In addition, the literature has discussed the benefits of using mobile devices in the classroom, such as anywhere and anytime access to learning resources, better methods of collaboration and communication, individualized learning and differentiated instruction (*eg* Eschenbrenner & Nah, 2013; Santos, 2013; Kukulska-Hulme & Traxler, 2005).

Despite the benefits, Traxler (2010b) reminded that:

> Student devices present a major challenge to many of the institutional practices and procedures associated with ICT and 'conventional' desktop e-learning. It is easy to say that education should embrace student devices but not easy to say how. This is part of the paradox. (p156)

The challenges often discussed in the literature are associated with network infrastructure, network security, technical support, equity issues and classroom disruptions. The purpose of this chapter is to present a review around these key challenges. This is followed by a review of a case study implemented at a higher education institution within the United Arab Emirates to illustrate how these challenges occur in practice when adopting personal devices in the classroom. Based on the review and the practical example provided, the chapter expects to discuss potential strategies to help minimize the challenges.

Bring Your Own Device

Contrary to educational institutions providing students with mobile technology, the main concept behind a BYOD programme is that students will use their personal mobile devices in teaching and learning practices. This model allows a wide variety of devices with different operating systems and applications. The Abilene Christian University, for instance, issued iPhones and iPods to a group of students and faculty to carry out learning activities (Perkins & Saltsman, 2010).

Lin and Rivera Sánchez (2012), on the other hand, discussed the implementation of a mandatory SMS student response system in a Singaporean University where students used personal mobile phones to participate in weekly and graded classroom quizzes. According to the authors, all students owned a mobile device making the project implementation feasible. Therefore, when HE institutions embark on a BYOD initiative, it means they will be explicitly implementing a policy on relying on student mobile technology (Hockly, 2012).

As argued by Traxler (2010b), educational institutions cannot afford to ignore the use of students' mobile devices in education. These are students' everyday tools that they carry with them all the time. As stated by Cisco (2012):

> Students can use their mobile devices to respond to multiple-choice questions, allowing professors to collect active feedback within minutes. Users can also access online applications such as MATLAB and Blackboard for anytime, anywhere learning using their preferred devices... This capability, combined with the fact that wireless access is available in more far-flung areas of the campus, is improving convenience and promoting a richer learning experience. (p3)

Kukulska-Hulme and Traxler (2005, p26) observed that mobile technologies for learning and teaching

> ...open up new opportunities for independent investigations, practical fieldwork, professional updating and on-the-spot access to knowledge. They can also provide the mechanism for improved individual learner support and guidance, and for more efficient course administration and management.

While the BYOD programme offers opportunities for HE institutions ranging from educational opportunities to reduced technology costs (*eg* Traxler, 2005; Stoerger, 2013), it also presents challenges (Dahlstrom & diFillipo, 2013; Traxler, 2010a). In the following sections, this chapter discusses key challenges associated with bringing students' personal mobile devices to the classroom.

Key challenges
Network infrastructure

A BYOD programme requires a change in the institutional network infrastructure. A robust infrastructure is needed to support a wide range of wireless enabled mobile devices (Dede & Bjered, 2010; Cherwell Software, 2012). Research has shown that lack or limited internet connectivity can cause disruption to mobile-based learning activities.

For example, Nykvist's (2012) case study on the use of BYOD in teaching reported that the institution network was not initially built to handle an extreme load of wireless mobile device users. The study indicated that when multiple classes were running at the same location, saturation could quickly be reached and students found it difficult to obtain the IP address or encountered an extremely slow transfer of data.

Similarly, Stav, Nielson, Hansen-Nygard, and Thorseth (2010) found that students had difficulties in completing learning activities due to technical problems associated with reduced network capacity. The authors recommended providing sufficient capacity in the wireless network and proper location of access points.

Many institutions will probably need to upgrade their network capacity and performance by increasing bandwidth, adding access points, and boosting their network management capabilities (CDW-G, 2012; Fritschi & Wolf, 2012) to handle high number of devices and data transfer. One challenge, according to Dahlstrom and diFillipo (2013, p. 3), is

> Maintaining and upgrading infrastructure to accommodate more devices and technologies that cross paths with IT domains, predicting what the next technology will be in order to proactively be ready to accommodate it.

A further challenge is that making improvements in network capacity imply that universities must support the costs of maintaining and sustaining wireless access (Melhuish & Falloon, 2010). Campbell *et al.*

(2013, para 23) believe that to '...enable an infrastructure that is scaled sufficiently and flexible enough for BYOD...' financial investment is needed. Dede and Bjered (2010) added:

> Anytime, anyplace learning ... calls for a new wired/wireless infrastructure that allows students to access the internet, their digital content, and their learning communities from whatever device they happen to have... This requires investment in a mobile broadband infrastructure that complements and augments conventional wired computers... (p.13)

Network security

A further challenge that institutions need to consider is related to network security. In other words, allowing students to connect their personal mobile devices to the institutional network can expose sensitive information (diFilipo, 2013). HE institutions have been dealing with security issues since they started issuing laptops to students. However, the number of mobile devices that students currently bring to university campuses has exacerbated the existing security (diFilipo, 2013).

A BYOD programme represents a dramatic shift for many institutional information technology (IT) departments used to controlling which technology students and faculty could use (Violino, 2012). Such an approach enables IT personnel to manage network and information access privileges to maintain the level of data security (Emery, 2012). Markeelj and Bernik (2012, p.103) stressed that 'The usage of mobile devices can't be restricted just because they represent an information security risk, but we should use this technology wisely.'

Several security risks related to BYOD have been discussed in the literature. For example, the loss of a mobile device that is unprotected could mean exposure to personal or corporate data that users might have stored in that device. A further risk is that mobile devices can communicate with various networks concurrently, regardless of the firewalls. If a mobile device is connected to an institution's network as well as a public network, an unprotected path to the institution's central information system can potentially be opened, creating a security issue. A mobile device can become a gateway to an institution's private data (Markeelj & Bernik, 2012).

Markeelj and Bernik (2012) observed that there is no available system to enable institutions to monitor the performance of their information system in regard to accessing and transferring data via mobile devices. However, institutions can educate students and faculty about security practices and network polices as well as remind them about responsibilities as users (CDW-G, 2012). Poe and Garfinkel (2009, p180) pointed out that:

> Understanding the technology of wireless networking itself, however, is only partially the way to think about wireless security ... users should be able to participate in the development and implementation of security policies... More importantly, we can engage student in classroom (or digital) discussions about the role of individual responsibility in ensuring that wireless environments are safe spaces for productive exchange and learning.

Furthermore, the literature has suggested several strategies that can be implemented to secure corporate data as well as other sensitive information (*eg* Markeelj & Bernik, 2012; Poe & Garfinkel, 2009). For example, a widely-discussed strategy is to require students and faculty to register their devices with the IT department. The network will only provide access to the registered devices (referred to as Mac address registration).

Many universities use this strategy as a way to protect their wireless networks. For example, as part of its security system, the University of South Florida in the United States requires students to register their devices with the IT department (see www.usf.edu/it/class-prep/wireless. aspx). When students register their devices, it enables the IT personnel to track or monitor a wireless user through its Mac address. A further strategy includes implementing private segregated networks for mobile device users which prevent them from accessing corporate data (CDW-G, 2012).

IT support

According to Traxler (2005), mobile learning creates a demand for support structures and its development is dependent on the institutional capacity to provide such support. A study by Smith, Salaway and Caruso (2009), for example, suggested that if the number of mobile device users increased, then the institution's IT department would be overwhelmed with demands for technical support for those devices.

However, supporting multiple mobile devices with different models and operating systems can be more complicated than supporting a range of identical devices purchased and maintained by IT staff (Sangani, 2013). It would be much easier to support multiple mobile devices if they were from the same manufacturer, had the same software and were configured exactly the same (Sangani, 2013). This scenario would be possible if institutions were offering the devices to students which are not the case with a BYOD model.

Traxler (2005) noted that:

> ...the perception amongst IT support staff that the whole area of handheld computers, their platforms and their applications is too personal, fluid and diverse to ... support at an institutional level in the way that PC provision is supported... This kind of attitude will inhibit experimentation and progress... (p 184)

Quinn (2012, p101) stressed that a 'top issue is whether to support learner-owned devices...' Campbell *et al* (2013) noted that if HE institutions expect students to use their own devices in the classroom, it creates an obligation to provide support for those devices. However, others have indicated that students should be responsible for repairing their faulty/damaged mobile devices (CDW-G, 2012; Hockly, 2012).

According to CDW-G (2012), IT support should assist users accessing the network, although this can become a challenge due to the variety of operating systems and platforms. The University of British Columbia, Faculty of Medicine, which embraced a BYOD model, clearly states in their guidelines that students are responsible for repairing their own devices (see http://med.ubc.ca/files/2012/02/FoM-BYOD-Student-Guidelines.pdf).

Researchers like Alden (2013) believe that students are quite comfortable with using their devices, and can learn informally how to work them (Kukulska-Hulme, 2010). Alden (2013) feels, however, that students may occasionally need technical support to perform certain tasks such as downloading or using applications. A study by Ramsden (2005) on the use of Personal Digital Assistant (PDA) did raise concerns regarding IT support for students and faculty within the current supporting structure. The author suggested a supporting structure with an emphasis on a student-to-student network type.

Equity

A BYOD programme may widen the digital divide. When students' personal mobile devices become an institutional requirement in teaching and learning, all students must have access to a device and wireless (Dede & Bjered, 2010; Traxler, 2010a; UNESCO, 2013). Beckmann and Martin (2013), for example, indicated that during the implementation of learning activities, the instructor unintentionally disadvantaged students who did own a mobile device.

Therefore, institutions must ensure that not a single student is disadvantaged due to a lack of available technology (Cherwell Software, 2012). In this respect, Kinash, Brand and Mathew's (2012) study indicated that in order to ensure all students could access a mobile technology, each was assigned to a loan scheme whereby an iPad was available for both university and home use. A further strategy to avoid equity issues is discussed by LaMaster and Stager (2012, p6):

> Those without phones teamed up with their neighbours. By the end of the period, all 27 students were working on their assignments collaboratively on personal devices. And they have done exactly what we educators always dream of: They assessed their learning needs and found the right tools to satisfy those needs without adult intervention.

Although mobile device ownership among students is widespread, one cannot assume that all can afford the latest technology, or devices may be less powerful compared to others'. As such, learning activities must be compatible with all mobile devices (Curtis, 2012).

Schepman, Rodway, Beattie and Lambert (2012), for example, described a multi-platform solution as a necessary condition for mobile learning. The authors noted that it is advantageous to use technology which enables mobile learning on hardware that students already own and that utilizes relatively generic software which can be tailored to different tasks. Johnson (2012, p85), while referring to equity issues at school level, added:

> When selecting library e-books, online databases, learning management systems, and e-textbooks, part of the criteria must be how accessible these materials are on a wide a range of operating systems.

Moreover, when planning outside class activities, instructors must be aware of any limitations that may raise inequity issues, such as students who do not have an available or sufficient data plan for their mobile devices (Nykvist, 2012). Campbell *et al* (2013) stated a further equity issue:

> ...if BYOD does not become established within higher education... Learners' experiences of a sophisticated, agile, and personally responsive computing ecosystem reflecting their own growing powers of judgment and creativity, powers linked to the their own developing identities, will be destructively absent from their experience of school ... thus depriving both learners and teachers of the experiences they need in order to thrive in a truly complex world. (Para. 9)

Classroom disruption

Although personal mobile devices are viewed as potentially supporting teaching and learning, they can also disrupt lectures (Sharples, 2002; Fang, 2009). HE institutions may face faculty resistance to use students' devices in the classroom. Research has shown that mobile devices are often seen as sources of distraction, cheating and inappropriate use of the technology (*eg* Sharples, 2002; Mueller, Wood, De Pasquale, & Cruikshank, 2012; Geist, 2011).

For example, Geist (2011) indicated that many instructors considered mobile devices as distraction during the lectures as students would not pay attention because they were often browsing the internet or accessing social media. Burns and Lohenry (2010) further indicated that most of the faculty and students agreed that mobile phones in the classroom were a source of distraction. Mobile phones are considered distracting because of problems with ringing, texting messaging, or multitasking (Fang, 2009).

While Scornavacca, Huff and Marshall (2009) reported that students occasionally used social media during class activities, the overall experience of using personal mobile devices was positive. The authors felt that positive results can be achieved by encouraging students to bring their personal devices to the class. In order to minimize disruptions, Sharples (2002) suggested that instructors could either attempt to prohibit the use of mobile technology in class or, alternatively, use those devices with full knowledge that there will be disruptions which need to be managed. However, as observed by Dyson, Trish, Smith and Wallace (2013, p 411), banning mobile devices from educational institutions and classrooms '...prevents students from benefiting from m-learning, benefits that have been well documented in the literature...'

Several strategies have been discussed in the literature to minimize distractions caused by mobile technology ranging from implementing policies to etiquette (*eg* Burns & Lohenry, 2010). Bugeja (2007), for example, indicated that some universities are relying on educational campaigns to make students more aware of classroom etiquette. Fang (2009) added that rather than seeing distraction as a challenge, instructors should see it as an opportunity to reflect upon and modify their instructional approach.

Many instructors, however, may not know how to integrate these devices into teaching and thus need training. To make good use of mobile devices in the classroom, instructors need to understand their educational value (Naismith & Corlett, 2006) and how to integrate these tools into the classroom teaching (Mueller, *et al.*, 2012). Furthermore, institutions should organize training to both instructors and students on proper use of mobile technology in the classroom (Sangani, 2013; Fang, 2009). In particular, educating students regarding the use of mobile technology in the classroom is paramount for successful BYOD implementation (Burns & Lohenry, 2010).

Case illustration

This section reviews the main findings from a case study (Santos, 2013) to illustrate the challenges discussed in the above sections. The study was conducted at a higher education institution in the United Arab Emirates. It investigated the implementation of quizzes in the classroom supported by students' personal mobile devices as well as explored the implications of bringing those devices to the institution.

Study participants consisted of 19 Emirati female undergraduate students enrolled in a 15-week educational technology course within the Bachelor of Education programme. A staff member from the IT department also took part in this study. Mix methods of data collection were adopted as a means to achieve triangulation. The study adopted a commercial web browser response system (SMART Response) which is compatible with multiple mobile devices.

Network and security

Santos (2013) reported that the current institutional network infrastructure could only support the number of students participating in the study. Results suggested that there was a need to increase the network capacity to accommodate a higher number of devices. However, the study indicated that to increase the network capacity some money needed to be spent. This agrees with others who have discussed financial costs involved in making improvements in the network infrastructure to accommodate the BYOD model (*eg* Campbell *et al.*, 2013).

Santos also showed that to justify the costs of increasing the wireless bandwidth and access points at the institution, there must be teaching and learning outcomes related to the BYOD programme. In this respect, the literature has shown the benefits accrued of using mobile devices in teaching and learning practices (*eg* Lundin *et al.*, 2010; Scornavacca *et al.*, 2009). For example, Stoerger, 2013 (p478) found that:

> The majority of students claimed that the mobile devices were beneficial to the learning process and helped them understand concepts covered in the class... Moreover, students noted that the integration of mobile activities into the curriculum was a good use of their time and supported their learning outside the classroom...

Furthermore, Santos (2013) quoted an IT staff member who demonstrated awareness that soon the institution would need to provide internet connectivity to students' personal mobile devices:

> I would say within 18 months here we would have to be providing access to the students somehow... When I say access, I mean connectivity. So at a basic level, you are going to have to provide connectivity... Otherwise you would become irrelevant...(Santos, 2013, 11)

Similar to others (*eg* diFilipo, 2013), study by Santos (2013) reported concerns over network security. It showed that a guest account was used as a way to protect the institution network in case students participating in the study abused or shared the password with anyone outside the study. The study suggested that the institution would create a segregated network and have students registering their personal mobile devices with the IT department as strategies to protect the network. However, findings revealed that to create a segregated network, there was a need to increase the bandwidth to accommodate more devices (Santos, 2013), which in turn required financial investment.

IT support

The above review on IT support to personal mobile devices suggested mixed results with some arguing that IT support is needed while others believing students can support their own devices or little support is required (*eg* Traxler, 2005; Alden, 2013). Santos (2013) illustrated that students did not require IT support while participating in the quiz activities. Only a few students had technical problems, mainly related to the password to access the wireless guest account, and they figured out how to solve technical problems by themselves.

Similar to ideas discussed in the literature (*eg* CDW-G, 2012), Santos suggested that IT support for mobile devices is complex due to a variety of devices and operating systems. According to findings, IT support would be more related to connectivity or access to network and distribution of applications to mobile devices.

Equity

Santos (2013) showed that equity issues emerged right from the beginning of the study. According to the results, although all students owned mobile devices, only a few had subscriptions to a local internet service provider. In other words, most of the students could only have internet access on their mobile devices when they were able to connect to a Wi-Fi.

At the time of the study implementation, students did not have access to the institution wireless network. In order to implement the mobile-based quizzes, Santos indicated that the institution provided the participating students with a wireless guest account. This action, in turn, seemed to have created two classes of users within the institution in which one group had access to the Wi-Fi while other students did not.

Norris and Soloway (2011, p77), although addressing a case at school level, reported a similar pattern in which a particular institution inadvertently created two classes of users: 'There were those who could afford the data plan associated with the iPhone and those who could not...'

Furthermore, a closer examination of Santos' (2013) findings suggests a further equity issue. It seemed that only a group of students who participated in the study was benefiting from using advanced technologies to support learning in the classroom. On a positive note, and in supporting of researchers (*eg* Curtis, 2012) who indicated that learning activities must be cross platform, the study showed that the web-based response system enabled all the Emirati students to access the quizzes in the classroom. The only requirement was that students had internet on their personal mobile devices.

Disruption

Santos (2013) did not report disruptive behaviours caused by having students' personal mobile devices in the classroom. The literature, however, has shown that mobile devices can disrupt classroom teaching (*eg* Mueller *et al.*, 2012; Geist, 2011). According to Santos' findings, the guest account provided to the students required a password every time they wanted to access the wireless. The study suggested that the process of accessing the wireless that resembled a 'hotel type experience' may have discouraged students from using their mobile devices after completing the in-class quizzes.

Concluding remarks

This chapter has discussed key challenges associated with using students' personal mobile devices in the classroom. To effectively implement a BYOD programme, all institutions need to carefully consider their current network infrastructure to accommodate a variety of mobile devices. As noted by UNESCO (2013, p35), 'Most mobile learning opportunities depend on reliable connectivity to the internet and other communication and data networks.'

In addition, network security becomes more challenging when there is a multi-device environment. Implementing security measures and upgrading network implies considerations for financial costs. While BYOD is seen as reducing costs, these are hidden costs that need to be taken into account. Institutions must be attentive of equity issues by putting in place strategies to ensure that all students have access to a mobile device, internet connectivity and are able to participate in organized activities in and outside the classroom.

Violino's (2012, p 41) recommendation to schools not to '… rush into a BYOD program without researching and addressing issues such as access controls, security and support' equally applies to HE institutions. Pilot studies such as that by Santos (2013) should be conducted to test the BYOD initiative to help advance understanding on how to deal with the challenges discussed in this chapter and others that may emerge.

Furthermore, pilot studies could include faculty that are more comfortable with using mobile devices in the classroom to experiment with the BYOD concept. Outcomes could be shared with other faculty, IT staff and others through workshops. The pilot may illustrate the development of strategies and written policies to deal with network security and disruptions caused by the use of personal devices in the classroom.

However, developing policies may not be enough. Both faculty and students need to be educated with regard to network security practices. In addition, as observed by Geist (2011, p806; 810), it is important to communicate policies regarding when and how to use personal devices in class. Geist found that

> Students maybe be unaware that the use of cell phones affects teaching... Awareness foster courtesy and professionalism necessary for optimal teaching and learning. (p 806, 810)

The review suggested mixed results related to IT support for students' personal mobile devices. HE institutions should develop clear policies on how or whether they will provide support for personal mobile devices and make those policies available to students. Building on Ramsden's (2005) ideas of creating a support structure based on students instead of relying on IT support, institutions could promote a student network supporting system based on mobile device models and operating systems. Alternatively, if practical, train and assign IT personnel to support major mobile device models or operating systems used at the institution. While Santos (2013) revealed that IT support was not required, more studies are needed to validate the results.

Outcomes of this review suggest potential strategies to help minimize the challenges associated with a BYOD model. More studies investigating these key challenges are recommended. Studies could, for example, include different groups of students, and focus on formal and informal learning.

References

Alden, J. (2013). Accommodating mobile learning in college programs. *Journal of Asynchronous Learning Networks*, 17(1), 109-122.

Beckmann, E. A., & Martin, M. D. (2013). How mobile learning facilitates student engagement: A case study from the teaching of Spanish. In Z. L. Berge & L. Y. Muilenburg (Eds). *Handbook of mobile learning* (pp. 534-544). London: Routledge.

Bugeja, M. J. (2007). Distractions in the wireless classroom. *Chronicle of Higher Education*, 53(21), 1-4.

Burns, S. M., & Lohenry, K. (2010). Cellular phone use in class: Implications for teaching and learning a pilot study. *College Student Journal*, 44 (3), 805-810.

Campbell et al. (2013). The wild-card character of bring your own: A panel discussion. Retrieved from www.educause.edu/ero/article/wild-card-character-bring-your-own-panel-discussion

CDW-G (2012). Bring your own device [White paper]. Retrieved from webobjects.cdw.com/webobjects/media/pdf/Solutions/K12-BYOD.pdf?cm_sp=21CenturyClassroom-_-Resources-_-BYOD+K12

Cherwell Software (2012). BYOD - an educational revolution. [Web blog comment]. Retrieved from www.universitybusiness.co.uk/?q=features/byod-%E2%80%93-educational-revolution/5227

Cisco (2012). University embraces bring-your-own-device with wireless network. Retrieved from www.cisco.com/en/US/prod/collateral/wireless/C36-698193-00 University_Embraces_Bring Your Own Device.pdf

Curtis, J. (2012, November, 23). Bring your own device (BYOD). [Web log comment]. Retrieved from www.jisc.ac.uk/blog/bring-your-own-device/

Dahlstrom, E., & diFillipo, S. (2013). Consumerization of information technology/BYOD. EDUCAUSE. Retrieved from net.educause.edu/ir/library/pdf/ECRP1301.pdf

Dede, C., & Bjered, M. (2011). Mobile learning for the 21st century: Insights from the 2010 wireless EdTech conference. Retrieved from isites.harvard.edu/fs/docs/icb.topic1116077.files/!Wireless%20EdTech%20Research%20Paper%20Final%20March%202011.pdf

diFilipo, S. (2013). The policy of BYOD: Considerations for Higher Education. Retrieved from www.educause.edu/ero/article/policy-byod-considerations-higher-education

Dyson, E. L., Trish, A., Smith, R., & Wallace, R. (2013). Toward a holistic framework for ethical mobile learning. In Z. L. Berge & L. Y. Muilenburg (Eds). *Handbook of mobile learning* (pp. 405-416). London: Routledge.

Emery, S. (2012). Factors for consideration when developing a bring your own device (BYOD) strategy in education. Retrieved from scholarsbank.uoregon.edu/xmlui/bitstream/handle/1794/12254/Emery2012.pdf

Eschenbrenner, B. & Nah, F. F. (2013). Mobile technology in education: Uses and benefits. *International Journal of Mobil Learning and Organization*, 1(2), 159-183

Fang, B. (2009). From distraction to engagement wireless devices in the classroom. EDUCAUSE Quarterly, 32 (4). Retrieved from www.educause.edu/ero/article/distraction-engagement-wireless-devices-classroom

Fritschi, F. & Wolf, M. A. (2012). Turning on mobile learning. Illustrative initiatives and policy implications. France: UNESCO Publications.

Geist, E. (2011). The game changer: Using iPads in college teacher education classes. *College Student Journal,* 45(4), 758-768.

Hockly, N. (2012). Mobile Learning: What is it and why should you care? Retrieved from www.academia. edu/2050979/Mobile_learning_What_is_it_and_why_should_you_care

Johnson, D. (2012). On board with BYOD. *Educational Leadership,* 70(2), 84-85.

Kinash, S., Brand, J., & Mathew, T. (2012). Challenging mobile learning discourse through research: Student perceptions of Blackboard Mobile Learn and iPads. *Australasian Journal of Educational Technology,* 28(4), 639-655.

Kobus, M. B. W., Rietveld, P., & van Ommeren, J. N. (2013). Ownership versus on-campus use of mobile IT devices by university students. *Computers & Education,* 68, 29–41.

Kukulska-Hulme, A. (2010). Learning cultures on the move: Where are we heading? *Educational Technology & Society,* 13(4), 4-14.

Kukulska-Hulme, A., & Traxler, J. (2005). Mobile teaching and learning. In A. Kukulska-Hulme & J. Traxler (Eds.), *Mobile learning: A handbook for educators and trainers* (pp. 25-44). London: Routledge.

LaMaster, J., & Stager, G. (2012). Point/CounterPoint. Should students use their own devices in the classroom? *Learning & Leading with Technology.* 39(5), 6-7.

Lin, J., & Rivera-Sánchez, M. (2012). Testing the information technology continuance model on a mandatory SMS-based student response system. *Communication Education,* 61(2), 89-110. doi: dx.doi.org/10.1080/03634523.2011.654231.

Lundin, J., Lymer, G., Holmquist, L. E., Brown, B., & Rost, M. (2010). Integrating students' mobile technology in higher education. *International Journal of Mobile Learning and Organisation,* 4(1), 1-14.

Markeelj, B. & Bernik, I. (2012). Mobile devices and corporate data security. *International Journal of Education and Information technologies,* 1(6), 97-104.

Melhuish, K. Falloon, G (2010). Looking to the future. M-learning with the iPad. *Computers in New Zealand Schools, Learning, Leading, Technology.* 22(3) 1-16.

Melton, R. K., & Kendall, N. M. (2012). The Impact of mobilization in higher education. *The Global eLearning Journal,* 1(4), 1-11.

Mueller, J., Wood, E., De Pasquale, D., & Cruikshank, R. (2012). Examining mobile technology in higher education: Handheld devices in and out of the classroom. *International Journal of Higher Education,* 1 (2), 43-53.

Naismith, L., & Corlett, D. (2006). Reflections on success. A retrospective on the mlearn conference series 2002-2005. mLearn 2006: Across generations and cultures. Banff: Canada.

Norris, C. & Soloway, E. (2011). Tips for BYOD K12 programs. Critical issues in moving to "Bring Your Own Device." District Administration. Retrieved from www. districtadministration.com/article/tips-byod-k12-programs

Nykvist, S. S. (2012). The trials and tribulations of a BYOD science classroom. In Y. Shengquan (Ed.) Proceedings of the 2nd International STEM in Education Conference (pp. 331-334). Beijing Normal University, Beijing: China.

Perkins, S., & Saltsman, G. (2010). Mobile learning at Abilene Christian University: Successes, challenges, and results from year one. *Journal of the Research Center for Educational Technology*, 6(1), 47-54.

Poe, M., & Garfinkel, S. (2009). Security and privacy in the wireless classroom. In A. C. K. Hea (Ed). *Going Wireless: A critical exploration of wireless and mobile technology for composition teachers and researchers* (pp. 179-195). New Jersey: Hampton Press.

Quinn, C. N. (2012). *The mobile academy: mLearning for higher education*. US: Joseey Bass.

Ramsden, A. (2005). Evaluating a low cost, wirelessly connected PDA for delivering VLE functionality. In A. Kukulska-Hulme & J. Traxler (Eds). Mobile *learning: A handbook for educators and trainers* (pp. 84-91). London: Taylor & Francis.

Sangani, K. (2013). BYOD to the classroom. Engineering and Technology Magazine, 8(3). Retrieved from eandt.theiet.org/magazine/2013/03/byod-to-the-classroom.cfm

Santos, I. M. (2013). Integrating personal mobile devices in teaching: The impact on student learning and institutional support. *Learning & Teaching in Higher Education: Gulf Perspectives*, 10(2).

Schepman, A., Rodway, P., Beattie, C, & Lambert, J. (2012). An observational study of undergraduate students' adoption of (mobile) note-taking software. *Computers in Human Behavior*, 28, 308-317.

Scornavacca, E., Huff, S. & Marshall, S. (2009). Mobile phones in the classroom: If you can't beat them, join them. *Communication of the ACM*, 52(4), 143-146.

Sharples, M. (2002). Disruptive devices: Mobile technology for conversational learning. Retrieved from www.tlu.ee/~kpata/haridustehnoloogiaTLU/mobilesharples.pdf

Smith, S. D., Salaway, G., & Caruso, J. B. (2009). The ECAR study of undergraduate student and information technology. Retrieved from net.educause.edu/ir/library/pdf/EKF/EKF0906.pdf

Stav, J., Nielson, K., Hansen-Nygard, G., & Thorseth, T. (2010). Experiences obtained with integration of student response systems for iPod touch and iPhone into e-learning environments. *Electronic Journal of e-learning*, 8(2), 179-190.

Stoerger, S. (2013). Becoming a digital nomad. Transforming education through mobile devices. Z. L. Berge & L. Y. Muilenburg (Eds). *Handbook of mobile learning* (pp. 473-482). London: Routledge.

Traxler, J. (2005). Institutional issues: Embedding and supporting. In A. Kukulska-Hulme & J. Traxler (Eds). *Mobile learning: A handbook for educators and trainers* (pp. 174-187). London: Taylor & Francis.

Traxler, J. (2010a). Will student devices deliver innovation, inclusion, and transformation? *Journal of the Research Center for educational technology*, 6(1), 3-15.

Traxler, J. (2010b). Students and mobile devices. *ALT-J- Research in Learning Technology*, 18(2), 149–160.

UNESCO (2013). UNESCO policy guidelines for mobile learning. Retrieved from unesdoc.unesco.org/images/0021/002196/219641e.pdf

Violino, B. (2012). Education in your hand. Community College Journal. Retrieved from www.ccjournal-digital.com/ccjournal/20120809?pg=40#pg40

Chapter 8

Kids can

Yasemin Allsop

Introduction

With the rapid technological developments in recent years, computer and video games are currently the most discussed controversial topic in digital learning. Perhaps this is due to the numbers of hours children are spending in front of screens playing their favorite games. However educators have started to see the power of this new medium and explore ways to use computer games to support learning within schools.

Parallel to learning with playing computer games, there is also an increasing interest in children creating their own games and its educational value. This has flourished through the recent influences of constructivist theories on technology-supported learning, where learners actively build knowledge through experiment and discovery. The ease of having access to a vast range of game design programs online and the ability to create digital games without any knowledge of technical skills has also motivated this interest.

Previous studies into children's game-making practices focused on the impact on specific learning areas such as; literacy skills (Good and Robertson, 2004, 2006), story telling and writing skills (Dyer, 2008), skills in the areas of mathematics, science, art and computer literacy (Yatim and Masuch, 2007); some studied as part of game literacy, teaching students to learn to be critically, creatively and culturally accomplished individuals (Buckingham and Burn, 2007).

There were also some studies looking at children developing their thinking skills through game design activities. Papert (1998) used programming as a way to promote learning general thinking skills. He described programming as a construction tool for personal expression and knowledge construction, which empowers students to explore the psychological and cultural aspects of learning.

Jonassen (1996), defined computers as cognitive tools, when used with constructivist learning environments, it activates critical thinking and learning. Jonassen (1999) describes technology as 'the designs and environments that engage learners'. He also talks about how learners learn the most when they become the designer of the learning materials, rather than just learn from it. Kafai (1995, 1996) studied children's game design activities and suggested that game design is a context for children to practice and develop transferable skills such as planning, mathematical thinking and problem solving.

Dyer (2008), focused on a number of games-making projects for primary school children that aimed to develop students' storytelling and writing skills based on the curriculum. As a result Dyer explains that creating digital games motivates learners to achieve; increases self-esteem; provides opportunities for collaborative learning; develops problem solving; develops students ability to observe, question, hypothesize, test and facilitate metacognitive reflection.

There is no doubt that technological advances are changing not only the way we communicate but also the way we think and learn both individually and socially. What is remarkable is the way our brain responds to these technological innovations. Research in neuroscience suggests that our malleable brain is developing new capabilities and strategies. This innovation is not only affecting the adults of today but also the children of the digital age.

Children's interactions with the new technologies, either through playing games or designing their own games, is gradually transforming their own internalized thinking along with how they conceptualize learning in a social context. There has been a shift in understanding the anatomy of thinking and learning from a ready-static perspective to an interactive-dynamic experience. The students are no longer passive learners waiting to be taught; they are the head engineers of their mind lab where they design and control their thinking process sometimes alone, sometimes in partnership with the facilitator – teacher, parent, friend or computer, which leads to learning at anytime, anywhere.

However defining the context of how this change impacts on the thinking pattern of a child is still a vague area. The main difficulty is how we can observe the child's mind and take an image of their mental activities whilst making games, as thinking is not always visible. Their game designs could give us information on whether they are able to use the software to create a game. However it doesn't explain the steps in the cognitive process such as how they solved the problem, the strategies they used, the steps they followed and so forth. This chapter aims to explore this further.

Defining the focus

It is appropriate to suggest that digital game-making can be seen as a learning space to develop children's thinking, as it engages learners with constant problem-solving activities. However there isn't much information on whether this affects the foundations of the way the child thinks. Hence the question, 'Do digital game design activities impact on children's thinking patterns for learning and how?'

While this is a very complex question to answer, it is nevertheless a very important one as it is directly linked to the way the child learns. One way of finding an answer is to explore one's cognition, basically entering into the mind of a child. 'Cognition' as an umbrella term includes all the mental activities that lead to gaining, storing, connecting and transferring of knowledge and skills.

It can be seen as a brain's thinking function to design solutions for problems. Thus, if we are to understand children's thinking processes when designing their own games, the interrelation between thinking, learning and metacognition needs to be explored, as they are all strands of one's cognition. The following section will explore this relationship, which I call 'think-to-learn-to-think', as it is not only interrelated but also a continuous, overlapping process at times.

Think-to-learn-to-think...

It is apparent that the thinking element of game design activities is becoming a focus, as there is a growing emphasis on teaching children critical thinking skills so that they will become successful learners. Thus, defining what thinking is and how best to teach it with technology is still hazy. One of the biggest misconceptions in this area is thinking as a function is mostly evaluated through specific learning outcomes, rather than studying the process of cognitive activities in one's mind.

In a closer look thinking, as the main foundation of cognition, can be seen as the process of making constant connections between what we know and what we understand of concepts to develop further meanings. The firm bond between thinking and learning extends this definition further. According to Perkins (1992, 2003) learning is a consequence of thinking and successful learning depends on making thinking visible.

Thinking isn't only a mental process as it involves dialogue with 'self' but also with 'others'; likewise learning cannot be merely defined as the process of gaining knowledge. Learning and thinking are profoundly interrelated motions, overlapping at times. Thinking is, indeed. partly a mental process to learn, through the inward and outward effects of one's actions in the physical world which constitutes the skills of enquiry, creative thinking, reasoning, information processing and evaluation (National Curriculum, 2004).

A's to learning, it can also include developing the ability to think critically and to be analytical, to use information effectively, to make decisions, to think imaginatively, creatively and critically (Jessel, 2012). Noticeably, both notions include many similar skills. However having these skills doesn't alone guarantee that the student will learn. Learning is extensively derived on how well students can transfer and apply these skills to different learning contexts.

Bransford *et al.* (2000, p55) states that the transfer of the skills and knowledge is possible when learning involves more than simple memorization or applying a fixed set of procedures. Foremost, the student needs to understand the concepts and become expert in the skills, then know how and when to apply the skills to new situations. Although these steps look very straight forward, it is only viable when one develops the ability to understand and reflect their own thoughts, in other words metacognitive skills (Flawell, 1979; Fisher, 2005).

Cross & Paris (1988) defined metacognition as the knowledge and control children have over their own thinking and learning activities. Students can improve their learning by being aware of their own thinking and regulating their learning activities. The heart of metacognition is to be able to think inwards and organize the mental activities in mind, by visualizing the steps through conversations with 'self'.

This is a very important point, as when a child is asked to 'think', it basically directs them to use their internal voice to talk with 'self'. Thus, it looks like being part of a cognitive process; metacognition is a high level thinking skill on its own. Sternberg (1998, p17) states that metacognitive skills are driven by motivation which activates learning and thinking skills, then feeds back into the metacognitive skills, enabling one's level of expertise to increase. According to Sternberg these processes involve planning, evaluating and monitoring problem-solving activities and allocating cognitive resources appropriately is central to intelligence.

Method

The data was collected for a period of six months using participant observations, informal conversations, in-depth interviews, learning journals and video interviews for a wider scale research that had more extensive focus than here. However, for the purpose of this study children's before, during and after game design 'thinking maps' and video recordings of group discussions will be analyzed to gain an understanding of their mental activities when making their own digital games. A class of 30 children aged 10/11 were taught how to design digital games using 'Alice', which is a freeware object orientated 3D game design environment.

Thinking maps

Before the game design sessions started the children were given a blank sheet of paper and asked to explain how they think when they learn in any subject. They were not given any specific layout, so that they could reflect their own thinking context and style freely rather than using a set framework. They were asked to keep their thinking map during game design activities with them so that if there was any alteration that they wanted to make they could annotate directly onto it. At the end of the project, the children were asked to draw another thinking map to show their thinking for the learning process during the game design activities.

Group discussions

There were two discussions held on separate occasions: one during the game design project and one at the end of the project. Each lasted for 40 minutes. The discussions were video-recorded and focused on the children's view of the thinking process when making computer games in comparison to other activities in relation to learning.

Studying the children's thinking maps

Ujvara's thinking map

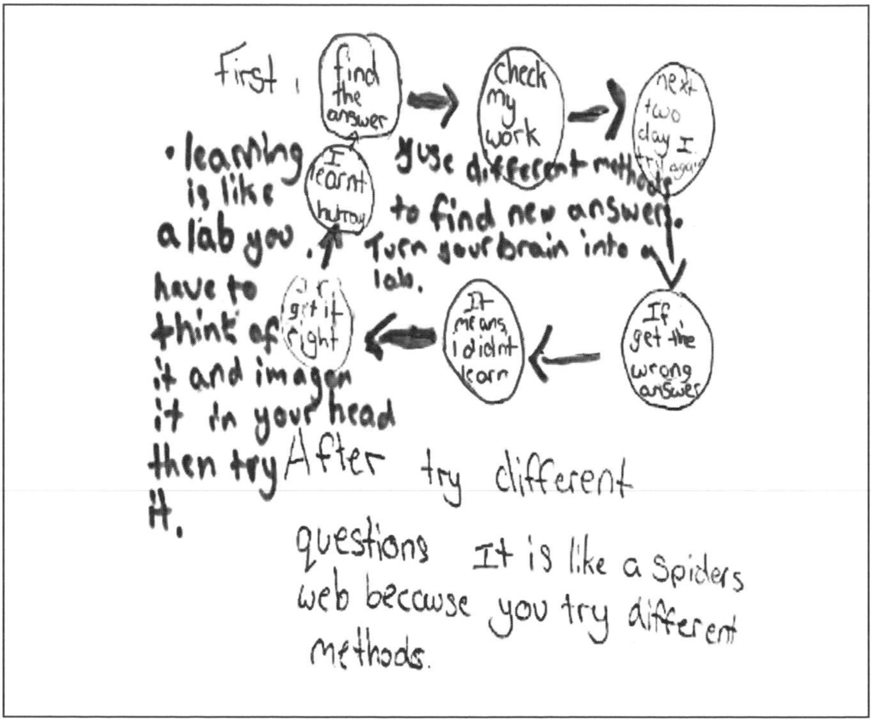

Figure 1: Ujvara's pre-project thinking map.

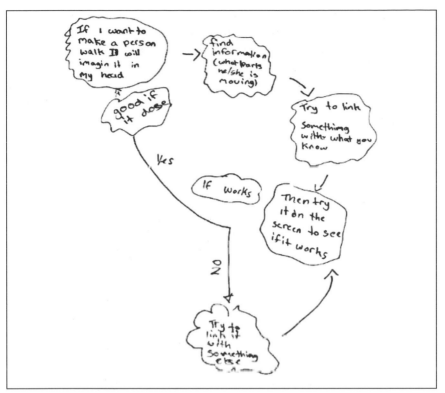

Figure 2: Ujvara's after-project thinking map with annotations.

In her thinking map before the game design activities (Figure 1), Ujvara drew out the process as a continual diagram and described it as a 'spider's web'. Her thinking started with an answer straightforward, then checking if her answer was right. It gets interesting, as she talks about remembering the concept again and being able to use it in couple of days' time.

She ends her map by suggesting that if she doesn't remember how to answer after couple of days she did not learn but if she does, she defines this as she did learn. Underneath her diagram she also wrote the word 'concentrate' and 'think different things'. She annotated her map during game design and she had written

> Learning is like a lab; you have to think of it and imagine it in your head then try it out. Use different methods to find answers. Turn your brain into a lab.

Her thinking map after the game design (Figure 2) has a different layout but is still drawn as a continual process. She starts with imagining the task in her mind: 'If I want to make a person walk, I will imagine it in my mind.' She then looks for the information required to accomplish the task. She links what she has found to what she already knows. She tries out her design on screen to see if it works. If it doesn't she suggest linking different information.

Helen's thinking map

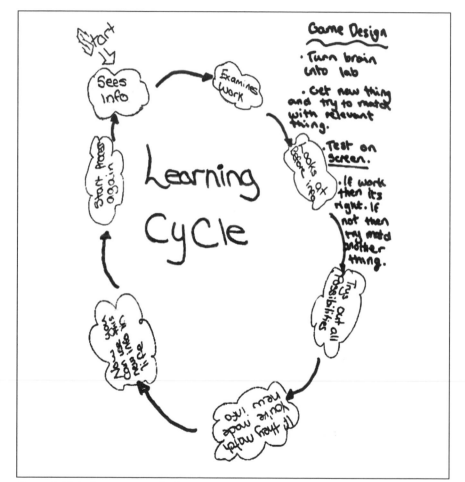

Figure 3: Helen's pre-project thinking map.

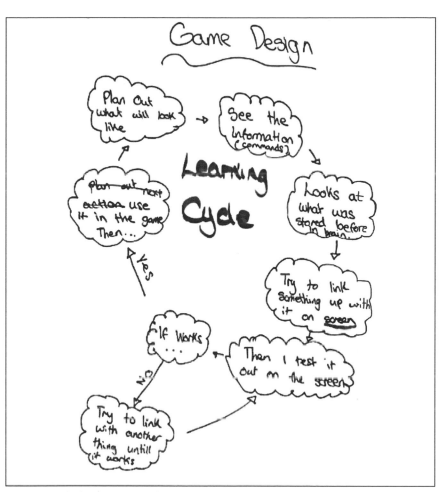

Figure 4: Helen's after-project thinking map with annotations.

Helen's thinking map has a continual circular layout. She marked the 'Start' point clearly. Her starting point is receiving information. Examining the work, looking at the prior knowledge, trying out all the possibilities, if they work you gained new information, which you can use in life, followed this. Then she starts the process again.

What is remarkable is that in her 'during game design thinking map' she also mentioned turning her brain into a lab. She mentioned trying different ideas/methods (engineering), testing on the screen and if it doesn't work try other things. Her thinking map after game design was also a continual circular cycle. She started the process by planning her game 'what it would look like', then looking at the information on the game program, such as commands (explore), then checking what she already knows and if she could link that with something on screen.

She then moves onto the testing stage (experiment). If it doesn't work, she then suggested linking another thing until it did work. If it works then it can be used in the game. When she was asked to explain this during group discussion her answer was

> Let's say I used codes; if for example I wanted to make the girl walk towards the car OK, I create the methods and the properties and function, maybe a variable, I don't know, I might need it, so together I create a line of codes. If this works, the girl moves where I want her to move, then I can use it when I make maybe a zombie move.

What this actually tells us is that she uses codes to program the object to move to a target point. She experiments with codes to conceptualize the action 'move' using a trial and error method. She then stores this concept in her mind to use another time when in a similar situation. She constantly checks her design for errors and makes corrections to manipulate the object/s to create the desired action.

This is a very complex activity and requires one's ability to analyze their internalized thoughts, visualize the effects of their thoughts on the actual design, then reflect on it by applying their thoughts onto the design itself using sets of codes.

Insaaf's thinking map

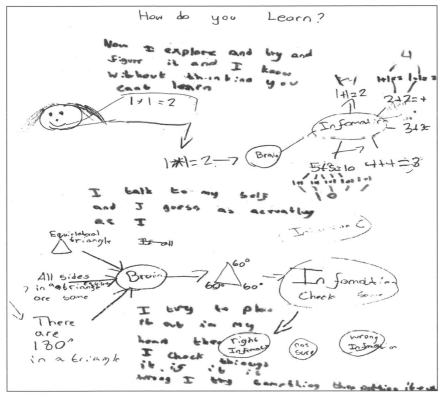

Figure 5: Insaaf's pre-project thinking map with annotations.

When compared to those of the two girls above, Insaaf's map (Figure 5) before the game design is not in a circular cycle. He uses examples to explain his thinking rather than listing the steps. He places his brain at the centre of problem-solving and shows how different information related to a problem has been connected and checked. He classifies some information right, some as wrong, placing a not sure option in the middle. His alteration on the map during the game design has textual explanations.

He starts with: 'Now, I explore and try and figure it and I know without thinking you can't learn.' His second sentence is: 'I talk to myself and I guess as accurately as I.' His final sentence says: 'I try to plan it out in my head then I check things, if it is wrong I try something, then putting it right.'

Note 'talking to self' and 'planning in the head' was first mentioned during game design activities. This doesn't mean he did not use these functions before, but it seems as though he is now aware of his own thinking and able to reflect upon his mental activities.

His after game design thinking map (Figure 6), has four linked boxes with text in them, although it is not circular. He starts with trying out

what happens if he clicks on the buttons on Alice (explore); then he uses the information he gained from trying out to plan what to do (engineer);

then he tries out his plan/s to create a final game (experiment/ then elicit). If he came across a problem, he tries stuff out until he gets it right (error

checking/evaluate). His thinking sequence is clearly mapped out and his final step tells us that he is engaged with the activity because when he

comes across a challenge/issue he doesn't give up, but tries out different possibilities until he finds the solution.

Figure 6: Insaaf's after-project thinking map.

Mahin's thinking map

In his before game design map (Figure 7), Mahin places the brain at the centre of his diagram. He then has sentences pointing out from the brain in numerical order. He first looks at the question (area of a square given as an example). He looks at the numbers. Then he calculates it. If he got the correct answer, he knows that he has solved the problem. He then revises it to make sure that he understands it. He added 'The logic helps in math as well as Alice' to his map during game design.

When he was asked to explain this; his answer was

> Well, it is really logic isn't it, if you can understand things, like connecting what you know and make sense of things, then you can solve any problem, could be in maths, like algebra, or in Alice like you want the space man to fly. You can do it if you can understand it, then you kind of know it.

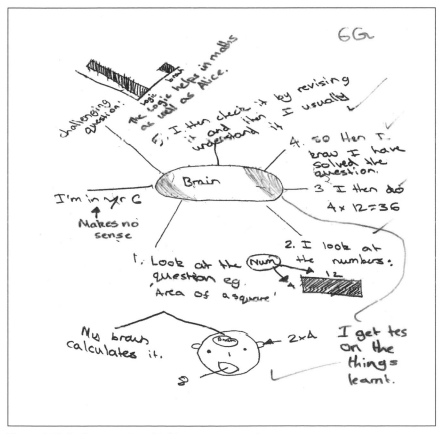

Figure 7: Mahin's pre-project thinking map annotations.

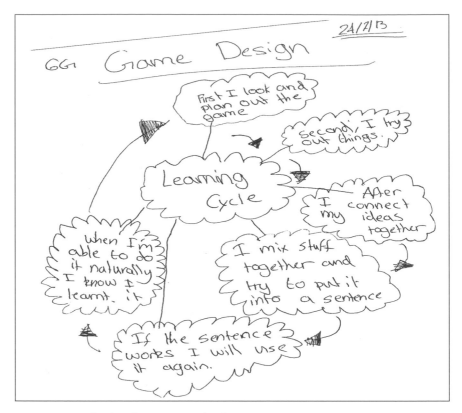

Figure 8: Mahin's after-project thinking map.

His after game design thinking map (Figure 8) had a different layout. He placed 'Learning cycle' at the centre. His mental activities were placed around these words and linked via arrows which show a type of continual cycle. He suggested that he first look and plan out the game (engage/ engineer), then he try out things (explore). This is followed by connecting his ideas, mixing stuff and putting into a sentence (coding- experiment). If the sentence works, he uses it again. When he can do this (coding) naturally he describes it as learning.

Mahin's thinking process starts with engineering ideas, and he then moves onto explore and experimenting. Once he is sure that his coding can make his idea happen, he uses this to design his game (elicit).

A conversation with children on thinking and game design

Although it is not possible to share all of the points made by the children here, there were some comments definitely worthy of a mention. The children thought that they had to do more when designing computer games because there wasn't always someone sitting next to them to help them. One child expressed this as:

> I think you have to link ideas because there isn't always a teacher besides you all the time, and not everybody knows game design. Teachers know maths and literacy because they learned to do that, I think you have to link ideas and think outside the box because you don't always have help.

Many of them compared game design with learning a new language. One child said:

> Maths, English is the language we understand. We know what 5 + 5 means. In Alice at the beginning we don't understand what it means, then we learn to do things. If you want something to move without you controlling it, you don't know because it is a different language. It is a coding language. You have to think deeper.

They also discussed how, as they learn to understand this language, they used similar codes to program the objects to do different actions.

> But you don't need to learn each movement as a different sentence. You could use the same coding for different actions. It could be like just adding stuff. When you're swimming you could just do move forward then move up or out, so you don't create all different, you need to add one more. Basically you need to know if you can use previous coding for another stuff.

When they were asked about the 'thinking sequence' during game design, a wide range of mental activities were involved. However 'imagining, visualizing' were the most mentioned words. Some of their comments were:

> I think about the motion in real life. When I think about swimming, I think about like I move my arms up and down.

> When you do maths, let's say a word problem, the answer is usually in the question. But in Alice you have to start from beginning and make an imaginary world and you have to make something to solve the problem.

> Sometimes you visualize it.

I imagine the game before I make it. If I make a game where it is a car game, in a city, first I make the scene-imagine the city, then the car and I think about what to do with it.

They also mentioned the word 'lab' quiet often. They talked about the virtual lab (lab in mind) and physical lab (the program) and how they connect them through design in mind then test on screen.

You turn the program into a lab, because you try out things on it. When you press 'play', you are basically testing, it is a real-physical lab really.

I use my mind lab, my virtual lab to match it with realistic lab. I plan it in my virtual one then test it using the program.

I test it out in my mind. If it is not realistic, then I won't try on my design, because I know it won't work.

I try to design the movements in my mind but I try out on the program, because the codes are on the program, not all in my mind.

I kind of visualize it in my mind. It is like pressing the 'play' button, but making it as you go. Like I need to make the man move forward, so that the other one can talk. You go to the real program to make it real.

One interesting point came out when they discussed the link between thinking and learning. One child described the process using another scientific example: 'It is like electricity and a light switch. They need each other to turn on the light. With only electricity you couldn't do something, you need the switch to turn on the light'. When another child asked; How do you apply this to game design? Her reply was; 'Switch is learning, electricity is thinking as it keeps going, never stops. Then another child asked: 'What is the light bulb then?' Her answer was: 'The light bulb is the end result, the solution, like your game design.'

Defining a model for think-to-learn-to-think cycle, 6E model

Although this was a small study it provides us with some interesting insights into children's thinking for learning processes during game design activities. The study will continue into the coming years, where the concept will be developed in further depth.

At this stage it is still very beneficial to share the main cognitive activities the children reported when making their own digital games. The study of children's Pre-during-after project thinking maps and the explanations they shared during group discussions suggests that their thinking sequences were altered during and after game design activities. Some of the changes noticed were:

Their drawings which represent their thinking processes had a clear layout with a continuous cycle.

Visualising, imagining the solution before testing on screen was included as a main mental activity.

Turning brain into a 'lab'. Many children talked about using their mind as a virtual lab to plan and test their design.

Talking to 'self'. Quite a few children mentioned having a conversation with themselves when planning their game or trying to find a solution to a problem.

Naming 'thinking map' as 'learning cycle'. Although drawing a 'thinking map' to show their thinking process was discussed at the beginning, many children labeled their map as a 'learning cycle'.

The thinking sequence that the children drew when making digital games had a similar pattern. The most frequently mentioned functions were motivation, exploring (Alice, design ideas), testing (ideas-design), checking for error and decision making (deciding a game idea, deciding which code to use). What was noticeable was how the majority of the children drew their thinking process as a circular continuous cycle which had the flexibility to allow them to move in between different steps as they needed. The main stages for think-to-learn-to-think cycle can be suggested as engage, explore, engineer, experiment, elicit and error check/evaluate.

Engage

Engagement is the core trigger for thinking. Without it, the process of thinking cannot come forth. In every step of the thinking sequence, from creativity to decision-making, children need to retain their attention to proceed to the next stage. Their engagement with the activity, sometimes alone, sometimes collaboratively with their peers or in partnership with their teacher, is the key element for laying the foundations for the thinking process. Although engagement seems to be the starting point for thinking, it is a continual motion, connected to each and every one of the arrays of the thinking system.

During the six months of the project, the majority of the children were completely engaged with the tasks, some longer than others. There were, however, a few students who from time-to-time became disconnected from the task, one reason for which could be a lack of cognitive resources to cope with the complex problems.

There are some strategies that teachers could use to support learners. They could encourage peer or whole class discussions to identify the main areas that children are having problems with and allow the group to design solutions collaboratively. They could also use questioning to encourage the learners to think aloud and deeper to check out if there is an error in their design.

Explore

Once the child has engaged with the activity, they then start to explore the interface of the medium used which they then extend it through exploring ideas and possibilities. When I first introduced the Alice game design program to the children, they spent around 30 minutes randomly clicking on the character and object files, methods, functions, and events. They then looked at the videos available on the Alice website and on YouTube.

Before even understanding how the program functions, they had a conversation with their friends on possible narrations for their games. Some of them also tried to copy the tutorials to find out more about what they could do. So it can be said that exploring occurs in two motions: learning about the mechanics of the medium (interface); and knowing what they could manifest with it (narrative).

Engineer

After exploring the interface of the game design program and the possibilities that they could manifest with it, the children start to engineer their own design ideas. During the Alice project, the way they did this was very individual. Some planned their game ideas on paper using a storyboard; some just discussed it with their partner and then directly started to design.

There were a few who walked around the classroom to see what others were working on. It was notable that during this stage the interaction between the learners in the classroom was minimal. Their focus and communication was more internalised than social. There were also some discussions around whether it was technically possible to turn their ideas into a design and how they could know this.

Experiment

This is the stage where testing, trying out, takes place. The children check if their ideas can be transformed into a design. They connect their ideas to the design through constant dialogue, thinking (dialogue with 'self' and 'others'), and action (dialogue with design) before turning these into reality using software. The children had many ideas, some of which they could turn into a design but some they couldn't. This didn't mean it wasn't possible; they just were not able to design a solution, so they moved onto another idea.

For example, one child wanted to have a multi-player car racing game. He managed to be able to have the cars controlled one at a time, but he couldn't find a way to have them controlled by different players using different computers, so he decided to explore ways of having the cars controlled by two players using the same computer. This is quite a fascinating action as it allows children to re-think their problems and design workable solutions. What a life skill to have.

Elicit

This can be seen as the decision-making part of the thinking process. After testing out their ideas and possibilities the children select the ones they like and then develop into a game. In our project this stage was the longest one. It was also firmly linked to the experiment stage.

This project made the children understand the importance of deciding carefully and making the correct choice. Every time they made the wrong choice they had to experiment with different ideas. Their issues with the decision-making stage became more visible towards the end of the project, where some were very close to completing a game, some still trying out other ideas. In a way, it made them aware of how wrong decisions impact not only on the outcome but also causes time-management issues.

Error check/Evaluate

When designing their games, the children often used the trial method to code. They constantly checked for errors but also evaluated to see if their coding was correct for the action they wanted to create. They reported that they automatically started to check if their design was correct, without even having a problem. They also stated that it is easier to realize your mistake when you are making a game without anyone telling you, because the game will not work. They compared this with a maths lesson when they said: 'Until your teacher tells you, you don't really know you have made a mistake! It is not always easy to see.'

Conclusion

The study into children's thinking for learning processes gives us information about the mental activities that the learners performed. What is significant is that, although most of the children's thinking processes followed a similar sequential pattern, the order of steps varied a number of times. This might be related to cognitive resources and previous experiences that the child had prior to the activity.

Another interesting point was their view on how game design impacted on their minds. They talked about using their mind as a lab to plan, visualizing solutions, testing ideas on the screen, checking for errors constantly, and thinking deeper as help was not always available. They suggested that their brain was more active during game design activities as they had to do the most of the work without much support.

They described this as 'thinking deeper' and 'thinking faster', which might be seen as extended cognition. Remembering the focus question at the beginning (do digital game design activities impact on children's thinking patterns for learning and how?) it is clear that there is a firm link between game design activities and the way the child thinks.

It can be suggested that, whilst making games, children transform their mind into a lab where they can develop and test their designs through thinking (dialogue with 'self' and 'others') and action (dialogue with design) before turning these into reality using software. This is a continual and constant 'making sense' process, where children can exercise their planning, decision-making, organizing, testing and evaluating skills that are a foundation to learning in many areas. The core of this process revolves around the teacher, learning space/task and the student's ability to regulate their own learning through ongoing monitoring and evaluating (metacognition).

This chapter provides us with a starting point to understand children's thinking process when designing their own games and I hope it will continue in the coming years to explore the context of their thinking further when making their own computer games or designing computer programs.

References

Bransford, J. D., Brown, A. L., & Cocking, R. R. (Eds.). (2000). Learning and transfer (Chapter 3). *In How people learn: Brain, mind, experience, and school* (pp. 51-78). Washington, DC: National Academy Press.

Buckingham, David & Burn, Andrew (2007): Game Literacy in Theory and Practice. *Journal of Educational Multimedia and Hypermedia*, 16(3), 323-349.

Cross, D. R. & Paris, S. G. (1988). Developmental and instructional analyses of children's metacognition and reading comprehension. *Journal of Educational Psychology*, 80(2), 131-142.

DfES (2004) *National Curriculum Thinking Skills*. Retrieved May 23, 2013, from www.bucksict.org.uk/KeyStage3/CourseMaterials/IncreasingProgress/Resources%20for%20session%201/ho%201.5.pdf

Dyer, G. (2008). *Making Digital Games … an exploration of game authoring in primary schools*. Retrieved June 12, 2013, from www.det.nsw.edu.au/media/downloads/detawscholar/scholarships/yr08/june/gdyer.doc

Fisher R. (1998), Thinking about Thinking: developing metacognition in children. *Early Child Development and Care*, Vol 141 (1998) pp1-15. Retrieved June 12, 2013, from www.teachingthinking.net/thinking/web%20resources/robert_fisher_thinkingaboutthinking.htm

Flavell, J. H. (1979). Metacognition and cognitive monitoring: A new area of cognitive-developmental inquiry. *American Psychologist, 34,* 906-911.

Jessel, J. (2012). Social, cultural and cognitive processes and new technologies in education in Miglino, O., Nigrelli, M. L., & Sica, L. S. *Role-games, computer simulations, robots and augmented reality as new learning technologies: A guide for teacher educators and trainers* Napoli: Liguori Editore

Jonassen, D., & Reeves, T. (1996). Learning with technology: Using computers as cognitive tools. In D. H. Jonassen (Ed.), *Handbook of research in educational communications and technology* (pp. 693-719). New York: Simon & Schuster Macmillan.

Jonassen, D. (1999). Designing constructivist learning environments. In C. Reigeluth (Ed.), *Instructional design theories and models: A new paradigm of instructional theory* (Vol. II, pp. 215-239). Mahwah, NJ: Lawrence Erlbaum Associates

Kafai, Y. B., & Resnick, M. (Eds.). (1996). *Constructionism in practice: Designing, Thinking, and Learning in a Digital World*. Mahwah, NJ: Lawrence Erlbaum

Kafai, Y. B. (1995). *Minds in play: Computer game design as a context for children's learning*. Mahwah, NJ: Lawrence Erlbaum

Papert, S (1998). *Does Easy do it? Children, Games, and Learning*. Retrieved 25 June, 2013, from www.papert.org/articles/Doeseasydoit.html

Robertson, J. and Good, J. (2004). Children's narrative development through computer game authoring. In *Interaction Design and Children 2004 Conference Proceedings*, pp. 57-64, New York: ACM Press.

Sternberg, R.J. (1998, April). Abilities are forms of developing expertise. *Educational Researcher*, 27 (3), 11-20

Yatim, M.H.M. and Masuch, M. (2007). *Educating Children through Game Making Activity*. Paper presented at Game in Action, Göteborg University, Sweden.

Chapter 9

Musings on technological changes in a teaching and learning environment

Dawn Seddon

Introduction

In recent years we have seen computer (and more specifically, wireless laptop) technology become increasingly sophisticated and more widely used by the general population. It would logically follow that there are great benefits to be reaped from using such tools within the educational sector, especially in the light of instant access to a wealth of materials and endless communicative possibilities using resources such as the World Wide Web, social networking sites blogs and wikis and from a motivational standpoint.

After teaching language classes for a number of years and observing the way students learn, watching their interactions and also by engaging in numerous discussions with colleagues, I am left contemplating the question of whether or not language learning using technology is actually as effective as envisioned.

Individual laptops were introduced in the Higher Colleges of Technology, United Arab Emirates, to replace computer labs and more traditional language labs. The main aims of the shift, it was argued, were to empower learners with individual portable learning tools that could be used within the classroom, and outside for self-access and independent study. Additionally, each student having individual ownership would ensure they could log and store their work securely. In addition it was claimed teachers would have access to a wealth of tools at any time without the need for a dedicated computer laboratory.

So, I decided to look a little more deeply into this 21st century progress through assessing student and teacher perceptions of the effectiveness of laptop use in English language classes. Based on my preliminary discussions, it can be ascertained that in-class laptop use can be both conducive to and detrimental to language learning. This may be due to teacher perceptions of the value of ICT – those who embrace and wish to promote its use, versus those who are more resistant and sceptical about its actual benefits – or to how far students are willing to learn new tools in addition to actual second language learning.

Very often, innovations regarding the institutional use of the latest technology are imposed top-down by management as they are assumed, by their progressive nature, to be the 'better path' to enabling more efficient learning. Nevertheless, such initiatives are usually embraced rather than challenged, or rejected, though many practitioners hold elements of doubt at the onset of implementation and may initially 'fear' change with the majority adopting the initiative after sometime, a minority remaining resistant (Rogers, 2003).

What particularly gripped my interest in pursuing this topic further was that, this semester (beginning in January 2012), the shipping of the designated laptops ordered for our new students failed to happen on schedule. When students finally received their 'essential tools' we were already eight weeks into the semester, at midway point. After initial panic and uproar about how our learners were going to be seriously disadvantaged, resourceful English teachers went about teaching their lessons 'unplugged'. After years of metaphorically 'leaning on the laptop', learning was, nevertheless, taking place effectively – results were largely unaffected and students were positively engaged using more 'standard' methods.

This was, of course, all noted purely by observation so further research seemed necessary to ascertain how students and teachers actually perceived the value of the laptops after they were eventually introduced. My research was conducted well into the semester when students and teachers could make reasonable comparisons as to how learning was occurring. Fundamentally, I am interested in discovering how we can help learners learn best. To do this effectively requires looking at learning preferences and questioning what is going on within the classroom.

The foundation programme at The Higher Colleges of Technology is a four tier pre-degree intensive English Language programme that aims to bring learners to an IELTS band of 5.5 within a two-year time frame. Learners placed in level one are typically false beginners or lower elementary at a CEFR level of A1. Students come from an education system in which they have English instruction from primary school, but this seems to be largely ineffective. Most students arriving with very limited communicative language and display acquired fossilised error patterns arising from predominantly structure-based instruction.

Additionally, their world knowledge is limited, probably partly due to social, family and religious restrictions. It is not clear how much computer or IT training students receive prior to coming to the college. For some, this could be their first experience of working on a laptop and many may not be familiar with the English keyboard or commands. A few come from homes with no internet access, though this tends to be a minority from very conservative backgrounds.

For most, however, the college will be the only place where they can freely access social media – sensitive content is generally blocked by the government (other than in educational establishments) and there may be family-imposed restrictions on accessing social networking sites, messaging and email, especially as my students were all young Muslim women.

Learners are typically in the 18-26 age range and in the current cohort there are students who are new (recent school leavers), and those who are repeating the level. Classes are homogenous in nature so a study across classes should produce typical or representative results. Students follow the same curriculum and classes are roughly the same size (between 14 and 20 in a class). Those repeating the level will have had one semester more exposure to laptop use than new students, but not necessarily with any greater success.

Each class typically has one or two teachers who teach integrated skills over 20 hours weekly, over a 20-week semester. Teachers are native speakers of English from the UK, Ireland and North America. All are very experienced, have worked in various locations around the world and hold at least a TESOL/ELT Diploma (most have Masters Degrees).

While there is no denying that computer technology has become more sophisticated and user-friendly which has, in turn, opened up numerous possibilities for exploration in the ELT classroom, there is currently quite considerable debate as to whether in-class laptop use is as effective as we might presume. Reading current articles, I have discovered that there are two main polarised standpoints: either those who see laptops as interfering with concentration and impairing effective learning; and those who view laptop technology as essentially enriching and indispensable in technologically aware, current educational practice and in classrooms promoting student autonomy and communicative authenticity.

Murray (2008) talks about how technology tools have changed as rapidly as the pedagogy that supports their use. Over the past 20 years the focus in the ESL/EFL classroom has been predominantly on communication and providing learners with authentic communicative opportunities. She points out that technology has evolved to offer a range of such opportunities and therefore it would be logical for English teachers to exploit this.

Nunan (1988) turned the focus of ELT on encouraging learner autonomy and learner-centeredness – the use of the laptop PC could thus be the perfect vehicle for the motivated learner. Levin, Tamar, Wadmany and Rivka (2006/7) go further to suggest that those teachers whose philosophy support student-orientated learning and Constructivist approaches are probably those who are first to promote new technology in their classrooms.

The Apple Classrooms of Tomorrow (2001) also emphasises that technology has enhanced better student-centred practises and helped significantly in empowering the learner. Indeed, the use of laptop/wireless technology (when exploited competently) can encompass the whole pyramid of the revised 21st- Century Bloom's Taxonomy (Anderson *et al.*, 2001) to include everything from 'remembering' to 'creating', fully supporting 'higher-order thinking' strategies.

Murray (2008) promotes ICT as a tool that helps learners to organise, edit and review, especially in writing. Murray also points out that the use of tools facilitates communication, extends boundaries beyond the classroom and promotes independence. Those, such as chat programmes and online discussion boards, all provide authentic communicative opportunities.

However, Kim and Rissel (2008) in their research found that teachers often underutilise ICT because of their own beliefs about the place of computers in learning. Nevertheless, they state that many teachers see the distinct advantages of using tools such as discussion boards especially in reducing the fear of face-to-face participation in live discussions involving more reserved learners.

For others, it is the very nature of such tools (chat, social networking sites *etc*) that leads to inefficiency and off-task behaviour which effectively impairs learning. Fried (2008) conducted research indicating that students using laptops in class spent a large amount of time multi-tasking and were significantly distracted by chat and social communications outside the learning environment. Fried (2008) goes further to state that:

> the use of laptops was negatively related to several measures of learning. The pattern of the correlations suggests that laptop use interfered with students' abilities to pay attention and to understand (the lesson).

Fried also quotes other research on cognitive interference which has shown that performance speed is reduced, and errors increased, due to distraction from pop-up messages and unrelated periphery overload on the screen. With lower level learners, this is especially true – even the interface of a programme in English, to a beginner, can pose significant confusion and raise panic which detracts considerably from the task in hand.

While email and instant messaging can certainly be seen as purposeful tools promoting real world opportunities for authentic communication, Lauricella and Kay (2010) suggest that they can also be detrimental in the classroom when used recreationally within the class.

In their research on laptop effectiveness, Lauricella and Kay (2010) received comments from students that key distractions were also web surfing, watching movies and playing games on their laptops in class, with 70% of students spending 50% of class time on non-lesson focused activities.

Reflecting on these viewpoints, it figures that if a teacher is committed and convinced that using technology befits and enriches sound pedagogy and can scaffold tasks carefully for the learners, many of these negative implications may be eradicated. Similarly, the reverse is also true, as indicated by Ghasem and Hashem (2011) who state that; '...language teachers should carefully consider new strategies in teaching, but ICT without correct strategies cannot help us in the classroom.'

In order to assess the situation from different perspectives and thus reap a more accurate overview of what is happening with teaching and learning, I decided to use three main instruments of enquiry. These were questionnaires, one directed at students and another for teachers, plus 'field notes' from a live observation. After some discussion with colleagues who became interested in what I was investigating, one proffered some feedback from one of his classes regarding a task giving the students a choice of using a laptop or not. This supported my main research, so I have also included it here (full permission granted).

The logical starting point for an enquiry regarding how learning takes place would be in asking the students. To find out how students use laptops and ask about some of their preferences, I adapted the *Laptop Effectiveness Scale* (LES) implemented by Lauricella and Kay (2009) which looks at the academic (classroom based) and non-academic (recreational) uses of laptops by students in further education.

Given the level of the students being surveyed, I decided 'closed' yes/ no response questions were probably the best starting point, so little ambiguity could interfere. To add further to clarity, I also had the questions translated into Arabic and questions were kept simple and direct. The final three questions were based on prior observations of what may (or may not) cause student reticence or frustration where laptop use is the issue. In the second part of the questionnaire, the objective was to acquire more qualitative responses and to determine more individual opinions, so I introduced more open-ended questions which were kept to a minimum in order to not overload or confuse the students.

The teachers' questionnaire

The teachers' questionnaire was more complex and involved than the student version, for obvious reasons. I asked eight teachers whether they would participate and obtained three full responses. My assumption, based on the comments from one colleague, is that at the conclusion of the academic year, teachers were too busy to give their time even though completing the survey would only take approximately 20 minutes.

All teachers were given the option of return by email or printing a paper copy. Two chose the version which would retain anonymity; one returned by mail. While the questionnaire did generate a wealth of detailed, albeit more casual, face-to-face discussion afterwards, I have left these comments out of this research as these were 'enriching' discussions between colleagues which, on the basis of ethics, I have not gained explicit permission to reproduce.

The questions are based on common experience with laptops in the specific curriculum, expectations and common practices. The main aim was to find out what teachers actually do in their classes; what they find useful; and what reservations they have about integrating laptop use into their English classes.

The first section refers specifically to tools or programmes that are commonly used within the college system and their applications:

Teacher questions, Part A

How do you use laptops with your classes?

Please indicate

    a. Which tools you currently use and frequency (0=never, 5=very frequently).

    b. How useful you think this tool is (0=of no use, 5=extremely useful)

1. Communicative Uses

Tool, programme, use	Frequency of use	Valuable?
Email correspondence with students	0 1 2 3 4 5	0 1 2 3 4 5
Students send homework to teacher	0 1 2 3 4 5	0 1 2 3 4 5
BB Vista discussion boards	0 1 2 3 4 5	0 1 2 3 4 5
Other:	0 1 2 3 4 5	0 1 2 3 4 5

2. Independent Study

Tool, programme, use	Frequency of use	Valuable?
ILC/Library & Learning Site	0 1 2 3 4 5	0 1 2 3 4 5
Global Beginner E-workbook	0 1 2 3 4 5	0 1 2 3 4 5
Clarity (tensebuster)	0 1 2 3 4 5	0 1 2 3 4 5
Other language games/programmes/site Name:	0 1 2 3 4 5	0 1 2 3 4 5

3. Language Production

Tool, programme, use	Frequency of use	Valuable?
Word processing – typing; editing, error correction	0 1 2 3 4 5	0 1 2 3 4 5
Presentations; PowerPoint, Movie Maker…	0 1 2 3 4 5	0 1 2 3 4 5
Voice recording; Voice thread, voice recordings on BBVista etc	0 1 2 3 4 5	0 1 2 3 4 5
Other:	0 1 2 3 4 5	0 1 2 3 4 5

4. Resources

Tool, programme, use	Frequency of use	Valuable?
Online dictionary	0 1 2 3 4 5	0 1 2 3 4 5
Translation tools	0 1 2 3 4 5	0 1 2 3 4 5
You Tube/videos	0 1 2 3 4 5	0 1 2 3 4 5
Other:	0 1 2 3 4 5	0 1 2 3 4 5

5. Reading

Tool, programme, use	Frequency of use	Valuable?
Webpages and Webquests (authentic)	0 1 2 3 4 5	0 1 2 3 4 5
ESL Reading Sites/Progammes	0 1 2 3 4 5	0 1 2 3 4 5
Graded Readers – with sound files	0 1 2 3 4 5	0 1 2 3 4 5
Other:	0 1 2 3 4 5	0 1 2 3 4 5

The second section gives opportunity to comment about actual classroom experience using laptops:

Teacher questions, Part B

1.	Have you used laptops for tests and quizzes this semester? If so, what is your experience? Positive/negative? What are the advantages/drawbacks?
2.	From your experience, do you see laptops as aiding student focus or providing a source of distraction?
3.	Do you think your students enjoy using their laptops?
4.	What factors (if any) do you think make students reluctant to use laptops on a day to day basis?
5.	Do you think your students had adequate ICT skills before starting the course?
6.	How do you think laptops are helpful in class?
7.	How do you think laptops are not helpful in class?
If you are teaching a new section (or returning students new to level one)...	
8.	Do you think your students have been disadvantaged by their laptops arriving late into the semester?

Live observation: 'field notes'

Questionnaires, while supplying valuable data, only show part of the picture. Frequently they yield subjective responses, especially where open-ended questions are employed and may not be truly indicative of what is happening in the real situation. While this study is essential about *perceptions*, I determined that a more complete picture would be obtained by integrating an element of live observation within the study.

This is not to say that note-taking during live observation does not have its pitfalls. In discussing action research methods, Wallace (1998;57-59) suggests the idea of 'field notes' and indicates that taking notes while teaching is not as common as it probably should be among language teachers probably since:

> ...the necessity of maintaining discipline and the sheer complexity of interaction (with learners) leaves little time for taking notes. (p 58)

Furthermore, he indicates pertinently that the drawbacks of such a method would be that a teacher's intensive involvement in the lesson itself would mean that important observations would be lost and recall possibly impaired. (Wallace, 1992:58)

In order to minimise this interference, I asked my colleague/supervisor to observe my class, paying attention to interaction and engagement with laptop-based and non-laptop based activities in the context of a regular class.

Here are the focus points for the observation:

Observation Point		
Non- laptop focused activities	Student engagement	
	Interaction	
	Language production	
Laptop focused activities	Student engagement	
	Interaction	
	Language production	
Could the laptop-based activities have been done just as successfully without a laptop (or better)?		
Was too much time taken to set up the laptop-based activities? (i.e. teaching the ICT tool/IT sub skills)		
Was the laptop use at any point counterproductive? (e.g. for students with weak IT skills, students with no laptop, technical problems etc)		
At which points of the lesson did students display off task behaviour?		

Observation/field notes table

Notes were taken as the lesson progressed over a 1hr 40 minute block. The observer's notes were returned to me after the lesson and discussed. Ideally this could have been repeated, with different classes and teachers, across a variety of activities using both wireless technology and more standard practices. I suggested to other colleagues that they might do this with their classes, but no one decided to go ahead, probably for the reasons preciously indicated by Wallace (1992).

Student task response and feedback questionnaire

During the initial stages of my research, colleagues were actively engaged in assisting me through the process. One teacher, who did not take part in the questionnaire, independently devised his own mini-research for his class, the results of which were shared.

For this, students were given a writing activity and offered different ways of completing the task – either using pen and paper, writing using word processing or sending directly to the teacher using email. After completing the task, students were questioned as to why they chose the particular method. The questions were structured to allow simple responses, with multiple options:

Foundations Level 1 (F03) Writing Assignment: 'My Hometown, Neighbourhood & Home'

Please tick ONE of the boxes:

I wrote the essay:

On paper, with a pen/pencil ☐

On my laptop, as a Word document ☐

On my laptop, as a real email to my teacher ☐

If you wrote it on paper, why did you do that? (You can tick more than one):

I prefer (like it better) to write on paper, because I can plan it and see it easier ☐

I don't like using a laptop/computer to write essays etc. ☐

I sill have trouble typing/using my new laptop ☐

I forgot to bring my laptop ☐

If you used your laptop (typing a Word document or email), why did you use it? (You can tick more than one):

I don't like writing on paper (by hand/pen) ☐

I know how to use my laptop and I prefer it to writing by hand ☐

I think a piece of writing (e.g. an essay) looks better if it is typed, not written by hand ☐

Using your laptop means you get help with spellcheck, you can delete mistakes ect. ☐

I don't like my handwriting / I have difficulties writing by hand, so I like typing better ☐

I think I will learn English better, now that i have my new laptop:

Yes, I agree Maybe/perhaps ☐ I don't know ☐

No, I don't agree ☐ I don't have a laptop yet ☐

Thank you.

Student preference feedback.

It should be noted that this particular class was a new (rather than repeating) section who had recently received their laptops, and had thus become accustomed to completing tasks by hand. The teacher gave the raw data (the completed questionnaires) to me after which I analysed the responses.

Student questionnaire responses

Sixty-four questionnaires were collected. All students completed the eight 'yes/no' questions with 60 completing part two which required more open-ended responses.

All respondents claimed to own a laptop with 92% of the sample (59 students) saying their teachers actively request them to use laptops in English class. 97% of students were positive about laptops helping them to learn English, but this seems to be restricted to in-class use for a few as not all (81%) indicate that they use a laptop or computer at home for English practice.

This chart shows student responses to the first four questions in the survey:

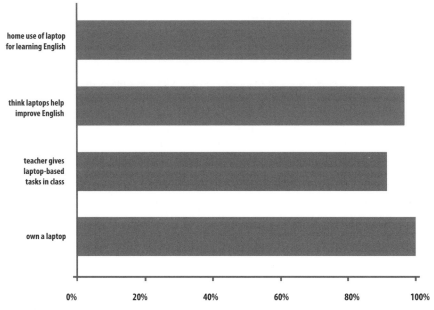

Foundations students; laptop use and learning English.

The second chart shows the distribution of responses to the following four questions that are concerned with student experiences and preferences regarding using a laptop.

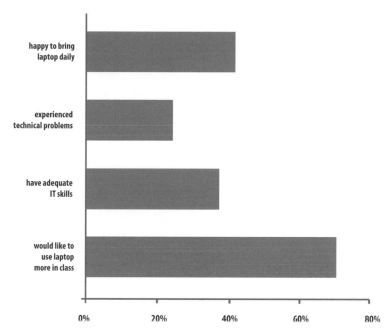

Student experiences with laptops.

These questions generated a variety of responses, with some students indicating that they were not absolutely happy with the idea of increasing the frequency of laptop use in lessons, though 73% would like to use their laptops more. A relatively large number of students (69%) felt that their IT skills were not enough to manage using a laptop in English classes – only 39% said they thought their current level of IT competence was adequate.

Preference for the laptop does not seem to be majorly affected by technical problems preventing students from participating in a lesson, with only 30% reporting such issues. The main issue, however, seems to be student reluctance to bring their laptop to class each day with fewer than half (44%) indicating that they would be happy to do so.

In the second section requiring open-ended responses, of those who answered, many gave general non-committal responses and many answers were repeated (probably owing to student insecurity and discussing what they would write). However, there were several things to be gleaned from what students decided to say.

In relation to using the laptop outside class, most students responded that they would use it to complete homework set by the teacher, or to 'find' answers to homework. Similarly, a majority indicated that outside class they were more inclined to use their laptop recreationally, citing the following activities:

Surfing the web.

Watching movies.

YouTube.

Searches using Google.

Chatting.

Seven students do not use their laptop outside class at all.

The things that students enjoyed in class were using a translator, or translating tool and having easy access to an online dictionary. Using the internet was also popular, but for what purpose was not made explicit. Students are also happy that teachers can explain things simply using data shows, quick searches and pictures. Many learners expressed that they enjoy using practice activities for grammar and vocabulary which give instant feedback/marking.

Negative comments related to not feeling comfortable using the keyboard and being held back by slow typing speeds. Technical issues such as freezing, sticking keys and slow internet connections were also mentioned as were other hardware problems. One student just wrote that using computers in class is 'boring'!

Teachers' responses

As indicated, only three completed forms were received, but those who did partake supplied interesting and detailed responses. These were individualised and indicate that each teacher has his/her preferences as to how laptops should be used.

One example of this is that two of the three have not used Blackboard Vista discussion boards at all, not viewing them as valuable, while the other saw this as the most valuable tool and used it most frequently. Email correspondence was also under-utilised, but viewed by one teacher as useful. Only one teacher asks students to email homework, but one other indicated that she would have used email more if laptops could have been introduced earlier in the semester. These findings are surprising and indicate that the full potential of the communicative uses of the laptop are not put into practice.

Teachers view the course book ICT component (Global Beginner e-workbook) as very useful and use it frequently with classes. This matches what students seem to enjoy doing. There is virtually no communicative use here, but these materials allow students to work independently, review their work and receive instant feedback. One teacher commented that they exploited these materials by creating a weekly online plan that students could follow at their own pace, noting that this was extremely effective when used in-class, rather than as homework/independent study.

All three teachers found the ability to use voice recording programmes and tools within Blackboard Vista and Web 2.0 tools such as Voice Thread very useful, but there appears to be some differentiation of use and opinion where word processing tools are concerned.

None of the teachers either extensively use, or see the value in, translation tools although this is what the students indicate as valuable for their own use. Obviously, this has a great deal to do with teachers attempting to move students away from translation methods towards greater self-reliance though one teacher uses an online dictionary frequently.

Teacher comments gave best insight. All three teachers have been reluctant to attempt integrating testing templates using educational technology due to there being a backlog in receiving the laptops and getting students acquainted with them. This was seen as too time-consuming and disruptive, as well as there being glitches with software programmes which potentially compromise the reliability of results.

While noting the benefits of laptops, two of the teachers viewed laptop use as more distracting than useful. This said, teachers indicate that if the students are properly engaged in the activity this is minimised. All teachers agree that they believe students enjoy using the laptop as it provides a different focus. One teacher indicated that she felt some students have become over reliant on translation, copy/paste and spell checker tools.

Teachers express that they frequently hear complaints from students that the laptops are too heavy to carry around, which makes them reluctant to bring them daily. This correlates with the student response with 66% of students not wishing to bring their laptop each day. This seems to be the major negative response, with other factors being students who find on-screen reading challenging and those who are unable to access online materials at home.

All teachers see the value of the library self-access materials as part of the ICT component of the course. There is a strong feeling that students should be given some instruction in basic IT skills, possibly bilingually before being expected to function in English on a laptop. One teacher points out that students are operating with commands and interfaces in another language using specific vocabulary that should be at least pre-taught, making simple tasks such as navigating an additional challenge.

Field notes

Whilst observing a class in action, several key points were noted. Students were seen to be fully engaged in the non-laptop focused activities at the beginning of the lesson but when the word 'laptop' was mentioned, students were sent into a flurry of activity which could be interpreted as unfocused. While not intentionally disruptive, the unpacking, plugging-in and logging-on meant students were missing necessary instructions and I was left to repeat and review several times, despite instructions to wait.

It was at this point that students first lapsed into Arabic to check and clarify with each other. This interfered with what was, up to that point, an English-only zone with all learners completely focused on the task. The setting up of the activity took a total of ten minutes, to teach the process and 'walk' students through the necessary steps of searching and compiling a basic picture show, supported by target sentences, in PowerPoint.

Even then, things were unclear and a lot was demanded in the teaching situation: dealing with students who were confused; unintentionally off-task; operating the wrong programme due to misunderstanding; or encountering various technical difficulties such as:

Missing system drive.

No wireless signal or slow connection.

Experiencing a long start up time.

This interlude of 'troubleshooting' was compounded by students with very weak IT skills being unable to cope with simple file management and navigating the keyboard. The observer noted that the students' lack of basic IT skills was definitely hindering the activity.

In this particular activity (making a slide show of photos from an imaginary holiday, leading to a communicative activity talking about the experience), it was intended that the use of the internet to search for pictures and the simplicity of inserting them into a slideshow would enable an activity that would otherwise be difficult to attempt due to limited knowledge of other countries, coupled with the inability to supply authentic photographs or anecdotes.

While this was to some extent jeopardized by the difficulties handling the tool, the possibilities of having a resource more readily at hand than, say, brochures opens up possibilities for a more enriching classroom experience when learners pre-equipped with the necessary IT skills.

Teacher's 'student choice' questionnaire

Surprisingly, all 14 students who were given the choice to complete the writing task either on the computer or by handwriting chose to handwrite on paper. The reasons for choosing this method are:

- I prefer to write on paper, because I can plan it and see it easier [14]
- I don't like using a laptop/computer to write essays etc. [9]
- I still have trouble typing/using my new laptop [10]
- I need more training in how to use my laptop [8]
- I forgot to bring my laptop [8]

Interestingly, all students claim simple preference as the reason not to use the laptop, with more than half expressing that they just don't like it. The other reasons fall into the bracket of 'computer anxiety', either having difficulties with typing or with feeling less competent on the computer due to insufficient preparation or training. With eight students 'forgetting' to bring their laptop to class, this reinforces the previous findings that the students prefer not to carry equipment to class on a daily basis.

Discussion

The results indicate that there is a measure of reticence from both students and teachers in fully embracing the integration of various types of technology in general English classes. The late arrival of laptops seems to have geared the focus back to more standard ELT teaching and learning.

While students reportedly enjoy the shift of focus offered by ICT-based tasks, when given the choice, these lower elementary learners still feel more comfortable using traditional methods. This is probably a matter of keeping within their comfort zone. This is further compounded by feeling held back by lack of knowledge of the keyboard and being slowed down either by this lack of practice, or by technical issues.

Teachers are sceptical about the real benefits of spending a lot of time 'teaching the tool' where students are (or claim to be) lacking the basic IT skills necessary to fulfil tasks. There is a general feeling that if students had foundation training, teachers would be more eager to integrate ICT/laptop use in their classes.

Actual use of laptops is heavily weighted to games/activities where students work individually rather than exploiting communicative uses or using authentic up-to-date information. My assumption is that teachers feel students either have not had adequate training or that students are not ready linguistically to take on such challenges. This is compounded by the paradigm that teachers themselves may feel 'behind' or challenged by ever-developing technology and would benefit from focused training themselves.

In practice, a lot of groundwork needs to be done to ensure efficient class use of laptops as indicated in the live observation where a large amount of time was consumed by troubleshooting and offering individual assistance. Such issues may also contribute to teacher reluctance as they further complicate classroom management when off- task behaviour interferes with lesson objectives. This ranges from students who forget laptops (and so are unable to participate properly) to those 'multitasking' on chat/social networking sites in Arabic who are neither engaged or focused.

Further questions

The research was not as broad as I had intended due to the fact that only a few teachers responded – this does not give enough scope to properly evaluate the wider picture of teacher attitudes to laptop use, nor a fully comprehensive overview of the application of laptop-based ICT. Had a wider sample been obtained, we may have seen a more varied picture. Nor does it assess elements of teachers' own 'computer phobia' as an explanation of why some have restricted use of or negative views about using laptops with lower levels. This became apparent as a possible influencing factor on student behaviour while the study was in progress.

It would be beneficial, given time, to repeat the process of research with a different cohort where the issuing of laptops was not delayed, as this probably had some impact on all areas of enquiry. Phinney (1991) when addressing computer-assisted writing in ESL, indicates that through research it was shown that at least one semester was needed for positive changes to take effect.

Additionally, with limited time allocated to the implementation of laptops, negative responses could have been anticipated due to frustration and lack of pre-training. Student responses may have been more positive had teacher attitude been different. As Hyland (1993) pointed out, improvements in student performance when using CALL/ICT are not due to the computers but the teachers who direct the task, reiterating that 'support is a critical variable in... success [of integrating computers]'.

Nunan (1992;58) states that many criticisms of ethnographic research come from the fact that studies cannot be properly analysed by outsiders if they wish to replicate the enquiry. Here we are dealing with a very specific group of learners who are not representative of other learners worldwide. This study by no means supplies an adequate picture of how learners and teachers view laptop use outside the specific area of focus. Therefore, an analysis of other influencing factors could also enrich the enquiry were it to be re-investigated.

Recommendations

A year after I commenced this research, the decision was made that the Higher Colleges of Technology to replace laptops with iPads in order to move with technological advancements and provide a youth-friendly tool to aid language learning . However after one year of iPad experimenting it was decided to abandon their mandatory usage and invite students to bring their own device (BYOD). However since this the introduction of BYOD it has been decided to revert to Lap-Top use for the new academic year.

In using any device, be it a PC, laptop or iPad, there are key issues to be addressed. Hyland (1993) made recommendations that are still relevant;

> Students need to be familiar with the keyboard and software.

> Computer/laptop activities must be properly integrated into the ELT curriculum.

> Opportunities for collaboration and peer support must be provided.

> Learners must be offered *explicit* preliminary instruction in using the tool for the specific purpose it is intended in the English class. (Hyland; 1993)

Although many students and teachers still hold reservations about the usefulness of such technology in the classroom, and with current research indicating counterproductive behaviour in laptop-based classrooms, there is no denying that a complete shift back to traditional methods is highly unlikely. It is, therefore, our duty in embracing this move forward to ensure that students benefit fully from the range of communication possibilities offered by wireless technology. This can only be done through the provision of training, for both students and teachers, in using the tool before it can be properly exploited in English language lessons.

The tool without the pedagogy, and thorough support, is ineffective and is unlikely to lead to better language learning. Moreover, it is also imperative that designated technology does not replace good classroom practice, but rather enhance it. Additionally, while accommodating for learning needs, mobile/wireless technology is not a 'fit all' solution: teachers must continue to accommodate for all learning styles and personalities, with full awareness of learner preferences and behaviours.

References

ACOT (Apple Classrooms of Tomorrow Project). Softweb Resource Centre. April 2001 World Wide Web: www.softweb.vic.edu.au/research/pdf/NAV30_2. pdf

Anderson, L. W., Krathwohl, D. R., Airasian, P. W., Cruikshank, K. A., Mayer, R. E., Pintrich, P. R., Raths, J., & Wittrock, M. C. (2001). *A taxonomy for learning, teaching, and assessing: A revision of Bloom's Taxonomy of Educational Objectives* (Complete edition). New York: Longman.

Fried, CB (2006) *In-class laptop use and its effects on student learning* in Computers & Education 50 (2008) 906-914.

Ghasem, B and Hashemi, M (2011) *ICT: New Wave in English Language learning/ teaching.* Procedia Social and Behavioural Sciences 15. 3098-3102.

Hyland, K(1993) *ESL Computer Writers: What can we do to help?* System, Vol.21 No. 1 pp21-30. Pergamon Press Ltd, Great Britain.

Kim, H and Rissel, D (2008) *Instructors' Integration of Computer Technology: Examining the Role of Interaction* Foreign Language Annals Volume 41, Issue 1, pages 61–80, Spring 2008.

Lauricella, S and Kay R (2009) Appendix A – The Laptop Effectiveness Scale faculty.uoit. ca/kay/papers/les/AppendixA_LES.pdf

Lauricella, S and Kay, R (2010) *Assessing laptop use in higher education classrooms. The Laptop Effectiveness Scale (LES)* Australian Journal of Educational Technology 26(2) 151-163.

Levin, Tamar, Wadmany, Rivka (winter 2006/7) *Teachers' Beliefs and Practices in Technology-based Classrooms: A Developmental View.* Journal of Research on Technology in Education 39 157-181.

Murray, Denise E (Dec 2008) *From Marginalisation to Transformation: How ICT is being used in ESL learning today.* International Journal of Pedagogies & Learning 4.5: 20-35.

Nunan, D (1988) *The Learner-Centred Curriculum: A Study in Second Language Teaching.* Cambridge University Press.

Nunan, D. (1992) *Research Methods in Language Learning.* Cambridge University Press: UK.

Phinney, M (1991) Computer Assisted Writing and Writing Apprehension in ESL Students. In Dunkel, P (ed) Computer Assisted Language Learning and Testing: Research Issues and Practices. New York. Newbury House.

Pickering, K., McAvoy, J., Campbell, R & Tennant, A (2010). *Global Beginner Coursebook with eWorkbook.* Macmillan.

Rogers, E. M. (2003). *Diffusion of innovations* (5th ed.). New York: Free Press

The Council of Europe (2001). *Common European Framework of Reference for Languages: Learning, Teaching, Assessment.* Cambridge, CUP.

Wallace, M.J. (1998) *Action Research for Language Teachers.* Cambridge University Press: UK.

Glossary

CALL	Computer Assisted Language Learning
CEFR	Common European Framework Reference
EFL	English as a Foreign Language
ELT	English Language Teaching
ESL	English as a Second Language
HCT	Higher Colleges of Technology, United Arab Emirates
ICT	Information and Communication Technology
IELTS	International English Language Testing System
IT	Information Technology
PC	Personal Computer
TESOL	Teaching English to Speakers of Other Languages

Chapter 10

21st Century Learning from a 3rd Century BC Perspective

Lawrence Burke

"The most effective way to destroy people is to deny and obliterate their own understanding of their history." George Orwell

No-one seems quite sure what 21st century learning means or what kinds of skill set is to be defined as 21st century skills within an educational framework. There's lots of speculation and argument about what ought to be included. In fact everyone-from children, to parents to corporations and governments all have an opinion on what 21st century skills are and how they should be included in a school curriculum. In his insightful, well-argued essay Haywood asserts, and rightly so, that within the framework of 21st century learning we must face up to the existential human condition and offer an inclusive set of values and ideas which embody intercultural awareness and spirituality. (Haywood, 2014)

One of the fundamental premises underlying the current discourse on 21st century learning is that schooling at all levels needs to be restructured in a way which meets the demands and challenges of the 21st century. Yet this poses a conundrum for everyone-especially policy makers and curriculum designers- because no-one quite knows how to prioritize these demands and challenges, and quite frankly the most pressing ones, like climate change, the continual exponential increase in youth unemployment, the widening global gap between the rich poor and dispossessed, geo-political tensions; especially in the Middle East and South East Asia, religious sectarian strife and war are the ones most often excluded from any clearly defined set of 21st century investigative curriculum learning outcomes or enquiry based learning objectives within an educational framework. Haywood takes up this argument again and it's worth quoting in its entirety:

> "A particularly insidious approach to existential questions is to view them uniquely from academic perspectives, allowing for psychological, anthropological, historical or sociological insights but failing to respect the authenticity that students feel their personal engagement with these experiences deserve. I once visited a school which operated in a context where the national curriculum in religious studies was a mandated component of the curriculum, only to find that an internal report which stated "there is no evidence to show that Christian Studies and Islamic Studies leave room for the issue of global mindfulness". The same report went on to suggest that "The language belonging to critical, analytical and speculative methods is embedded in proper Religious Studies scholarship – but in our school we teach exclusivism, indoctrination, catechesis and supersessionism". What a missed opportunity to engage teachers and students on a genuinely inclusive intercultural project! " (Haywood, 2014)

However, a counter claim to Haywood's argument might be the content, ideals and secular values embedded in the International Baccalaureate learner profile. It does attempt to offer through the key domains of learning (affective, cognitive and psychomotor) a set of teaching and learning standards which aims high in terms of secular, liberal ideals, although on a practical level may appear more of a wish list of the type of character one could hope to have developed having graduated as an IB learner:

Inquirers *They develop their natural curiosity. They acquire the skills necessary to conduct inquiry and research and show independence in learning. They actively enjoy learning and this love of learning will be sustained throughout their lives.*

Knowledgeable *They explore concepts, ideas and issues that have local and global significance. In so doing, they acquire in-depth knowledge and develop understanding across a broad and balanced range of disciplines.*

Thinkers *They exercise initiative in applying thinking skills critically and creatively to recognize and approach complex problems, and make reasoned, ethical decisions.*

Communicators *They understand and express ideas and information confidently and creatively in more than one language and in a variety of modes of communication. They work effectively and willingly in collaboration with others.*

Principled *They act with integrity and honesty, with a strong sense of fairness, justice and respect for the dignity of the individual, groups and communities. They take responsibility for their own actions and the consequences that accompany them.*

Open-minded *They understand and appreciate their own cultures and personal histories, and are open to the perspectives, values and traditions of other individuals and communities. They are accustomed to seeking and evaluating a range of points of view, and are willing to grow from the experience.*

Caring *They show empathy, compassion and respect towards the needs and feelings of others. They have a personal commitment to service, and act to make a positive difference to the lives of others and to the environment.*

Risk-takers *They approach unfamiliar situations and uncertainty with courage and forethought, and have the independence of spirit to explore new roles, ideas and strategies. They are brave and articulate in defending their beliefs.*

Balanced *They understand the importance of intellectual, physical and emotional balance to achieve personal well-being for themselves and others.*

Reflective *They give thoughtful consideration to their own learning and experience. They are able to assess and understand their strengths and limitations in order to support their learning and personal development (International Baccalaureate Organisation, 2005-2013)*

As noble and as well thought out as these ideals are, they do not reflect the existential condition of human-kind in a way that makes the competencies within the IB learner profile attainable, measurable and achievable as a set of 21st century skills within an educational context. In addition they are for the most part hard-pressed to be defined as having been achieved once a student passes through any one of the 3 IB curricula. Interestingly enough, they are not dissimilar to the kinds of values education attempted by religious schools and institutions over the centuries which placed a higher emphasis on moulding character rather than free thinking independent individuals; "give me a child at 7 and I will show you the man" while often attributed to the Jesuits, is more often a reflection of the powerful ideological factors –regardless of the historical context- which shapes the human character and underpin the day-to-day practices within education.

One of the inherent problems with the secular nature of the IB learner profile, and any other kind of character forming education process for that matter is that it attempts to impose values rather than allow for the discovery, acceptance and integration of them into a learner's life. For example, the secular values inherent in the IB learner profile are in essence no different from the overarching goals within the values education of Christians, Muslims and Jews in their faith based schools, and the IB learner profile in a faith based school will not be allowed to undermine the ethics and morality embedded in the respective Holy books of the said faith based schools, except for perhaps the concept of risk-takers being brave in "defending their beliefs".

It could also be argued that as a 21st century skill set the IB learner profile is simply a liberal thinking framework which assumes it is far superior to all previous and future ones. The irony of course is that it is no different from any one of the numerous pedagogical theories and frameworks, or educational or social policy objectives of previous generations which assumed the right to claim the *Gnosis* of the age within a public or private educational system. "You cannot teach a man anything" remarked Galileo, "you can only help him find it within himself" (Science & Engineering Encyclopedia) has a strong resonance with the pedagogy underpinning the ideals of a 21st century skill set within the IB learner profile.

The renowned educator, the late David Purpel took up very similar themes to Haywood (Haywood, 2014) and the IBO in his quest for a skill set that could offer a transformative set of values in response to the unsettling times of the 20th and 21st century. He broke down the layers of meaning in the debates, discussions and arguments about educational reform, to reveal our human vulnerability and fear to bringing about serious change in educational curriculum. Central to his thesis was the belief that human beings have to work towards goodness. It is not innate. Our capacity for self-deception can lead us into all sorts of trouble as a species. If education is for the betterment of humanity why, Purpel asks, are we facing catastrophic consequences through the human development of our planet? Purpel argues that our mechanistic metaphor of the universe enabled us to deceive ourselves into believing we can conquer and subdue all of nature [including human nature] with little if any consequences.

"We as educators have for the most part been able (willingly) to separate our concern for education from our discussion of our most serious and profound matters. What is the meaning of life? How do we relate as a family, nation people? What is a just and fair way of distributing rights and responsibilities? How do we make appropriate moral choices?" (Purpel, 1989)

Notwithstanding the extraordinary efforts made by most students and teachers, he challenged the status quo in education through asking what difference education really makes in society. How is education contributing to positive social transformation? He argued that if we look through the lens of compartmentalization we can see that some domains of human effort are a testament to what we are able achieve. Aspects of the arts, sports, sciences, humanities, and religion, to name a few, shed light on our capacity for goodness, compassion, tolerance, understanding, love and cooperation. But, if we adjust our lens we see the whole picture. A landscape ruined through war, conflict, greed, deforestation, conflict and savage competition.

Purpel argues that there are no simple solutions to the kinds of existential crises facing humanity. However he did warn how the opportunists are seizing the moment to push their own social and political agenda in educational reform. In particular he argues that a vacuum left by the rejection of any sound moral and spiritual understanding is leading the way for Rightist groups, together with conservative politicians and corporations, to set the agenda for changes in the process of schooling. In terms of defining 21st century skills these changes, insofar as they have any impact are superficial and deal more with textual authority/power/ control issues, rather than seriously analyze the assumptions, which underpin our educational aims and objectives. Only a critical inquiry, founded upon an incisive analysis of these assumptions will enable us to reform education in the 21st century.

Purpel illustrates the contradictions in the values which infuse the post-modernist 21st century educative process as a comparison between an individual's potential and possibility or the inflexibility and nexus of power between vested interest groups and governments:

Transformative Values	Institutionalized Values
Community	Individual
Worth	Achievement
Equality	Competition
Compassion	Sentimentality
Responsibility	Guilt
Democracy	Authority/Power/Coercion/Control
Universalism	Ethnocentrism
Humility	Arrogance
Commitment	Alienation/Displacement/Complacency
Faith	Reason
Professional Responsibility	Self Deception

(Purpel, 1989, pp. 31-61)

His analysis of the dichotomy produced through the inherent contradiction in values promoted and institutionalized in schools, colleges and universities and those made manifest through actions and behaviours, is perceptive, insightful and instructive about the consequences of our actions as teachers and administrators in the 21st century. His argument is still relevant and shows that contradictions in values create chaos, instability, confusion and frustrations for all involved in the multifaceted process of 21st century education. We end up applying simple solutions, to complex problems. It is easier to discuss curriculum reform, electives, student behaviour, codes of conduct, assessment procedures, exam results, sporting prowess, student and staff morale and building maintenance, rather than address the core issues confronting people daily like, youth and adult unemployment, environmental degradation, spiritual impoverishment, war, famine, and the exponential growth of poverty as an accepted condition of 21st century living. Purpel suggests that in denying these stark realities we legitimate a false consciousness, which leads us into self-deception and the delusional belief that a fundamental seismic shift is occurring in the way we think and behalf and we are on the cusp of a secularized 21st century digital era where humankind is the master of his destiny. In other words, 21st century teaching and learning skills will see the fulfillment of Francis Fukuyama's prophecy of reaching the endpoint or *Omega* of our social and cultural evolution as a species (Fukuyama, 1992)

Some of the themes within frameworks offered by the IBO, Terrence Haywood and David Purpel are to be found in a other models put forward as encompassing essential skills for teaching and learning in the 21st century too. Several are premised upon an unshakeable, evangelical like faith in technology as the pinnacle of human learning. The assumption is that our world is being molded and redesigned by technology and as such technology will be able to answer some of our most profound questions in life like *Who are we? Why are we here? And where are we going?* Technological 'literacy' (I would argue it's a skill rather than a literacy) is being given precedence over Purpel's transformative values because the argument is that digital citizenship will replace our independent notions of belonging to specific countries, cultures and religions with their inherent ethical frameworks, values and specific moral world views. The International Society for Technology in Education's (2012) agenda and its inflexible stipulation on student, teacher and administrator behavior for 21st century learning is not dissimilar to the madness associated with the agenda of the Social Sciences in the 19th century as envisioned through the works of Claude-Henri de Saint Simon (de Saint Simon, 1964), Prosper Enfantin (Enfantin, 1830) and Auguste Comte (Comte & Martineau, 1853). These three men claimed that it was possible to effectively measure and understand all of the underlying principles of human behaviour thereby directing a society to be reorganized within the paradigm of behaviourism. We now know that this simply wasn't correct, and dare I say we'll find out, probably under the most difficult of circumstances, that attempts by ISTE to transform societies and cultures through technology and digital learning will suffer a similar fate.

A number of private and governmental *think tanks* have entered the debate on what should and shouldn't be a skill set in 21st century learning too. The Metiri Group (Metiri Group, 2013) argues for digital learning, inventive education and higher order thinking skills (it's odd that they don't seem to know we do teach these skills already). On the other hand, The Organization for Economic Cooperation and Development unlike some of the alternative 21st century frameworks discussed hasn't lost sight of the axiom that education is firstly a social, communicative process which emerges from within the foundations of literacy. It takes a more balanced approach arguing for equilibrium within the uses of educational technology and collaborative learning, and learning by doing, founded upon the principles of effective development of positive interpersonal human relationships (Organisation for Economic Cooperation and Development, 2005).

One of the more radical partnerships between governments, the private and educational sectors is the *Partnership for 21st century skills*. Their agenda is also founded upon a technological utopian model in which the future will be an interconnected, globalised world where individuals will collaborate and work together to continue to sow and reap the unprecedented advancements of the digital age. However, a worrying underlying premise in this model is that not everyone will be accepted into this brave new world of digitalized being and existence. There's a lack of any reference to social justice as a value to ensure a compassionate response to the gross inequalities within the social classes across the globe, already evident in the technological age through the inequalities in how children are educated and how millions will always be disconnected from the envisioned digitalized world order. One of their key arguments is that learners who do not or are not able to embrace the partnership's model of 21st century teaching and learning will simply be left behind (Partnership for 21st Century Skills, 2013). And it is this fiercely competitive, institutionalised way of learning which Purpel vehemently opposed, and in some respects the IBO attempts to redress through its character forming learner profile.

One of the more enlightened frameworks for the concept of 21st century learning is the European Parliament and the Council of the European Union's key skills for life-long learning. It outlines eight skills areas:

Literacy	Competency
Linguistic	Communication in mother tongue
Linguistic	Communication in a Foreign Language
Numeracy, Science & Technology	Mathematical competence & basic competencies in science & technology
Multi-media	IT & digital competence
Critical	Learning to Learn
Communicative	Social & Civic competencies
Empowerment	Sense of initiative and entrepreneurship
Cultural	Cultural awareness and expression

(ec.euorpa.eu, 2006) The most striking features of this set of 21st century skills is that it recognizes and utilizes a vast body of knowledge from the past and builds on it, unlike the Metiri Group and the Partnership for 21st century skills which appear to eschew learning from previous centuries under the misguided and mistaken belief that humanity is about to reach its highest evolutionary point as a knowledge seeking species via technology.

In analyzing the various frameworks and arguments put forward about teaching and learning in the 21st century it is apparent they are premised on the false assumption that this century (still only in its infancy) is somehow disconnected from previous ones and therefore how we prepare current and future generations through education must be based upon hitherto recently discovered and perhaps as yet unknown pedagogies. Hence perhaps the explanation for the exponential increase in the use of the term *multiple literacies* which have as their core foundations post-modernist views on technology, art, culture, politics, economics and philosophy.

Advocates of multi-literacies argue for a kind of multi-modal way of teaching and learning in the 21st century. They claim that because of the rapid technological changes and the interconnectedness of our world through digital and social media; teaching and learning must include the visual, linguistic, mathematical, logical, audio, spatial, and symbolic use of the body through movement. In other words pedagogical frameworks of multi-literacies will transform 21st century learning into a relevant set of skills designed so that students utilize self-discovery and exploration to facilitate communication and support and help co-create meaning in their lives. This should all sound very familiar to anyone up to date on the development and inventiveness of pedagogical theories throughout history:

Theorist	Theory	Description
Ausubel (1918-2008)	Subsumption Theory	Mechanism by which new material presented in academic settings (lectures) can be integrated into existing mental structures.
Bandura (1925-	Observational Learning Theory	Behavior can be learned through observation of others.
Bruner (1915-	Constructivist Theory	Individuals actively construct knowledge by comparing new ideas or concepts with their current knowledge (schema or mental models).
Comenius (1592-1670)	Pansophism *(universal knowledge)*	The idea that learning, emotional, and spiritual growth are interwoven. Proposed teaching through stimulation of the senses, not merely through memorization. Considered the "Father of Modern Education."
Dewey (1859-1952)	Learning by Doing	Learning occurs through experience.
Erikson (1902-1994)	Socioemotional Development	Erikson's "Eight Stages of Man" describes a series of crises individuals pass through at different ages. The stages begin with "trust versus mistrust" in infancy and continue through a series of paired outcomes for each age through older adulthood.
Festinger (1919-1989)	Cognitive Dissonance	Inconsistencies between behaviors and beliefs motivate people to change.
Freud (1856-1939)	Levels of Consciousness	The mind operates at different levels: conscious versus unconscious. He further subdivided the mind into the id (primitive motivations), ego (logical portion of the mind which acts to satisfy the id - when possible), and the super-ego (the conscience).
Paulo Freire (1921-1997)	Critical pedagogy	Social class and knowledge are key determiners of success or failure in life
Gagne (1916-2002)	Conditions of Learning	For different kinds of learning (motor skills, verbal skills) different conditions are needed, so different strategies should be used
Gardner (1943-	Multiple Intelligences	Each individual possesses seven distinct and measurable forms of intelligence: linguistic, logical-mathematical, spatial, body-kinesthetic, musical, intrapersonal, and interpersonal.
Kohlberg (1927-1987)	Stages of Moral Development	Pre-Conventional - based on self-centered interests Conventional - based on conformity to local expectations Post-Conventional - based on higher principles
Locke (1632-1704)	Tabula Rasa	The idea that individuals are "blank slates" on which teachers could "write" knowledge. A forerunner of behaviorism.

Maslow (1908-1970)	Hierarchy of Needs	Humans naturally strive to satisfy needs. The five levels of needs, from lowest to highest, are: physiological, safety, love, esteem, self-actualization. Lower level needs must be satisfied before the individual can move on to satisfy higher level needs.
Miller (1920-	Information Processing Theory	Short term memory can only hold 5-9 "chunks" of information at a time. A chunk can be any meaningful idea like a word, an identifiable image, or a digit.
Pavlov (1849-1936)	Classical Conditioning *(Behaviorism)*	The association of new responses with existing stimulus-response pairs. Classic example is pairing the ringing of a bell with presentation of food to dogs. After repeated pairing, the dogs will salivate upon hearing the bell (even if food is not presented). Original stimulus (S) response (R) pair is food -- salivate. New S-R pair is bell -- salivate.
Piaget (1896-1980)	Genetic Epistemology	Developmental stages of child development: 0-2 years: "sensorimotor" - motor development 3-7 years: "preoperation" - intuitive 8-11 years: "concrete operational" - logical, but non-abstract 12-15 years: "formal operations" - abstract thinking
Rogers (1902-1987)	Experiential Learning	Two types of knowledge: academic and experiential. Unlike academic knowledge, experiential knowledge is acquired to meet the needs of the learner, usually to complete an important, real-life task. Example: Learning to drive a car.
Skinner (1904-1990)	Operant Conditioning *(Behaviorism)*	Learning is the result of changes in behavior. As stimulus-response cycles are reinforced, individuals are "conditioned" to respond. Distinguished from Connectionism because individuals can initiate responses, not merely respond to stimuli.
Socrates (469 BC- 399 BC)	Socratic Dialogue	The oldest and most reliable pedagogical method of fostering critical thinking skills by asking questions rather than giving answers
Thorndike (1874-1949)	Connectionism *(Behaviorism)*	Learners form associations or connections between a stimulus and a response. Through trial and error, rewarded responses would be strengthened.
Vygotsky (1896-1934)	Social Development Theory and ZPD	Social interaction is critical for cognitive development. Related to this is the idea of a "Zone of Proximal Development (ZPD)." Some skills, an individual can perform independently. Other skills can be performed if the individual has assistance. Skills that can be performed with assistance are said to be within an individual's ZPD. The ZPD is the theoretical basis for scaffolding.

Watson (1878-1958)	Behaviorism	Proposed that most human learning and behavior was controlled by experience (not genetically pre-determined). Believed the only behaviors that should be studied are the "observable" ones.
Wertheime (1880-1943)	Gestalt Theory	Some ideas can only be understood as part of a "bigger picture" Important in problem-solving.

(Adapted from Teacher's Garden, 2013)

The above tables describe an all-embracing and reliable overview of the development of key skills in teaching and learning over the centuries. It suggests that rather than seeking a new 21st century framework we ought to be building on this wide-ranging and far-reaching body of knowledge from the past. Because within it are the foundations of learning we seek and search for so desperately today. Problem solving, critical thinking, innovative and creative intelligences, along with risk-assessment, inquiry and analysis, civic knowledge and virtues, social responsibility, life skills, life-long learning, learning by doing, cultural and global awareness are already clearly and purposefully covered through the insightful and engaging bodies of knowledge covered by the twenty-four theorists cited above.

21st century learning is not dissimilar from the learning of previous centuries. However there is one distinct difference today in so far as 21st century teaching and learning has become a prisoner of the dialectic of those promoting an increasingly technology driven world and seems unable to break free.

Plato would have argued, as does Haywood (Haywood, 2014) that some educators, students, parents, and members of the corporate IT sector were for the most part untutored and unlearned about the history of education and educational theories. He would have instructed them using his analogy of prisoners chained in a cave, unable to turn their heads. All they can see is the wall of the cave, and behind them fires burn. Between the fire and the prisoners there is a road, along which computer programmers, software and app designers, book publishers, IT corporations and members of renowned institutions of learning walk. They hold up their products and gadgetry which cast deceptive shadows on the wall of the cave. The prisoners are unable to see the real objects that pass behind them. What the prisoners see and hear are shadows and echoes of augmented realties cast by objects that they do not see or fully understand. These prisoners would mistake appearance for reality. They would think the things they see on the wall (the shadows) were real; they would know nothing of the real causes of the shadows. Plato argued that *"if they could talk to one another, don't you think they'd suppose that the names they used applied to the things they see passing before them?"* (Cahn, 2012, p. 175) Plato's point is that the prisoners would be mistaken, because they would be taking the terms in their language to refer to the shadows that pass before their eyes, rather than to the real things that cast the shadows.

Likewise today when we argue and debate what are 21st century teaching and learning skills, we think we have created these as new and innovative ideas and concepts. But, we are wrong. We are only looking at their shadows through a glass darkly. The real referents to the concept of 21st century teaching and learning skills we cannot see until the chains are broken and we leave the cave of myths and shadows and seek out a clear and lucid understanding of the pedagogies upon which the history of teaching and learning is founded.

References

Adapted from Teacher's Garden. (2013, December 16). *Outline of Educational Learning Theories and Theorists*. Retrieved from Teacher's Garden.com: www.teachersgarden. com/professionalresources/learningtheorists.html

Cahn, S. (2012). *Classics of Western Philosophy 8th Edition*. Massachusetts: Hackett Publishing Co.

Comte, A., & Martineau, H. (1853). *The Positive Philosophy of Auguste Comte*. London: Chapman.

de Saint Simon, D. (1964). *Social Organisation: The Science of Man*. New York: Harper Torch Books.

ec.euorpa.eu. (2006, December 12). *Education and Culture Life Long Learning Program*. Retrieved from ec.euorpa.eu: ec.europa.eu/dgs/education_culture/publ/pdf/ll-learning/keycomp_en.pdf

Enfantin, P. (1830). *Doctrine de Saint-Simon*. Paris: University of Lausanne.

Fukuyama, F. (1992). *The End of History and the Last Man*. New York: Free Press.

GoodReads. Inc. (2013). *Cicero Quotes*. Retrieved from Goodreads.com: www.goodreads. com/author/quotes/13755.Cicero?page=3

Haywood, T. (2014). Finding a Place for Existential Intelligence in School. *International School Magazine.*

International Baccalaureate Organisation. (2005-2013). *IB Learner Profile Booklet*. Retrieved from www.ibo.org/: www.ibo.org/programmes/profile/

Metiri Group. (2013, December 16). *The Core Beliefs of Metiri*. Retrieved from Metiri Group: metiri.com/

Organisation for Economic Cooperation and Development. (2005). *The Definition and Selection of Key Competencies.* Paris: OECD.

Partnership for 21st Century Skills. (2013, December 16). *Framework for 21st Century Learning.* Retrieved from Partnership for 21st Century Skills: www.p21.org/our-work/p21-framework

Purpel, D. (1989). *The Moral and Spiritual Crisis in Education.* Granby, Massachusetts: Bergin & Garvey.

Science & Engineering Encyclopedia. (n.d.). *Galileo, Galilei (1564-1642).* Retrieved from DiracDelta.co.uk: www.diracdelta.co.uk/science/source/g/a/galileo%20galilei/source.html#.Uq8Et-9DGUk

The International Society for Technology in Education. (2012). *Digital Age Teaching.* Retrieved from The International Society for Technology in Education: www.iste.org/standards/standards-for-teachers

Chapter 11

Reflections around on-demand publishing

Clyde Coreil

The undergraduates I teach were born after the digital revolution had occurred. However, the revolution that is in progress and one that has been accomplished are utterly different. Last week, I realized this with the sharpness of a razor as I took out my box of prompts – high quality reproductions of paintings.

I said that students would have to memorize the contents of one of the works and then write a story about it outside the classroom. Each of them quickly took out a telephone-camera and took a picture of their chosen reproduction – much like they had been challenged to a duel and the phones were their pistols. I should have anticipated the electronic weapons, but then I am of another generation.

With this lesson in mind, I will talk about what the print-on-demand revolution in publishing has meant for me. There are two main reasons why I think you might be interested. The first is my personal perspective as having lived and worked before, during and after both sides of the digital gap. The second is that virtually all of the publishing I have done has been closely related to academia. I say 'virtually' because, right out of college, I went to work for a newspaper, and more particularly, for a quiet and patient editor who provided all of the journalism training I had missed as a devil-may-care English major who was above concern with any kind of gainful employment.

The above-it-all came crashing down the day after graduation: I needed a job and finally found one at the *Daily Advertiser* in Lafayette, Louisiana, USA. There, Vince Marino, my kindly editor, shared his invaluable store of information on such things as page design, story development, and shooting pictures with a huge press camera that forgave virtually every shortcoming in technique. Five decades have passed since then, and never have I held a job that offered no opportunity to use my brief training as a journalist. Those two years after graduation have probably shaped more of my approach to problems and situations than anything else.

At this moment, there are stored on my campus about ten boxes of gorgeous (sic), beautifully illustrated books that would grace any coffee table. They also work as the tenth volume of *The Journal of the Imagination in Language Learning*. We open these undistributed items as late requests come in. When they arrived from the printer, there were about 300 boxes, and I had to beg and borrow a room to store them in. If the digital revolution had been complete, I would have been spared this rather ignominious task: after all, I had edited the books and storage was details. That was not how the administrators saw it.

After ten annual volumes, I think that the *Journal* is done, finished. I am pleased, however, to say that all of the 125 articles we published are now available on a website named CoreilImagination.com. A great ride while it was going. But age and financing wrote their message clearly on the wall. I set modesty aside when I say with pride that this body of carefully-edited information is available at no charge of any kind. At least two entire master's theses have come out of this material, and I suspect more will as time goes by.

Meanwhile, back in the classroom, I had been assembling over the years a steadily- growing folder of handouts of increasing value – at least to me. I thought of organizing them in some fashion and submitting them to a publisher. The biggest drawback to that was that I would, in all probability, have had to sell the copyright. If I had found a publisher, I would also have had to make any changes that might have been suggested by a darling from some English department. I knew that scene very well.

Once past that editor, the company itself could have proceeded to publish or leave the manuscript on the shelf for as long as it might have chosen. It would have had extensive if not complete control of cover design, page layout, and the power to make any other decision based on sales and profitability. I might receive a royalty check once income had cleared expenses. When it chose to declare my book temporarily or permanently out of print, then that would be that.

This is a keen sticking point that comes to the forefront when considering, for example, *Mastering the International Phonetic Alphabet* (1970), an excellent arrangement of IPA sounds and blank lines that judiciously follow. This very slim volume has been out of print for at least 30 years. I tried to get permission to purchase the copyright or to make copies for my students.

Even that was impossible: the company that had published the original had been sold and re-sold and no one could find a copy of the copyright notice: at least that is what they implied. Not much money was involved, and no one was interested. So, I proceeded to do the illegal. I copied the yellowing and cracked pages, put them inside thin page protectors and now copy only enough for each member of the class.

I would imagine a similar fate awaits any book called 'old edition'. I could tell a few other choice stories of an older edition of *Bedford's Compact Introduction to Literature* and the bookstore at my college. In short, take my advice and do not attempt to buck the tide of bookstore's handling only the most recent edition. Such advice did not prevent another publisher – Oxford, no less – from essentially changing editions as the semester was beginning. The tales of woe are virtually endless. Often, there is no alternative: Amazon seems complicit despite its enormous bookselling capabilities.

A slight ray of hope is provided by what used to be derisively called 'vanity presses'. They are still in business to soothe the vain, but the business is utterly changed. With their print-on-demand technology, all they have to maintain is the equivalent of a CD disc or two. If I ask for a copy of a certain book that appeared under their logo ten years ago, they simply put the disc in the machine and a few minutes later out comes a freshly printed book that looks as good as the original. For them – or for the company I work with at least – there is no such thing as 'out of print'.

Forced by the necessity described above, I looked into these publishing houses. I was tempted by the very American policy of publishing virtually anything that had no glaring errors in punctuation or spelling. The most obvious shortcoming was the lack of prestige involved, and the concomitant, sometimes embarrassing, covers. These houses do have minimum principles concerning covers, font, layout and grammatical errors.

However, once these have been met, the editorial content is the author's responsibility. Before making a final decision as to which print/publish-on-demand company I would go with, I came very close to signing a contract with another company with a fairly well known name. Our talks came to an abrupt halt when I found out that that company did not accept returns from a bookstore that had ordered a few copies.

Normally, publishers have a policy that a book bought by a bookstore in anticipation of sales has the right to return unsold books to the publisher and be reimbursed for them. This publisher, however, did not have such a policy. If the bookstore bought a copy, that copy was theirs and could not be returned. I asked the manager at my college's bookstore if this would affect transactions. He laughed and said that there was no way in which he would order anything from such a publisher. "That's not the way business is done in bookselling," he said.

So I did not sign the contract but looked around for another company. The one that I found said that they took books back. The company also strongly advised that I read closely a 75-page booklet in which all aspects of their transactions with authors and bookstores and a lot of other things were specified. I read the book closely and was appreciative of their apparently above-board policy. If I were to do it again, such a booklet of specifications is the very first thing I would request. Everything I read came to pass exactly as they had specified.

The company I chose also has a record-keeping department which sends notices about profits and royalties to the US Internal Revenue Service every year. They issue a standard monthly report to authors about royalties, whether or not such royalties develop, which I suspect is not often. Depending on the type of sales involved, these range from 15% to 40% of profits. I, for one, am not particularly concerned about payouts: what I am interested in is the availability of my book, or books, for I now have two.

The students make payment directly to the bookstore or to the company and not to me. If I chose to have only one or none of my publications on hand in my office, no one would be upset. Sales would continue as a result of my company linking its professional website to that of Amazon.com and to Barnes and Noble at no extra charge. Virtually all other publicity is provided according to an almost painful cafeteria style of choices. You can get each specific part for a specified sum of money. For example, I recently published through the company a book entitled *Term Papers and Academic Writing: Setting New Parameters.* Because of the number of exercises with blank lines, I specified 8" x 11" format and paid for it.

The only publicity I chose was being placed on an international list. I also requested 40 advance reading copies for teachers, critics and such. For this listing, plus the copies, I paid a total of about $450. I could have smorgasborded additional items, but I did not. The basic cost for their setup of my book including paperback, full-colored covers and black-and-white internal photographs, was about $550. They followed my request for basic burgundy and a handsome color photograph I had taken of a tree against the blue sky. Since I had taken the picture, no additional copyrights were involved. They are sticklers for copyrights.

It is or great importance that they did not purchase my copyright: I retain full and complete ownership of it. If tomorrow I choose to withdraw my manuscript, they will honor such a request. Of course they will not allow me to retain use of the cover or other formatting feature. Fair enough. So that is that as far as expense is concerned; an almost bare-bones order such as mine cost me just under a $US 1000. I consider that to be quite reasonable considering that my book has been given complete listing and sneak-peek preview according to the well-known Amazon model.

Additionally, I made about eight black-and-white pictures of trees which were published inside the book. (One point of my newspaper training was not to have only text if a photograph was at all available. So, I bought several rolls of film and proceeded to take pictures of obliging trees. Those photos do indeed lighten the unconscious burden of text, as does the carefully-reproduced tables and underlines I had requested.)

The biggest single difficulty with the company in my experience was telephone contact: they clearly preferred emails, which were responded to within a matter of hours. The aspect of the publication that impressed me most was the professional look of the basically burgundy cover and the care with which the interior was done. If the author is careful, he or she will wind up with a book that is indistinguishable from those that are produced by more regular publishers.

Tables of contents were lined up and the design of the pages was a little more than I had hoped for. In short, I find it to be a reasonably good looking book. Now, if I had specified that I wanted a purple-and-yellow polka dot cover, I suspect that that is exactly what I would have wound up with. They specified a modest price range for novels. Since mine was considered a reference book, I was allowed to charge a slightly higher price. If I had wanted a CD, they would have arranged for one to be slipped into a pocket in the rear of the book. The wait was somewhat longer than I would have hoped for: a little over three months until it simultaneously hit Amazon and became available for sale. As author, I get a discount of approximately 40%.

I have sent it to several scholars, none of whom seemed in the least concerned with who published it. They evaluated it according to the content. Now, if the book had had polka dots on the cover, they probably would have done a double-take. But thanks to my experience and to my editor of long ago, that did not happen.

If you decide to do one of your own, be careful: not particularly about the honesty of the company, but about what you are presenting to the world – and the world will know about it before too long. There is little privacy in the digital age. I suggest that you have a friend or two comment on your project before sending it off. And don't expect roses to come back if you send off wilted dandelions. It's a little like a plump guy getting onto a quality scale: the heavy numbers will not be tinted.

Am I sorry about spending almost $US1000? No. I had complete confidence in what I was doing. If the company sells only to my students, I will still have no regrets. I will not have to do a great many handouts – they are all organized and present in the publication. And then there is always a chance that it could become the world's number one bestseller, and I would become a filthy-rich couch potato, famous throughout both hemispheres.

Would I advise you to do the same? I suppose I would, but I would ask you to think carefully: what you send off will be just about precisely what you get back. If you make a lot of silly jokes in the text, their being bound will not reduce the silliness. On the other hand, if you have something that you would value even more highly if it were published, please consider my pro- and con- comments and then proceed to do whatever you like. Forewarned is forearmed.

Chapter 12

Social media as an instructional tool

Yasmine Salah El Din

Introduction

The aim of this chapter is twofold: first, to investigate online feedback given by freshmen students on their peers' written work; and second, to examine this feedback within a framework of Speech Act Theory, focusing on direct and indirect acts.

Facebook was the medium used for students to send their work and receive feedback on it. Using Facebook as a social network tool for students to communicate their ideas would shed better light on the social strategies young people use to communicate with each other to convey their messages in an academic context.

It would also add to the body of limited research on using social media to enhance academic skills. An investigation of direct and indirect speech acts would make it clear to students themselves and to their peers the extent to which they are/should be polite, and direct/indirect in providing feedback, whether warm (positive) or cool (negative). Results of this research would also direct their attention to the appropriate ways to express their ideas in a meaningful and clear way.

Importance of providing feedback

Despite the arguments against providing students with corrective feedback on their writing (Truscott, 1996), many researchers have defended giving feedback, providing evidence against Truscott's arguments (Ferris, 1999 and Lee, 1997). Feedback continues to be expected by students as a way for them to understand their level in relation to their colleagues.

Feedback also teaches students skills that equip them to improve their proficiency level to the extent that they realize what they need to do as writers and how they can accomplish it in an effective way (Williams, 2003). Students expect to receive comments that would guide them in doing their rewrites, or in writing new compositions all together.

The three main areas that teachers usually provide students with feedback on are language, content and organization. Teachers typically use one, or a combination of two or three ways in providing students with corrective feedback on their grammatical errors. They either correct the surface errors, use a code to indicate the place and type of error without providing the correct form, and/or they may just underline the error without providing any indication as to the type of error they identified. As for content and organization, teachers mainly provide written comments on the ideas, their relevance to the topic, how coherent and well organized they are.

The present research investigated another type of feedback than that provided by teachers: namely that given by peers. Peer assessment has been shown by researchers to be an effective way of providing feedback on students' written work (Nendonca and Johnson, 1994). It has been shown to have positive effects on student achievement and attitudes (Topping, 1998).

First, it is not as threatening as feedback coming from an authority figure like the teacher. Second, if students are well trained, they can provide effective corrective feedback, including comments that could help a student improve his work. The third interesting point is that peers will sometimes capture an error that the teacher will have somehow overlooked.

Speech Act Theory

The present research used Speech Act Theory (SAT), with particular focus on the directness/indirectness attached to the comments given to students by their peers.

Although the term Speech Act Theory suggests that the theory deals with spoken discourse, in fact interactions between a speaker/writer and a hearer/reader fall within the scope of the theory (Horner, 1983). According to SAT, the locutionary act, *ie* what is said or written, does not necessarily determine the illocutionary act, the intention of the speaker or writer behind what was said or written. The theory contends that in uttering the string "That dog is dangerous", the speaker's intention might be not only to inform, but to warn the addressee as well. If you say "It's hot in here", you might be informing as well as requesting the hearer to turn on the AC or open the window.

Searle (1979) grouped speech acts under five categories:

> Representatives: a representative is an utterance that describes some state of affairs ("The sun rises in the east") by asserting, concluding, claiming, *etc.*

> Directives: a directive is an utterance that requires the hearer to do something. Requesting and ordering are two examples of directives.

Commissives: through a commissive, a speaker commits himself to doing something. Promising is one example of a commissive act.

Expressives indicate the psychological state of the speaker. For example, when congratulating or apologizing, the speaker expresses the way he feels about something.

Declarations: a declaration is an utterance that realizes change in a particular state of affairs. Christening a baby and firing an employee are examples of declarations.

Speakers and/or writers choose to be either direct or indirect in the way they want to convey their message, depending on several factors: the purpose of their speech or writing; who their audience are; as well as the intended effect they want to achieve by their speech/writing. Horner (1983) suggests that 'Sometimes writers declare their intentions directly in the opening paragraph, but sophisticated writers are often more subtle.'

Indirectness is a strategy implemented in spoken discourse in order to avoid or reduce conflict with interlocutors in personal interactions. We are usually 'indirect' because we want to save either our face, the interlocutor's, or both. Although some pragmatists do not necessarily find a correlation between indirectness and politeness, in the present study the word 'indirectness' often implies 'politeness'.

When one engages in a conversation, there is sometimes something one wants to do that goes against what the other party wants to accomplish. The same applies to writing. In order to save the conversation, or a piece of writing, politeness strategies are used. Indirectness is the most common of these strategies. I wanted to investigate the extent to which freshmen would use indirect or direct feedback via Facebook on their peer's written work

Participants

Thirty-two freshmen students participated in the study, over the span of the two fall semesters of 2012 and 2013. They were enrolled at the English Language Institute (ELI) of the American University in Cairo (AUC). The average age of the students at the time of conducting the study was 18. They mainly came from an English schooling background, either completing a high school American Diploma, an International General Certificate of Secondary Education (IGCSE), or an Egyptian government high school diploma (Thanaweya 'Amma). Two of the students had completed the French Baccalaureate, and one had completed her Abitur (German High School Certificate) prior to joining AUC.

Data collection instrument

Facebook was the main instrument that the researcher used to gather data for the study. All students had Facebook accounts, and the researcher had created a closed Facebook group to engage students in different academic reading and writing activities.

These activities included tasks like posting short passages to read; YouTube videos to watch prior to discussing a particular topic; posting assignments on a daily basis; posting problems with students' work for them to think about before they came to class to discuss them; as well as posting jokes, quotes, cartoons and/or puzzles related to language. The teacher also asked the students to post their own work, ask questions, respond to teacher's and each other's questions as well as give each other feedback on their work. This last activity is the focus of the present research.

Procedure

Carrying out the study took a full class session for each of the two classes, the first being during the first week of December 2012, and about ten days before the students were scheduled to have their final exam. The second time was during the third week into the fall semester, in September of 2013, when students had only written two compositions and the study was carried out when they were writing their third piece of writing. Each session (three hours) took place in a computer lab. Students were given an essay prompt and asked to develop the topic into a full-length essay, about 500 words. They did that in 80 minutes, the regular time given for them to complete an essay.

Then they were asked to send their work to the teacher as an attachment in an email message. The teacher posted all essays on the class Facebook group, giving each a number. The purpose was to make the essays anonymous so that they would not feel embarrassed if their work included many errors. All students in class were allowed to see each other's compositions. The students were then given a 20-minute break and when they came back, each student was assigned the task of reading two compositions and giving them feedback.

The feedback was supposed to cover five main areas: content; organization; vocabulary; grammar and mechanics. In 2012, because they completed the task towards the end of the semester, they were asked to provide a grade on each of the five areas. They had enough experience doing self and peer- evaluations on handwritten assignments, and it was not so difficult for them to do the same online.

In 2013, however, because the activity was carried out at the beginning of the semester, the students were not yet skillful at providing appropriate grades to their colleagues. That is why the teacher/researcher did not ask them to assign grades. Grades are not the focus of this research, since they were not required for one of the two groups of students under investigation. On the whole, the students' feedback comprised 58 posts in 2012 and 31 in 2013.

Analysis and results

Simple tallying of speech act types, with particular focus on direct/ indirect speech acts, was used for each of the two classes. The data yielded three main speech act types: representatives, directives and expressives, put in order of frequency of occurrence. Representatives, according to Searle (1979), are utterances that describe some state of affairs by asserting, concluding, or claiming something.

The representatives identified in the present data were divided into positive and negative representatives. Positive representatives were statements that indicated the student who wrote the feedback thought positively about something in the essay, while negative ones were expressed through statements indicating that the student did not like something about his/her colleague's work.

Two examples of a positive representative are 'adequate introduction with clear thesis statement' and 'your ideas and points are related to the thesis and to your body paragraph sentences'. Examples of a negative representative, on the other hand, are 'Paragraph 1 the counter argument is very short and weak' and 'there are some language mistakes'.

A directive is a request or an order addressed to a person to do something. In the present study, sometimes a directive was given directly and other times it was indirectly stated. In either case, the student who provided the feedback was asking the student writer to do something in future writing, in order to avoid a drawback that existed in their present work.

An example of a direct directive is 'Better proofread this again for a better flow of the essay'. An indirect directive is clear in statements like 'the second paragraph needs more development' and 'you need to work on enriching your glossary'. In these examples the form is that of a representative, but the illocutionary force is that of a directive; the intention is to tell the addressee 'Develop the second paragraph further.' and 'Enrich your vocabulary', respectively. One interesting example of a statement that has the form of a directive was 'keep up the good work'. In actual fact, the intention of the writer is to praise the author's work, which would be the indirect speech act in this case.

It is important to note that some of the statements given in the data could be classified either as a representative or an expressive. For example, the statement 'I can understand the ideas' is an expression of what the writer thinks and at the same time its function could be providing factual information from the perspective of the person giving feedback. However, for purposes of the research, when the statement clearly indicated how the student felt about the writing, starting with 'I feel', 'I like' or 'I guess', it was regarded as an expressive. Statements giving information about the writing without including the writer's feelings were considered as representatives.

Table 1 below illustrates the number of each of the speech acts identified in the corpus, covering both semesters. Note that in Fall 2012 the students gave feedback on their colleagues' work toward the end of the semester, so they had had more exposure to feedback given on their own writing, either by the teacher or by peers. As a result, they were more verbal and felt more comfortable giving feedback, which resulted in more statements, especially ones including negative comments on their peers' writing.

An interesting finding as well, as is clear from Table 1 is the number of direct directives given; in the fall semester of 2012 students felt rather sure what their peers had to do to improve their writing. In 2013, however, because the study was conducted during the first two weeks of the semester, students were more indirect than direct in expressing a need for something to be changed in the colleague's work.

One of the strategies used by students of both classes was hedging, in order to mitigate the effect of the criticism given. Examples of hedges were 'somewhat' and 'slightly', in the statement 'The ideas are slightly clear and the essay is somewhat organized.' This statement includes two hedges. The reason could be that the writer wanted to be polite in giving feedback to his peer, mitigating the negative criticism and therefore its effect on the addressee.

Another example of a hedge is 'a little bit' in the statement 'you need to work a little bit on language'. Many students were, consciously or unconsciously, aware of the need to be polite when conveying a message that might have a threatening effect on their addressee's face. This is particularly the case since everyone who belonged to the Facebook group, closed as the group was, saw the feedback given. There is also the possibility that students felt they needed to provide indirect/polite feedback because they were expecting their peers to be just as polite. So, they wanted their peers to reciprocate.

Speech Acts Identified in Student Peer Feedback

	Representative		Directive		Expressive	
	Positive	Negative	Direct	Indirect	Positive	Negative
Fall 12	45	51	14	12	4	4
Fall 13	37	27	2	11	9	3

Table 1.

Concerning whether the writer started the feedback with a positive or a negative comment, most of the feedback given started with a positive comment or a group of positive comments then moved to one or several negative remarks. The two types of feedback, warm and cool, or positive and negative, were most of the time separated with a forewarn, indicating to the addressee that what is to follow indicates a remark opposite in nature from what has been stated previously. Examples of forewarns are the words 'but' and 'however', illustrated in the example 'The content is good, catchy introduction and using a quote was a great idea, but you did not have a clear thesis statement and you are using too long sentences.'

Of all the comments posted by the 32 students, only three posts started with a negative comment. Two of these followed the negative comment with a positive one, while the third started with a negative comment, went to a positive one, and then ended with a negative comment. The general pattern, positive then negative, indicates that students were aware of the need to be polite in stating their opinion about their peer's work. They also probably learnt from the way their teacher, the present researcher, gave them feedback on their own writing. She typically found some positive aspects about their work that she praised, before providing negative feedback.

Concluding remarks

The present research attempted to explore the way freshmen students provided online feedback on their peers' academic writing. It is hoped by using Facebook as a tool for providing peer corrective feedback, light would be shed on the possibility and validity of using social media in an academic context.

Because of the limited number of students who participated in the research, results cannot be generalized to the population of freshmen students. More research is needed, with different proficiency levels, to reach more conclusive results. It would also be interesting to attempt to investigate the effect of online peer feedback on graduate students, mainly whether they employ the same or different strategies in giving feedback to their peers.

One limitation of this study, which could be incorporated in future research, is the fact that no interviews were conducted and this is perhaps a limitation of the medium of online feedback research. Focus-group interviews would help probe the issue of feedback further; students would provide reasons why they opted to begin their feedback the way they did rather than another.

It would also be interesting to ask the authors and writers to sit together and discuss the feedback. This would turn the feedback session into a more meaningful activity. Last, but not least, students need to understand that the ultimate goal for providing them with feedback, whether by the teacher or a peer, is to help them enhance their academic writing skills.

References

Ferris, D. (1999). The case for grammar correction in L2 writing classes: A Response to Truscott (1996). *Journal of Second Language Writing, 8*, 1, 1-11.

Horner, Winifred Bryan (1983). Speech-Act Theory and Writing. FFORUM: Essays on Theory and Practice in the Teaching of Writing. Upper Montclair, NJ: Boynton/Cook, 96-98.

Lee, I. (1997). ELS learners' performance in error correction in writing, *System, 25*, 4, pp. 140-149.

Mendonca, C. and Karen E. Johnson (1994). Peer review negotiations: Revision activities in ESL writing instruction. *TESOL Quarterly, 28,* 4, 745-769.

Searle, J. R. (1995). *Speech Acts: An essay in the philosophy of language.* London: Cambridge University Press.

Topping, K. (1998). Peer assessment between students in colleges and universities. *Review of Education Research, 68,* 3, 249-276.

Truscott, J. (1996). The case against grammar correction in L2 writing classes. *Language Learning,* 46/2, pp. 327-369.

Williams, J. G. (2003). Providing feedback on ESL students' written assignments. *The Internet TESL Journal, IX,* 10, October, iteslj.org/

Chapter 13

The educational time machine

Jon Orthmann, Reem Arafat and Nancy Fahnestock

Introduction

Imagine if you can a nomadic desert culture approximately 55 years ago before oil was discovered off the coast of Abu Dhabi. Now fast forward to today where the same culture is well-known for the tallest building in the world, modern airports, F1 racing, concerts, a shopping mall with an aquarium, another with an indoor ski slope and even perhaps the World Expo in 2020.

It is nearly impossible to imagine the changes that this small country, The United Arab Emirates (UAE), has undergone. It is a country where citizens make up a very small percentage of the population and where they are deeply traditional and follow an Islamic way of life. Given these visible signs of change it is inevitable there would be many more changes that are often not as distinct. This paper looks briefly at how education has changed in a relatively short timeframe for today's college level students.

Emergent classroom technology in many international institutions increasingly requires the use of laptops, iPads or some kind of mobile device, and the UAE is no exception to this trend. Even more impressive in the UAE is that this has been achieved despite the unique background of present-day college and university students and the incredible journey they have undertaken since beginning their educational experience. It is a distinctive background that is described briefly below.

Student background

In late 2005 the UAE set out to reform national education, primarily because a large number of teachers were not properly qualified to teach (Macpherson, Kachelhoffer and El Nemr, 2007). The curriculum was found to be ineffective: every day school culture was unsatisfactory thanks to reasons ranging from truancy and weak discipline. This was exacerbated by low levels of professionalism, low pay and status, resulting in a seeming lack of pride or integrity in the teaching profession. University students today would have been approximately mid-way through their educational experience when these changes began.

Before these changes they were taught mostly by Arab expatriates on short-term contracts who were viewed as easily replaced (Fahnestock, 2011). Fahnestock (2011) continued by suggesting that expatriate teachers were obliged to create a safe learning environment: safe in that they simply had the students working at their desks answering questions on handouts and doing other non-demanding tasks. The results of such unimaginative pedagogic activities were boredom, a dislike of learning and resentment (Pennycook, 1990).

Due to the pedagogic approach of many government schools, Barr (2007:9) suggests that:

> Emirati students leave school with well-developed 'surface' learning abilities which enable them to memorize detail and learn by rote for an exam, not all have learnt to master, or perhaps not even grasped the need for, 'deep' learning strategies which enable learners to put their learning to use, to criticize ideas, to solve problems, and to carry on learning. Put another way, surface learning can easily be forgotten the next day, but deep learning stays with the individual since it promotes real understanding and capacity.

As such, these students then enter colleges where they are suddenly exposed to a more innovative pedagogy where they are expected at times to explore and learn independently: where working on mathematics problems until you understand them is expected and rote memorization is of little, or no, use.

Rather than just completing assignments to gain a pass mark, today's students, armed with their mobile devices, are asked to evaluate their own learning and study as much as required to grasp certain concepts and then to go on and build on that knowledge independently. With few academic role models to turn to and coming from families where their mothers have little, or no, formal education, it is no wonder the students often fail to achieve their full potential.

External influences also affect the students' perception of the educational process. DeNicola (2005) argues that it is possible that the huge welfare system in the UAE has created a fissure in the work-reward relationship. For example, today it is common for poorly educated young men in the UAE to drive relatively new and expensive SUVs, when many students, and even graduates in other countries would struggle even to afford the petrol.

A brief look at this scenario makes it easy to see how colleges in the UAE could be setting their students up for further failure, or frustration, by asking them to make such a conceptual leap with their learning, when the pain of failure is largely intangible.

The program

The authors set out to explore the use of a program called ALEKS, an online mathematics program for students in foundations level classes at the Higher Colleges of Technology (HCT) in Al Ain. The acronym ALEKS stands for **A**ssessment and **Le**arning in **K**nowledge **S**paces, which is a web-based, artificially intelligent assessment and learning system. ALEKS uses adaptive questioning to quickly and accurately determine exactly what a student knows and does not know in any course. ALEKS then instructs the student on the topics he or she is most ready to learn.

As a student works through a course, ALEKS periodically reassesses the student to ensure that topics learned are also retained. There is an assessment once a week, under exam conditions, with the teacher present. If the students did not retain previously learned information, they are forced to go back and learn it again. ALEKS courses are very complete in their topic coverage and avoid multiple-choice questions.

An additional feature of the program is called quick tables, where the students work on their mental math skills. They were required to work for 15 minutes per day, six days a week on this part of the program, without a calculator. This counted as 20% of their final mark. When the entire program is completed and the student scores 75% in ALEKS, this is considered a passing grade, which is equivalent to a 60% HCT grade. Obviously the students are encouraged to get a higher mark, but this is the minimum allowed in order for them to move to the next class in their Bachelor's program.

This program is totally student-centered, meaning the students work independently on their device. However students are required to attend class four hours per week, with a teacher present. The teacher can assist the student if needed or the student may continue at his or her own pace. The students are required to answer questions and work problems and the concepts are introduced by written text.

There is no audio portion to the program. The students can request additional assistance and additional practice online or again ask their teacher for help with concepts they cannot grasp via the written text. Each class had approximately 20 students and the class was for one semester, which is 16 weeks long.

The use of ALEKS to deliver a foundations math class was piloted at Al Ain Women's College (AAW) in the fall semester of 2011 with four classes. Each class contained approximately 20 students. Several classes which were still using the traditional, teacher-centered, course material continued at the same institution. From spring semester 2012 onward delivery of this particular math course at AAW was done exclusively through the medium of ALEKS.

The package called, ALEKS Basic Math, includes topics from whole numbers, fractions, decimals, ratios, proportions & percentages, geometry, measurement, data analysis & statistics, real numbers and algebraic expressions & equations. This course is one of the Higher Education Math packages offered by ALEKS: the level of the topics generally aligns to topics students would first encounter in grades 8-10 in a US standards based curriculum to which ALEKS is aligned.

One unique aspect to this program is if the students worked ahead and finished the class early, they were not required to attend the remaining part of the semester. The overall goal of this study was not only to determine their level of success with the program, but to also define their level of satisfaction. A questionnaire was placed on the college portal and students answered questions on their laptops.

The findings

According to the responses, the students seemed to enjoy learning on their computers but because the program was written for native English-speaking students, this introduced an uncontrolled and unavoidable variable. They made comments about this in the evaluation at the end of the semester and these comments seemed justifiable. Aside from that, the other complaints were mostly aimed at the total student independence and it seemed from the data that they still wanted the teacher to teach at the beginning of the class, but then allow them to work on ALEKS independently after new concepts had been introduced.

Obviously this was not possible as each student is working at their own pace and the teacher cannot explain concepts to the entire class because they are all working on different concepts simultaneously. This is one of the benefits of ALEKS, as the weaker students do not hold the students with the higher skill levels back. It seems the students did not recognize this and that there is a more familiar or comfortable way for them to learn new concepts and that is for the teacher to explain them rather than reading about them on their devices.

Approximately 15% said they preferred to work totally on their own using ALEKS. Nearly half mentioned that they missed having a textbook and would have liked that in addition to the ALEKS program. One commented that he just wanted to use paper and pencil. They really liked the idea of being able to work ahead and finish early, yet surprisingly not all that many did so.

A very intriguing statistic was that approximately 85% of the students admitted they learned a lot using ALEKS. The following is not designed as an endorsement of ALEKS, but merely recognizes the finding in the data. As teachers in this institution for ten-plus years, we know the students well, and we know in traditional teacher-centered classrooms how much time students actively spend working. We know that in the past, if students could be bothered to do their homework it was often, although not always, copied.

However, using ALEKS, this does not benefit the student. In other words, if they indeed get someone to do the work for them online outside of class, this would ultimately be problematic for them when they returned to class. As the students are assessed weekly, again independently, based on what they are specifically working on, they would not be able to pass if the material they are being assessed on was completed by anyone else. Ultimately the program forces them to return to it and do so until they are able to pass under exam conditions. Obviously, they therefore have to learn more in order to pass.

One might argue that this is the case with any medium of content delivery, yet the use of ALEKS does make cheating more difficult. Admittedly it can still happen, but since the students are working at their own pace, it is very unlikely someone sitting beside them during the exam will be working on the same concept, much less the same type of problem. Furthermore, should that happen, the numbers are all randomized and the answers would not be the same.

In addition, in the traditional teacher-centered class, when the teacher is explaining a concept, the students are passively learning. The amount of time they actively work varies, but that is not so using ALEKS. Students must be actively working the entire time. This has to mean more learning is taking place. And also just working in class is not enough. Learners are forced to work outside of class (*ie* do their homework and understand it) or ALEKS does not give them credit for those concepts until they have passed them under exam conditions.

Therefore, if you equate the amount of time required to pass a math class using ALEKS as compared to a traditional, teacher-centered class, it becomes obvious that more work is required, but this ultimately leads to more learning. We accept that some students did not like it for various reasons and no doubt the increased workload was part of the reason. Yet despite this resistance the program is, in the final analysis, beneficial.

There were other comments, such as the grade requirements being set too high in ALEKS, yet these are equivalent to the teacher-centered classroom. They also complained that it was a really hard course, or that it takes a lot of time to do, yet that is a requirement of many courses. Some students complained that, when they took an exam and their grade dropped, they became frustrated, but if this happened then ultimately they did not retain the concept and it needed to be revisited.

This obviously does not happen in the traditional classroom so it is not a familiar way of learning, and it would seem their comments were again justified. However the authors agree that what ALEKS forces them to do was definitely necessary.

Conclusion

This is only a small-scale study conducted in one college and it obviously raises several questions as well as answering others. The results are inconclusive, but an argument can be made for further study of this program as well as researching how the students faired in their future studies.

Given all the changes to their short educational path, these students deserve a great deal of credit for persevering. Unlike their grandparents education is a major part of their lives and they recognize this and are working to better themselves and their country. The authors appreciate the opportunity to assist the students in their learning.

References

Barr, P. (2007). Working toward graduate outcomes. In P. Barr (Ed.), Foundations for the *future: Working towards graduate outcomes* (pp. 7-13). Abu Dhabi: HCT Press.

DeNicola, C. (2005). Dubai's political and economic development: An oasis in the desert? Thesis, Williams College, Williamstown, MA. May 10, 2005.

Fahnestock, N. (2011). Thesis for doctorate, University of Exeter, Exeter, UK.

Macpherson, R., Kachelhoffer, P., & El Nemr, M. (2007). The radical modernization of school and education system leadership in the United Arab Emirates: Towards indigenized and educative leadership. *International Studies in Educational Administration (ISEA), 35* (1), 60-77.

Pennycook, A. (1990). *Critical Pedagogy and Second Language Education system,* 18/3 Pp 303-314.

Chapter 14

The future is now, the future is flat

Julie Lindsay

In the emerging learning landscape supported by digital technologies, different modes of interacting and sharing provide a multitude of opportunities for everyone. Learning has never been as fluid as now. A mobile device in conjunction with ubiquitous wireless network access literally means we can learn anywhere, anytime, from anyone. Not only is this fact a catalyst for true analysis and subsequent changes in what we perceive as necessary schooling, but it ultimately means each individual can shape their learning pathway in such a unique way that no two learners need ever have the exact same experience. It also means that for those who do have technology access, we are now in the age of true 'personalized lifelong learning'.

The aim of this chapter is to share ideas and practices to do with connected and 'flat' learning in order to encourage a deeper understanding of collaborative working modes that can be embedded into current curriculum objectives and beyond. It also looks at the imperative of building strong learning communities in order to take learning global and makes a suggestion for the leadership styles and attitudes needed to foster this.

The proposition is that learning is global, has to be global and therefore classrooms must be 'flat'. This is about a shift in pedagogy, a shift in mindset, and an essential purpose for the integration of technology across the curriculum. In order to embrace global learning and flat learning teachers, school, and leaders need to adopt different leadership styles and modes, as well as focus on curriculum redesign and have connected learning as an essential infrastructure.

Connected learning

Connected learning is about not working in isolation but learning with and from others. It is through networking and interacting with others that a personal learning network (PLN) can be established. Digital communication is the key to PLN proliferation with tools such as Twitter, Facebook and other social and educational networks providing a means to frequent and meaningful exchanges.

According to George Siemens, the theory of connectivism[1] starts with the individual and the context within which people learn. The development of nodes for learning, the importance of being able to filter and synthesise information to form new knowledge, and the ability to do this in an almost cyclical way through the learning network is the key to understanding this concept.

Each learner, with the use of digital tools, is responsible for developing their own connection strategy and building a viable PLN. This goes beyond the immediate and usual school and work interactions. A strong PLN can provide uncountable resources and support across cultures, across countries and across generations. In addition, learners can find and join purposeful learning communities. These learning communities are made up of collections of people often already in the learners PLN, who come together for a purpose. This purpose may be ongoing, such as the iPads in education users group, or it may be for a short period of time like a professional development course, or a Grade 10 history class.

These professional learning communities (PLC) are important as they provide access to ideas and resources that go beyond what we have traditionally considered authentic and viable learning modes, such as books, articles, lectures, videos. To function, a PLC builds trust among its members, and is usually quick to self-moderate and filter what is not appropriate or necessary. A PLC extends the boundaries of learning beyond the immediate circle of interest and encourages involvement from the wider community through online practices including discussions, blogging, sharing multimedia. The sociability of online learning and PLC development is what builds a strong and viable community.

In his book, *Jousting for the new generation*[2], David Loader tells us 'Knowledge sharing among students can be a major source of content and pedagogy'. In flat classroom projects we say, 'Students are the greatest textbook ever written for one another'[3]. The new learning landscape is one where the quality of your PLN has a direct impact on the learning pathway. It is one where responsibility for curriculum, content and learning is equally shared among all learners of all ages. The scenario where networked and connected learning that builds communities of practice founded on collaboration is one also where everyone must have an openness and appreciation for new ideas, and a willingness to share without prejudice.

Flat learning

So, if connected learning joins us with others to support our learning, what then is 'flat' learning? It is not so different really, but takes a slight change in mindset to understand and embrace. In a 'flat' learning environment technology becomes the true enabler for connection and collaboration. It is through the power of technology that the power of people can be harnessed.

Technology tools are used to virtually eliminate the physical walls of the classroom or learning environment, bringing the world into the classroom and opening the classroom to the world. It implies discovery, engagement, collaboration and co-creation with others who are not in your physical learning space. Flat learning is important because it connects learners with the world and impacts the context in which we learn.

Flat learning is pedagogy supported by technology; in many ways it goes beyond just connecting: it is about global citizenship, and it is about breaking through stereotypes to accept others. Flat learning can change the world, as we know it – both locally and globally. More importantly, flat learning dictates active rather than passive learning as it assumes a responsibility on the part of the learner to connect through their PLN and to understand the consequences of those connections (cultural, social, political). It assumes a responsible, active learner will be a reliable contributor and collaborator and give to others as well as receive. Student-centred and personalised learning is a natural outcome of flat learning.

Flat learning uses emerging technology tools to scaffold the learning but goes 'beyond the wow' of initial engagement. However, true flat learning is not about the hardware or software, although these together provide access, build skills and foster engagement and excitement. It is about sustained connected pedagogy with distinct practices and habits that changes the learning paradigm.

Recipe to flatten your learning

Let us take a journey through strategies presented here as a simple 'recipe' to flatten the classroom, or to flatten the learning. This is an holistic approach to education in the digital age that includes, assumes, subsumes and embraces all other modes such as blended learning (and its sub-set, flipped learning), inquiry-based, challenge-based, project-based, problem-based, design thinking, visible thinking and many others in vogue now.

There are three essential steps to flatten the learning: step 1 connection; step 2 citizenship; step 3 collaboration. (Note, 'Flattening Classrooms'[4] shares seven steps to flatten your classroom as a broader and also valid model.)

Step 1: connection

Step into connecting yourself to your PLN and develop habits of lifelong learning. This includes daily workflow that sustains connections across the globe. It is important to understand there are no set working hours or set leisure hours anymore in a connected learning mode. Asynchronous interactions sustain community learning, while synchronous opportunities provide immediacy and currency to the learning.

A blend of both synchronous and asynchronous working modes means a truly globally connected learner can be working and learning at any time of the day or night. The reality is that a Skype call, for example, with the other side of the world means one of the participants at least is up early in the morning or later in the evening or night. Opportunities for these connections cannot be ignored and all teachers and students must develop a flexible schedule that is not intimidated by others who lack understanding and criticize the need for 'odd hours' to connect.

The use of 'push' and 'pull' technologies is a vital understanding to have when taking this first step to connect. In the current world where information overload impacts us all, being able to aggregate and syndicate information is essential. What is called Really Simple Syndication (RSS) allows us to push information out to others and to pull information to us, and to cluster this and organise in ways that helps us comprehend it. Why bother to write a blog post today if you cannot share this with others?

Sharing, for example, can be done via a tweet or other digital announcement, or via others subscribing to blog updates through their RSS reader. This brings the new blog post directly into an easily accessible format and can be used to access multiple authors. Social bookmarking is another tools for sharing favourite online sites and media, and is a way of connecting with a PLN and into PLC's through effective group creation. A tool like Diigo provides this facility.

Flattened learning through connecting includes creating a connection strategy in order to build a diversity of experiences for all learners. This connection strategy can include learning pathways for information, location and communication. Information involves PLN development, but is more than that. In its broadest sense it means making decisions, using solid research skills, vetting resources and then sharing and conferring with others.

Location refers to the scope of connection. It is important to cement connection practices through both local and global modes so that learning connects with the real world and is not an abstract theory. Communication in its broadest sense is about using technological and non-technological approaches to connect intra-personally and interpersonally. It is not all about the technology; it is about understanding how to harness connection strategies to relate to others as a person.

Finally, connection as a first step involves educators developing more 'entrepreneurial' skills and attitudes. A 'teacherpreneur' or 'edupreneur' is a teacher who sees an opportunity to make a profitable learning experience for students through the forging of partnerships as well as through innovation and customization to student learning needs.[5] Good teacherpreneurs, sometimes seen as renegades, are in fact connectors for learning. Teacherpreneurs lead the way in connected and flat learning modalities.

Step 2: citizenship

Connection is not enough on its own. In this recipe, citizenship is the second step to flatten your learning. This refers particularly to digital citizenship and a new enlightened model that includes further areas of awareness beyond technology itself. Citizenship brings to the fore all of the approaches to learning we need to be able to relate effectively through the use of technology.

It includes understanding how to connect with safety and privacy; copyright and legal aspects of learning online; essential habits of learning; and literacy and fluency. In addition, an 'enlightened' model of citizenship includes learners approaching online situations and opportunities through technical, individual, social, cultural as well as global areas of awareness.[6] This goes beyond usual simple structures for digital citizenship, and embraces a more global position for learning.

Citizenship also refers to taking an active role in digital learning. No longer is it relevant to learn 'about' digital citizenship without being immersed in digital activities. Both teachers and students need to feel the power of global connectedness, be involved in global discussions and projects so that they understand not only how to become a reliable and effective digital citizen, but also so they learn more about the world with a view to implementing action projects back in their local community. Friedman calls this 'glocalization', the ability to think global and act local.[7] Students and learners of all ages already harness the power of digital learning modes to learn with others and from others, not just about others. They are doing this in conjunction with a solid digital citizenship approach that supports connected learning.

Step 3: collaboration

Can we learn how to collaborate? If it is a required 21st century skill, and if technology supports more effective means of collaboration, especially in a flat learning context that is beyond the immediate – virtual and asynchronous – then educators need to not only teach it but employ and model it as well. This final step to flatten your learning includes understanding social and educational collaborations as well as collaboration that leads to co-creation. Global collaboration is vital to the classroom of now, and to the learner in a digital learning environment.

It is important to build a culture of collaboration and encourage the proliferation of learning communities. Students today must learn how to collaborate at a distance, and how to be effective communicators asynchronously to support this collaboration. Teamwork is still alive and well – but teams in a flattened classroom cross borders and traverse oceans.

In the actual Flat Classroom Project[8] students from mixed country teams collaborate on research, share their work via a co-authored wiki, then design and create an individual piece of multimedia to share their learning. This multimedia has an outsourced clip from another student, thereby making this a co-created product. The communication and collaboration skills needed to achieve this effectively in a global context are higher order. The results are exciting to see.

Embedding flat learning into the curriculum

It is one thing to follow the simple recipe above to flatten your learning (teacher, student, parent and others), but the real challenge, joy and power come from embedding flat learning into the everyday curriculum. What does this look like? How do you know if learning is flat? Flat learning must become ubiquitous, and part of the everyday learning workflow, but like all new pedagogy or methodology there is the case for creating opportunities that focus on connected, flat learning skills and habits in order to become more familiar with the technologies used and the processes involved.

As a workflow, you know your 'classroom' (virtual or real) is flat if:

You and your students expect to have regular if not daily conversations with teachers and students from other classrooms around the world.

You and your students communicate, collaborate and create products with other people from different countries and cultures that make a difference to the world.

In order to experience this flat learning, certain technologies provide better access than others. The Web 2.0 tools such as blogs, wikis, social networks and multimedia portals such as YouTube (video) or Flickr (image and short video) provide open access (or semi-closed access as needed) so learners can be connected and learn and share together. Other tools, although seemingly important from an organisation perspective, often do not. A school-based learning management system, for example, is usually 'closed' in nature, requiring permission to enter, and typically does not provide collaborative learning spaces for diverse groups or teams beyond the immediate school.

Tapscott in his book *Wikinomics*[9] refers to wikis as 'disruptive' technologies because they impact usual learning modes and patterns. Wikis, as with other Web 2.0 technologies, are innovations that have dramatically changed the course by which users connect, engage and relate with the world and transform society. A simple tool like a wiki allows for learner-centred initiatives, sharing of ideas and collaborative authoring online in ways that were just not possible before.

Re-designing curriculum to 'go flat'

There are some simple and effective steps that all educators can take to redesign curriculum in order to support flat learning. True flat and connected learning takes collaborative planning, within a school and community and with other schools and communities. Rich learning experiences supported by technology do not just happen, they must be carefully designed, planned and implemented.

A planned flattened learning experience takes time for the main stakeholders to share their needs and their circumstances and to integrate a divergent global learning adventure into the everyday curriculum. It is relatively easy to organise global interactions, such as one-off Skype calls, or traveling scrapbooks and so on – and there are many of these examples available now for educators to join and learn from. However the real challenge comes from embedding collaborative experiences across the curriculum so that from K-12 (and beyond!) students are required to work, at least for part of the time each year, in global collaborative teams, and more importantly are shown how to flatten their learning across all disciplines.

Let us review curriculum design objectives and necessary frameworks to embed local as well as global learning into the curriculum. To get started it is important to remember when we embrace flat learning in a global capacity we soon find out how different systems and schools have a variety of resources, capabilities and schedules. As a rule of thumb, if you think an activity can be done across the globe in two weeks with multiple partners, it will likely take twice as long as that or more.

Therefore curriculum that includes interactions at a distance must first be planned in terms of project design essentials such as aims, standards, required outcomes, team structures, assessment, timeframe or workflow and learning legacy (this refers to what will be left behind from the collaboration for others to learn from).

When designing flat classroom projects we then overlay this with the 'Seven Steps Design Principles', namely:

connection (how is this done?);

communication (modes, styles, tools);

citizenship (accepted working modes for effective learning being digital);

contribution & collaboration (clear expectations for all participants);

choice (different learning styles and access to resources);

creation (clear outcomes, including co-creation goals); and

celebration (reflection and assessment aims).

In addition to these design strategies other considerations include the role of social media, the choice of Web 2.0 tools, and the ability to actually choose tools that do not limit participation and make the learning 'unflat'. Building in rigor as well as relevance to the learning are key decisions to be made when designing a global collaborative experience and when embedding this into the curriculum. This is where the designers' PLN and PLCs come into the fore. If you have not had any interactions with classes in China, you may not know that Google and many other tools are blocked, but that it is still very possible to learn together, 'flat' and connected, through other software choices and modes of working. Working with a global community helps to address these challenges, collectively building bridges to solutions.

Leadership for flat learning and a global future
The impact of technology

Technology is part of the solution in meeting the needs of 21st century learners. Technology also supports individual sharing of the same vision and becoming empowered through alternative and virtual networking capabilities, using both synchronous and asynchronous communication techniques. According to Papa, technology leadership is more about pedagogy and human relations and less to do with the technology itself.[10] Therefore leadership to support technology is more about designing and implementing new strategies to help teachers and students recognize, understand and integrate technology with teaching and learning in the classroom.

The context of technology does not alter the fact that it is a leadership challenge (not a technology challenge) to develop a culture of cooperation and collaboration. If this is not already in place, the introduction of new technologies is not going to change that culture and make it cooperative. People must have the ability as well as the willingness to share knowledge by using technology, and be willing to make relationships that are not face-to-face.

The use of technology promotes transparency and accessibility. The Head of school is now more accessible, and other changes have taken place as to how people interact and with whom they interact on a daily basis. One goal is to move away from strategic leadership – where only leaders were encouraged to look beyond the organization for information and new knowledge, and move to a more flattened environment, with less hierarchy where everyone at all levels can be looking at, and should be looking out for, critical information.

What type of leaders will successfully support flat learning?

A new paradigm for educational leadership is needed to support place-based learning, connectivism and global outreach. A learning environment must have certain flexibility that all participants can consolidate as well as innovate within the learning community, and be able to break out of the 'bubble' that constrains true global independence and collaborative learning.

It is easy to say 'visionary' leadership is required to support flat and connected learning. In fact global standards, such as ISTE NETS.A include '...a shared vision for comprehensive integration of technology to promote excellence and support transformation throughout the organisation'.[11] In terms of implementing the vision however, we need to question what is the best way to allow (support?) students and teachers (all learners) to find their own voice and take charge of their learning? How do we promote a culture of sharing and collaboration and the mindset needed for flat learning that includes change and the change process as normal?

We are seeing now a new paradigm of educational leadership that must address school revitalization in a digital world. Online learning communities and the ability to connect globally are leveling the playing field to advantage learners; therefore education leaders must recognise teachers as providers of new forms of leadership. Support of the teacherpreneur, as a leader who takes all the best practices in education and latest advances in technology and uses them to blaze new trails in teaching and learning that focus on connection and collaboration is an important ongoing change we need to see.[12]

A typical teacherpreneur leader is a champion for change and realizers of the vision; is able to introduce new methods of publication and sharing; is adept at building and facilitating communities; is a researcher; innovates from within; has curriculum flexibility and autonomy; is able to work within and beyond the school culture; and takes on the roles of managers, directors, mentors, guides as needed.

School leaders can foster and support the teacherpreneur leader by encouraging customisation of learning experiences to local standards while being flexible to embrace the world through new curriculum approaches. They can also equip teachers to investigate new global relationships and design solutions for learning (flat learning) that support innovation and pedagogical excellence.

One new form of leadership that aligns with these needs is 'parallel leadership', a form of distributed leadership.[13] In this model teacher leaders and school principals engage in collective action to build capacity through mutual trust and shared purpose. For successful parallel leadership a professional learning community must be accepted as integral to organizational development with the core purpose of creating and sustaining 'new knowledge'.[14]

The importance of effective leadership

Connecting learners, connected learning leading to collaborative learning is a mindset, and relates to the school culture. Leadership that will impact this involves a shared responsibility via collaborative planning as a school community to take advantage of global learning. There must be support within the school for teachers who want to take risks and try new techniques and ideas. Otherwise serious and lasting change cannot be sustained. Connected learning promotes ownership of the learning pathway, and all stakeholders rely on effective leadership to not stifle creativity and collaboration.

Connected learning leadership framework

In a connected and 'flat' learning environment, and one that uses mobile and ubiquitous tools, a more integrated leadership framework is needed. This includes the three main stakeholders – school leaders, teachers as leaders and students as leaders. Rather than there be tension between all three groups, for connected and collaborative learning the playing field must be leveled with shared understandings and shared motivation to improve learning outcomes.

The role of the Head of school (and other designated leaders onsite and offsite) is to navigate a pathway from consolidation to innovation as a cyclical approach. They must blur the lines between physical and virtual learning and connected approaches using technology through being a 'learning concierge' and model best approaches to connecting, communicating and collaborating with the world. Above all, this leadership framework relies on a flattened hierarchical approach to leadership and promotes a parallel approach for sustained capacity, and a scenario where in fact leaders 'get out of the way of the learning' by fostering technology-supported and engaged rather than passive learning modes.

The role of the 'school' as such (all stakeholders working together) is to provide motivation, encouragement and accountability in the learning process; to provide the technology infrastructure for connected learning; and to create support for the most ideal conditions for learning possible, thereby limiting the friction and barriers to learning.

The role of the student is to be the main driving force behind their own learning and to be a reliable and responsible communicator, contributor and collaborator in online and face-to-face modes. As well as having a clear and ethical approach to using technology as a global citizen they must learn how to work collaboratively while maintaining individualism and be able to create and co-create content and share this through their network.

The role of the teacher has the same objectives as for the student but also includes being a learning architect by creatively reshaping curriculum and opportunities to take advantage of multiple connections and modes of learning. The teacher must also become a change-maker and teacherpreneur, and be able to find rich learning opportunities and share them with their students.

Concluding summary

Flat learning is not in the future, it is now. The digital revolution has provided a myriad of opportunities that will continue to change schools, and support learning connections and collaborations. Are teachers and school leaders ready to be connected and model best-practice global approaches? Are school communities able to go beyond the 'fear factor' of using technology and embrace a balanced, learner-centred approach that will benefit all? Those who are will move forward and provide alternative approaches to learning while encouraging global attitudes and understandings. These alternatives must include flat, connected learning modes.

Communities should be planning professional learning opportunities and flattening the experience of learning for all. One teacher with 25 students is an outdated model that is limited in concept and practice. Technology allows for teachers, students, parents, experts, and other valuable resources to join the learning community when needed. Growth can be exponential, especially with enlightened leadership modes in place.

We have the tools; we have the pedagogy, let's connect the world!

References

1-14 Loader, D. (2007). Jousting for the new generation.

Chapter 15

The impact of technology overuse on child sensory development

Cris Rowan

Introduction

Reminiscing about growing up in the 'good old days' is a memory trip well worth taking when trying to understand the issues facing the children of today. A mere 20 years ago, children used to play outside all day, riding bikes, playing imaginary games and building forts. Masters of creativity, children of the past manufactured their own form of play that didn't require costly equipment or parental supervision. Historically, children moved, touched and connected with other human beings a lot, and their visual and auditory world was largely nature-based and simple.

Prior to the explosion of technology, a child's sensory stimulation was *balanced,* allowing for adequate development and *integration* of the senses. As sensory integration is prerequisite to achieving foundation skills for school readiness, adequate sensory development plays a salient role in a child's ability to pay attention, print and read[1-2]. The rapid intrusion of 21st century technologies such as television, video games, movies, internet, iPads and cell phones, has created a sensory world that is vastly different from 20 years ago.

The critical factors for child development of movement, touch, human connection, and nature have taken a 'back burner' to the fast-paced, exciting virtual world of technology, with devastating consequences. The expertise of the occupational therapist in the areas of sensory processing and motor development brings them to the forefront as leaders on the impact of technology overuse on children.

This article discusses the intersection between sensory processing, motor development, and technology overuse, and details how occupational therapists can help parents, health and education professionals practice principles of balanced technology management to ensure optimal child health and academic performance.

Then and now

In the past, family time was often spent doing chores, and children had expectations to meet on a daily basis, fueling a child's inner drive and motivation to succeed. The dining room table was a central place where families came together to eat and talk about their day, and after dinner time became the epicenter for baking, crafts and homework.

Today's families are different. The 'big screen' has replaced the dining room table, and reality television has become the new age family. Prevalent overuse of technology is fracturing the very foundation of families and education systems as we know them, and causing a disintegration of core values that long ago were the glue that held families and schools together.

Where, 100 years ago, humans needed to move to survive, they are now under the assumption everyone needs technology to survive. Studies in 2010 by the Kaiser Foundation, and in 2008 by Active Healthy Kids Canada, showed that elementary aged children use on average 7.5 hours per day of combined technology use, with 65% of these children having televisions in their bedrooms, and 50% of North American homes having the television on all day[3-5]. 'Baby TV' now occupies 2.2 hours per day for the 0 to two year-old population, and 4.5 hours per day for three to five year-olds and is causally linked to developmental delays[6-8]. This situation has prompted France to ban its broadcasters from airing television shows aimed at children under three years of age[9].

Rather than hugging, playing, rough housing, and conversing with their children, parents are increasingly resorting to putting babies in bucket seats and toddlers in strollers in front of blaring televisions. Providing children with the latest video game, televisions in the car, and trendy iPads and cell phones, is creating a deep and widening chasm between parent and child.

The impact of technology overuse on developing children

Children now rely on technology for the majority of their play, grossly limiting challenges to their creativity and imaginations, as well as limiting necessary challenges to their bodies in order to achieve optimal sensory and motor development. Sedentary bodies bombarded with chaotic and intense sensory stimulation, are resulting in delays in attaining child developmental milestones, with subsequent impact on achieving basic foundation skills necessary for literacy [10].

Children's developing sensory systems have not evolved biologically to accommodate the sedentary, yet frenzied nature of today's technology. The impact of rapidly advancing technology on the developing child has resulted in increased incidence of physical, psychological and behavior disorders that the health and education systems are just beginning to detect, much less understand.

Fourteen per cent of Canadian children have diagnosed mental health disorders[11]. Between 1991 and 1995, prescriptions for psychotropic medications in the two to four year old toddler population, as well as in children and youth, tripled[12-14]. Eighty per cent of this medication was prescribed by family physicians and pediatricians[15]. Fifteen per cent of Canadian children are developmentally delayed[16], and 15% are obese[17]. Media violence has recently been classified as a public health risk due to causal links to child aggression[18]. A quarter of elementary children have been cyberbullied, and youth who reported being harassed online were eight times more likely to carry a weapon to school in the past 30 days[19].

Diagnoses of attention deficit/hyperactivity disorder, autism, coordination disorder, sensory processing disorder, anxiety, depression, and sleep disorder can be causally linked to technology overuse, and are increasing at an alarming rate[22-26]. Infants with low tone, and toddlers failing to reach motor milestones, are frequent visitors to today's pediatric physiotherapy and occupational therapy clinics[27].

Hard-wired for high speed, the young children of today are entering school struggling with self regulation and attainment of attention skills necessary for learning, eventually becoming significant behavior management problems for teachers in the classroom. Poor motor coordination of the hands and eyes is affecting children's ability to print and read[28], and for the first time in Canadian history, has resulted in a decline in literacy[29]. With research now showing access to 'green space' reduces attention deficit/hyperactivity disorder[30], and classroom movement improves learning ability[31], an urgent closer look by occupational therapists at the critical sensory and motor requirements for meeting developmental milestones is imperative.

Application of research knowledge by occupational therapists regarding the impact of technology overuse on sensory and motor development would assist in helping parents, teachers and health professionals to better understand the complexities of this issue, and help create effective strategies to manage balanced technology use.

Four critical factors for achieving sensory and motor developmental milestones

The four critical factors for achieving healthy physical, psychological, social and behavioral child development are movement, touch, connection to other humans, and access to nature[32-34]. Movement, touch, human connection, and nature provide the developing child with essential sensory input, integral for the eventual development of a child's motor and attachment systems.

When sensations of movement, touch, connection, and nature are deprived, devastating consequences occur. Young children require two to three hours per day of physically active, unstructured, rough and tumble play to achieve adequate sensory stimulation to their vestibular, proprioceptive, tactile, and attachment systems for normal development[35, 36]. These types of sensory inputs ensure normal development of posture, bilateral coordination, praxis, optimal arousal states and self regulation necessary for achieving foundation skills for eventual school entry.

Many of today's parents perceive outdoor play is 'unsafe', further limiting essential developmental components usually attained in outdoor rough and tumble play[37]. Dr Ashley Montagu, who has extensively studied the developing tactile sensory system, reports that when infants are deprived of human connection and touch, they fail to thrive and many eventually die[38]. Dr Montagu states that touch-deprived infants develop into toddlers who exhibit excessive agitation and anxiety, and may become depressed by early childhood.

Although Dr Montagu reports that the critical period for attachment formation is zero to seven months, connection to the human element is a biological need that is present for a whole lifetime. Sustenance of body, mind and spirit is achieved largely through human connection, without which human physical, psychological and behavior states become grossly impaired.

Studies show that exposure to nature acts on the parasympathetic nervous system to lower cortisol and adrenalin, and induce a state of calm where children are better able to pay attention and learn[39]. When children receive essential stimulation from movement, touch, connection, and nature, they are able to optimize their physical, mental, social and academic development and achieve species sustainability.

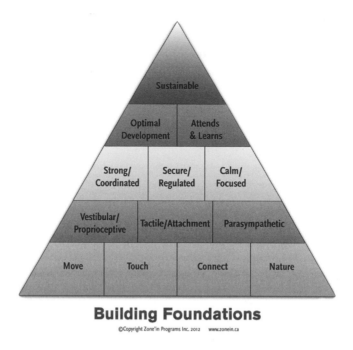

Building Foundations

©Copyright Zone'in Programs Inc. 2012   www.zonein.ca

Connection to technology is causing *disconnection* from self, others, nature and spirit

Technology overuse has had a devastating impact not only on children's sensory and motor development, but also on the development of a child's self identify, relationship to others, experience of nature, and sense of spirit. As children are *connecting* more and more to technology, society has witnessed a pervasive *disconnect* from self, others, nature and spirit.

Self development and identity formation follows the occupational therapy premise that 'you are what you do'. If all a child 'does' is watch television and play video games, then this experience is truly what they become. Little children often are incapable of discerning their sense of self from the 'killing machine' seen on violent television, video games and internet. Shy, lonely and in need of a friend, escaping to the virtual world of technology is causing an irreversible worldwide epidemic of psychological disorders in children.

Technology is also rapidly destroying what humans crave and love the most – connection with **other** human beings. Attachment or connection is the formation of a primary bond between the developing infant and parent, and is integral to that developing child's sense of security and safety. Establishing the infant-parent bond is best facilitated by close contact with the primary parent, lots of eye contact, and 'I see you' communication.

Family overuse of technology is gravely affecting not only early attachment formation, but also impacting negatively on child psychological and behavioral health. It appears that today's families have been pulled into the 'virtual dream', where everyone believes that life is something that requires an escape, and technology becomes the 'haven'. The immediate gratification received from ongoing use of television, videogame and internet technology, appears to have actually *replaced* the desire for human connection.

Nature is the 'mother' of all sensory experiences, and serves as an energy 'ground' for anxious or hyperactive children. Occupational therapists' training in sensory processing enables them to best describe the many positive sensory aspects of nature. The *smell* of grass and dirt stimulate the ancient olfactory system, resulting in relaxation and calming. The beautiful images of the sun reflecting off leaves and flowers, is intricately more *visually* complex, expansive, and therefore potentially interesting than any video game.

The *tactile* experience of wind on a child's face, or the feeling of rough bark when climbing a tree, is rich in sensory information. *Proprioceptive* input achieved through walking over uneven rocks on the beach, or auditory input from *listening* to the songs of sea gulls, or even the *taste* of gritty sand, all are sensory inputs that integrate to eventually help that child respond and adapt to their environment.

Last but definitely not least is **spirit**, the light in a child's eyes that let's everyone know that child is in an optimal arousal state, tapping into their inner drive, engaging in and performing skills to the best of their ability. Technology overuse may eventually results in 'death' of a child's spirit sense, observed by dull, cold eyes as the windows to the soul simply cease to exist.

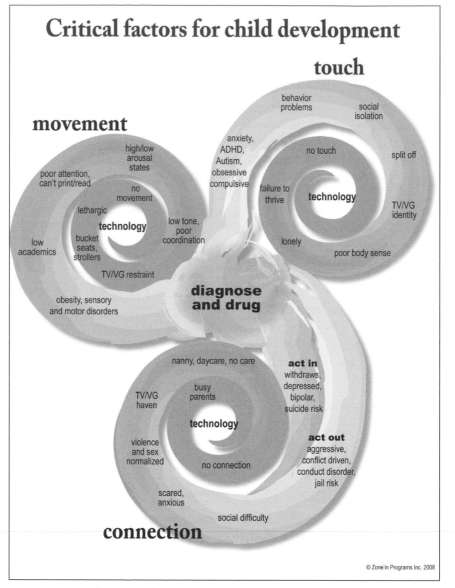

Critical factors for child development

© Zone'in Programs Inc. 2008

Sensory and motor system imbalance

Further analysis of the impact of technology overuse on the developing child indicates that while the vestibular, proprioceptive, tactile and attachment systems are *under* stimulated, the visual and auditory sensory systems are in 'overload'. This sensory imbalance creates huge problems in overall neurological development, as the brain's anatomy, chemistry and pathways become permanently altered and impaired[40].

A joint study by the British Columbia (BC) Business Council, and University of BC researchers with Human Early Learning Partnership, shows that just under 30% of BC children entering kindergarten are 'developmentally vulnerable' – lacking in those basic skills they need to thrive in school and in the future[41]. These children will go on to fail their grade 4 and 7 exams, and drop out of high school prior to completion. This study, entitled *A Comprehensive Policy Framework for Early Human Capital Investment in BC* states:

> Economic analyses reveal this depletion (in human capital) will cause BC to forgo 20% GDP growth over the next 60 years, costing the provincial economy a sum of money that is ten times the total provincial debt load.

Young children who are exposed to violence through television and video games are in a high state of adrenalin and stress, as the body does not know that what they are watching is not real[42]. Children who overuse technology have been reported to experience persistent body sensations of overall 'shaking', increased breathing and heart rate, and a general state of 'unease'. Occupational therapists might describe this state as a persistent hyper-vigilant sensory system, still 'on alert' for the oncoming assault from video game characters.

The effect of chronic states of high levels of cortisol (a stress hormone) emitted during video game playing on young children's sensory development is largely unknown. In the United States, the American Academies of Pediatrics, Physicians, Psychologists and Psychiatrists have joined with the American Medical Association in classifying media violence as a public health risk (second only to the impact of cigarette smoking on lung cancer), due to the causal correlation with increased child aggression[43].

One can't help but wonder if these children who are overexposed to violent media content will go onto develop a form of Post Traumatic Stress Disorder, as a child's body experience may be registering viewed media violence as 'reality'. While cyberbullying (a new threat to children who use the internet) happens primarily at home, children often act out subsequent aggression in school, creating an escalating and very worrisome situation for school administrations[44]. In his book *iBrain* Dr Small, a neurophysiologist, reports that technology's rapid intensity, frequency and duration of visual and auditory stimulation, has been found to result in a 'hard wiring' of the child's sensory system for high speed, with subsequent devastating effects on a child's ability to imagine, attend and focus on academic tasks.

An example of the detrimental impact of technology on child academic performance could be found in Dr Dimitri Christakis' research, which reports that each hour of television watched daily between the ages of zero and seven years of age equated to a 10% increase in attention problems by age seven years[45]. Additional studies by Dr Christakis in 2011 showed that when four year-old children were exposed to *Spongbobs*, a popular cartoon, they demonstrated a significant decline in executive function after only nine minutes[46], and when background television was playing, parents talked 90% less to their children gravely impacting speech and language development[47].

Another consideration for occupational therapists would be the impact of prolonged visual fixation on a fixed distance, two dimensional screen on oculomotor development, which is necessary for eventual printing and reading. With reference to sensory and motor development, there is a vast difference between oculomotor location on a variety of different shaped and sized objects in the near and far distance (such as experienced in outdoor play), as opposed to looking at a fixed distance glowing screen.

Online screen reading (as opposed to reading books), has been shown to result in significantly lower levels in reading comprehension, largely due to the 'fast factor' noted with screen readers[48]. Due to their knowledge of ocular physiology and function needed for printing and reading skill, occupational therapists can help schools to understand the ramifications of technology overuse on academic performance, and assist schools with managing balanced technology use.

Virtual futures

One has to ask: are the ways in which we are educating and raising our children with technology sustainable? Exposure to TV, cell phones and internet results in largely a sedentary child who will be at risk for obesity and diabetes, as well as early cardiovascular compromise such as heart attacks and strokes[49]. The new millennium child is often isolated from friends and family, spending a third of their life in a dark basement predominantly playing video games and/or watching pornography.

Studies show that children (primarily young boys) are initially exposed to pornography by the age of ten, and 40% of children aged ten to 18 years are active users of technology containing violent sexual imagery[50].

Often neglected by their parents, who are struggling with their own internet and cell phone addictions, 21st century children are demonstrating problematic behaviors and coping difficulties that are being readily diagnosed as mental illness. Children who watch more than the expert recommended one to two hours per day of technology, have a 60% increase in psychological disorders[51].

In the United States, a nationwide survey reported problematic use of video games was associated with lower scores on life satisfaction and with elevated levels of anxiety and depression[52]. Additional studies reported that both anxious and avoidant attachment styles, as well as depression and phobia, explained problematic internet use[53]. It is now estimated that one in 11 children aged eight to 18 years are addicted to technology[54].

Exposure to high levels of visual and auditory stimulation from technology overuse are resulting in visual and auditory over-responsivities, with consequent difficulty concentrating and paying attention in school classroom settings[55]. South Korea recently coined the phrase 'Digital Dementia' to describe what is becoming a worldwide phenomenon in youth, permanent memory loss and inability to focus, causally linked to technology overuse[56], and the Journal of Computers and Education recently reported that multitasking on a laptop poses a significant distraction to both users and fellow students and can be detrimental to comprehension of lecture content[57].

Developmental delay, obesity, mental illness, detachment, ADHD, and autism result in early death, relationship difficulty, and unemployment. The ultimate consequence of technology overuse is that 21st century, for the first time in the history of humankind, is witness to a generation of children many of whom will not outlive their parents.

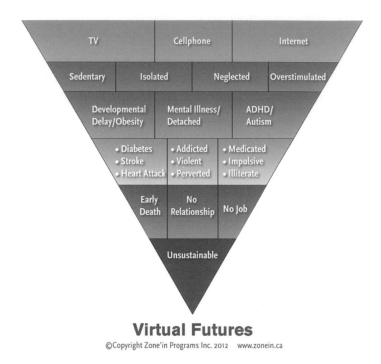

Virtual Futures

©Copyright Zone'in Programs Inc. 2012   www.zonein.ca

The role of occupational therapy in promoting balanced technology management

Pediatric occupational therapy is truly *the* salient profession specifically trained to bring together all the developmental components necessary to create a foundation for child health and learning. Occupational therapy scope of practice regarding technology overuse includes the traditional context areas of activities of daily living, education, leisure, play, and social participation.

The occupational therapist's ability to assess specific aspects of a child's sensory processing and motor development, and the relevant impact on performance skill components, will continue to place this profession in high demand now and in the immediate future. As technology overuse consultants in both the health and education sectors, occupational therapists can interpret researched-based information, perform standardized sensory and motor developmental assessments, and demonstrate excellent observational skills. These unique skills place occupational therapists in a crucial leadership position to help others learn how to balance technology use with what children need to grow and succeed.

The American Academy of Pediatrics issued a policy statement in 2001 recommending that children less than two years of age should not use any technology – yet toddlers zero to two years of age average 2.2 hours of TV per day (24)! The Academy further recommends that children older than two years should restrict usage to one hour per day if they have any physical, psychological or behavioral problems, and two hours per day maximum if they don't, yet parents of elementary children are allowing eight hours per day. It's important for occupational therapist to bring together parents, teachers and other health professionals to help society see the devastating effects technology overuse is having not only on children's physical, psychological and behavioral health, but also on their ability to learn and sustain personal and family relationships.

Occupational therapy is the profession that is best poised to raise this awareness, by providing programming to help society reverse the effects of technology overuse on children. Through fostering a sense of self, facilitating healthy relationship formation, using the art of play in an outdoor setting, and bringing forth a child's inner drive, occupational therapists can reverse this trend to over use technology. Facilitating vestibular, proprioceptive, tactile, and attachment sensory stimulation, and limiting visual and auditory sensory overload, the occupational therapist can help families and schools manage a balanced lifestyle.

Understanding and promoting healthy attachment between parent and child is already a part of every occupational therapy session. Through building skill and self confidence to promote occupational performance, occupational therapists can help children 'unplug' themselves from technology, easing the job of parenting and teaching. Using sensory and motor developmental practice frames of reference, and expert design and implementation of effective interventions, occupational therapists can help parents and teachers understand the profound effects of technology overuse on child development and academic performance.

Whether working in school or home settings, the occupational therapist is a future leader in the field of balanced technology management, where adults manage balance between activities children need to grow and succeed, with technology use.

Conclusion

While technology is an evolving 'train' that will continually move forward, the occupational therapist has expert knowledge regarding its detrimental effects. Immediate action taken toward balancing the use of technology with movement, touch, human connection, and nature, will work toward sustaining children, families and educational environments.

While no one can argue the benefits of advanced technology in today's world, connection to these devices has resulted in a disconnection from what society should value most, child health and academic excellence. Occupational therapists have the unique qualifications and skills to assess and treat children who overuse technology, to ultimately help bring the technology train back onto a healthy track. Occupational therapists can help create a sustainable future for every child.

References

1 Ayres JA. Sensory integration and learning disorders. California: Western Psychological Services; 1972.

2 Pelligrini AD, Bohn CM. The role of recess in children's cognitive performance and school adjustment. Educational Researcher. 2005; 34(1): 13-19.

3 Rideout VJ, Vandewater EA, Wartella EA. Zero to six: electronic media in the lives of infants, toddlers and preschoolers. Menlo Park (CA): Kaiser Family Foundation; Fall 2003.

4 Kaiser Foundation Report. 2010. Retrieved on April 30, 2010 from www.kff.org/entmedia/upload/8010.pdf

5 Active Healthy Kids Canada [2008 report card on the internet]. Available from: www.activehealthykids.ca/Ophea/ActiveHealthyKids_v2/upload/AHKC-Short-Form-EN.pdf

6 Christakis DA, Zimmerman FJ. Violent Television During Preschool Is Associated With Antisocial Behavior During School Age. Pediatrics. 2007; 120: 993-999.

7 Nunez-Smith M, Wolf E, Mikiko Huang H, Chen P, Lee L, Emanuel EJ, Gross, CP. Media and Child and Adolescent Health: A Systematic Review. Available online at www.commonsensemedia.org/sites/default/files/NunezSmith%20CSM%20media_review%20Dec%204.pdf

8 Zimmerman FJ, Christakis DA, Meltzoff AN. Television and DVD/video viewing in children younger than 2 years. Archives of Pediatric Adolescent Medicine. 2007; 161 (5): 473-479.

9 France pulls plug on TV shows aimed at babies [CBC online article Wednesday, August 20, 2008]. Available from: www.cbc.ca/world/story/2008/08/20/french-baby.html

10 Hancox RJ, Milne BJ, Poulton R. Association of television during childhood with poor educational achievement. Archives of Pediatric and Adolescent Medicine. 2005; 159 (7): 614-618.

11 Waddell C. Improving the Mental Health of Young Children. Children's Health Policy Centre, Simon Fraser University, Vancouver BC, Canada. 2007. Available at: www.firstcallbc.org/pdfs/Communities/4-alliance.pdf

12 Zito JM, Safer DJ, dosReis S, Gardner JF, Magder L, Soeken K, Lynch F, Riddle M. Psychotropic practice patterns for youth. Archives of Pediatric and Adolescent Medicine. 2003; 157(1): 17-25.

13 Mandell DS, Morales KH, Marcus SC, Stahmer AC, Doshi J, and Polsky DE. Psychotropic medication use among medicaid-enrolled children with Autism Spectrum Disorders. Pediatrics. 2008; 121 (3): 441-449.

14 Zito JM, Safer DJ, dosReis S, Gardner JF, Boles M, Lynch F. Trends in the prescribing of psychotropic medications to preschoolers. JAMA. 2000; 283: 1025-1030.

15 Goodwin R, Gould MS, Blanco C, Olfson M. Prescription of psychotropic medications to youth in office-based practices. Psychiatric Services. 2001; 52(8):1081-1087.

16 Hamilton S. Screening for developmental delay: Reliable, easy-to-use tools. Journal of Family Practice. 2006; 55 (5): 416-422.

17 Birmingham CL, Muller JL, Palepu A, Spinelli JJ, Anis AH. The cost of obesity in Canada. Canadian Medical Association Journal. 1999; 160:483-488. www.SPDFoundation.net

18 Huesmann LR. The Impact of Electronic Media Violence: Scientific Theory and Research. Journal of Adolescent Health. 2007; 41: S6-13.

Ybarra ML, Diener-West M, Leaf PJ. Examining the Overlap in Internet Harassment and School Bullying: Implications for School Intervention. Journal of Adolescent Health. 2007; 41:S42-S50.

19 Christakis DA, Zimmerman FJ, DiGiuseppe DL, McCarty CA. Early television exposure and subsequent attentional problems in children. Pediatrics. 2004; 113 (4): 708-713.

20 Paavonen E, Pennonen M and Roine M. Passive Exposure to TV Linked to Sleep Problems in Children. Journal of Sleep Research. 2006; Vol 15, 154-161.

21 Tremblay MS, Willms JD. Is the Canadian childhood obesity epidemic related to physical inactivity? International Journal of Obesity. 2005; 27: 1100-1105.

22 Children, adolescents and television. American Academy of Pediatrics, Committee on Public Education. Pediatrics. 2001; 107 (2): 423-426.

23 Children, adolescents and advertising. Committee on Communications, American Academy of Pediatrics. Pediatrics. 2006; 118 (6): 2562-2569.

24 Waldman M, Nicholson S, Adilov N. Does TV Cause Autism? Cornell University. December 2006. Available at: www.johnson.cornell.edu/faculty/profiles/waldman/autpaper.html

25 Jennings JT. Conveying the message about optimal infant positions. Physical and Occupational Therapy in Pediatrics. 2005; 25 (3); 3-18.

26 Braswell J, Rine R. Evidence that vestibular hypofunction affects reading acuity in children. International Journal of Pediatric Otorhinolaryngology. 2006; 70 (11): 1957-1965.

27 De Silva, S. 2006. Statistics Canada Centre for Education. Available at: www.statscanada.com

28 Kuo FE, Faber Taylor A. Children with Attention Deficits Concentrate Better After a Walk in the Park. *Journal of Attention Disorders.* 2009; 12; 402: originally published online Aug 25, 2008.

29 Rapport M Bolden J, Kofler MJ, Sarver DE, Raiker JS, Alderson RM. Hyperactivity in Boys with Attention-Deficit/Hyperactivity Disorder (ADHA): A Ubiquitous Core Symptom or Manifestation of Working Memory Deficits? Journal of Abnormal Psychology. 2008; DOT 10.1007/s10802-008-9287-8.

30 Nelson MC, Neumark-Sztainer DR, Hannan PJ, Sirard JR, Story M. Longitudinal and secular trends in physical activity and sedentary behavior during adolescence. Pediatrics. 2006; 118 (6): 1627-1634.

31 Insel TR, Young LJ. The neurobiology of attachment. Nature Reviews Neuroscience. 2001; 2: 129-136.

32 Korkman M. Introduction to the special issue on normal neuropsychological development in the school-age years. Developmental Neuropsychology. 2001; 20 (1):325-330.

33 National Association for Sport and Physical Education. NASPE Releases 34 First Ever Physical Activity Guidelines for Infants and Toddlers. February 6, 2002. Available at: www.aahperd.org/naspe/template.cfm?template=toddlers.html

35 Tannock MT. Rough and Tumble Play: An Investigation of the Perceptions of Educators and Young Children. Journal of Early Childhood Education. 2008; 35: 357-361.

36 Burdette, HL, Whitaker RC. A national study of neighborhood safety, outdoor play, television viewing, and obesity in preschool children. Pediatrics. 2005; 116: 657-662.

37 Montagu, A. Touching, the Human Significance of the Skin 2nd Edition. Harper and Row Publishers Inc. New York, NY; 1978.

38 Faber Taylor A, Kuo FE, Sullivan WC. Coping With ADD – The Surprising Connection to Green Play Settings. Journal of Environment and Behavior. 2001; 33(1):54-77.

39 Small G, Vorgan G. iBrain: Surviving the Technological Alteration of the Modern Mind. HarperCollins Publishers, New York, NY; 2008.

40 Kershaw P. British Columbia Business Council and University of British Columbia researchers with the Human Early Learning Partnership. A Comprehensive Policy Framework for Early Human Capital Investment in BC. 2009. Retrieved on April 30, 2010 from www.earlylearning.ubc.ca/documents/2009/15by15-Executive-Summary.pdf

41 Anderson CA, Gentile DA, Buckley KE. Violent Video Game Effects on Children and Adolescents: Theory, Research and Public Policy. Oxford University Press. New York, NY; 2007.

42 Anderson CA, Berkowitz, L, Donnerstein E, Huesmann LR, Johnson JD, Linz D, Malamuth NM, Wartella E. The Influence of Media Violence on Youth. Psychological Science in the Public Interest. 2003; 4:81-110.

43 Buchanan AM, Gentile DA, Nelson DA, Walsh DA, Hensel J. What goes in must come out: Children's Media Violence Consumption at Home and Aggressive Behaviours at School. Paper presented at the International Society for the Study of Behavioural Development Conference, Ottawa, Ontario, Canada. Available online at: www.mediafamily.org/research/report_issbd_2002.shtml

44 Christakis DA, Zimmerman FJ, DiGiuseppe DL, McCarty CA. Early television exposure and subsequent attentional problems in children. Pediatrics. 2004; 113 (4): 708-713.

45 Christakis, D.A. (2011) The effects of fast-paced cartoons. PEDIATRICS Vol. 128 No. 4 October 1, 2011, pp. 772 -774 (doi: 10.1542/peds.2011-2071).

46 Moje EB, Overby M, Tysvaer N, Morris K. The Complex World of Adolescent Literacy: Myths, Motivations, and Mysteries. Harvard Educational Review. 2008; 78(1):107-154.

47 Christakis, D. A., Gilkerson, J., Richards, J. A., Zimmerman, F. J., Garrison, M. M., Xu, D., Gray, S. & Yapanel, U. (2009). Audible Television and Decreased Adult Words, Infant Vocalizations, and Conversational Turns. Archives of Pediatrics & Adolescent Medicine. 163(6):554-558. Available at: archpedi.ama-assn.org/cgi/content/full/163/6/554#AUTHINFO

48 Tremblay, M.S., LeBlanc, A.G., Kho, M.E., Saunders, T.J., Larouche, R., Colley, R.C., Goldfield, G., Gorber, S.C. (2011) Systematic review of sedentary behaviour and health indicators in school-aged children and youth. *International Journal of Behavioral Nutrition and Physical Activity* 2011, 8:98 doi:10.1186/1479-5868-8-98

49 Wolak J, Mitchell K, Finkelhor D (2007). Unwanted and Wanted Exposure to Online Pornography in a National Sample of Youth Internet Users *Pediatrics* 2007;119; 247

50 Bristol University: School for Policy Studies News (2010). Available at: www.bristol.ac.uk/sps/news/2010/107.html

51 Mentzoni, RA, Brunborg, GS, Molde H, Myrseth H, Mar Skouveroe KJ, Hetland J, Pallesen S. Problematic Video Game Use: Estimated Prevalence and Associations with Mental and Physical Health. Cyberpsychology, Behavior, and Social Networking. 2011;110306113133023.doi:10.1089/cyber.2010.0260.

52 Shin S-E, Kim, N-S, Jang E-Y. Comparison of Problematic Internet and Alcohol Use and Attachment Styles Among Industrial Workers in Korea.

53 Cyberpsychology, Behavior, and Social Networking on May 19, 2011. doi:10.1089/cyber.2010.0470. Available at: www.liebertonline.com/doi/abs/10.1089/cyber.2010.0470

54 Gentile D. Pathological Video-Game Use Among Youth Ages 8 to 18. Journal of Psychological Science. 2009; 3(2):1-9.

55 Ben-Sasson, A., Carter, A. S. & Briggs-Gowan, M. The Development of Sensory Over-Responsivity From Infancy to Elementary School. *Journal of Abnormal Child Psychology.* (2010).

56 Sana F. Laptop multitasking hinders classroom learning for both users and nearby peers. *Journal of Computers and Education.* Vol 62, March 2013, 24-31

57 Digital Dementia: The memory problem plaguing teens and young adults, On Fox News, August 15, 2013, available at ht www.foxnews.com/health/2013/08/15/digital-dementia-memory-problem-plaguing-teens-and-young-adults/#ixzz2eE8KTuWR

Chapter 16

The need for inclusive accessible technologies for students with disabilities and learning difficulties

Simon Hayhoe

Introduction

This chapter discusses the philosophy of how assistive technology for people with disabilities and other forms of learning difficulties can be more inclusive. It looks at an educational model for analysing technologies and argues that the development of mobile learning has seen the evolution of inclusive technology.

It is the aim of this chapter to inform teachers and families of children with learning difficulties of approaches to integrating inclusive technologies in their children's education; to help adults who have disabilities and other learning difficulties choose the best forms of technology for particular situations; and also to contribute to a debate amongst educators and technologists as to the most effective future development of inclusive, assistive technologies.

This chapter is necessary in a book that reviews the future directions of education as many new technologies are being introduced into schools and colleges in wealthy countries while relatively little is known about their application in teaching and learning of students with difficulties in the school environment.

For instance, in the United Arab Emirates, Dubai's schools and government higher education institutions have introduced mobile tablet computers for all early years teachers in an initiative designed to make learning more independent and flexible[1]. Yet few studies of this initiative have been conducted either before or after implementation with students with disabilities. This is a pity, as technology in many instances has been found to help in situations seen in many Emirati schools.

For example, a recent study has found that icon-based interfaces, such as those found in tablet computers, can be helpful to students who speak English as a second language[2]. Furthermore, in many countries laws have enshrined a right to inclusion in education and similar cultural activities for students with disabilities, such as the 2010 Equalities Act in the UK and Americans With Disabilities Act 2008 Amendments in the US. Technology is a valuable tool in this process.

The chapter is broken into four sections. The first examines the study of educational technology, the integration of learning theories and modes of teaching with technology and how technology has been integrated into education through a model of Substitution, Augmentation Modification and Redefinition (SAMR). The second section describes what disability is, how accessible technology can support students with disabilities and learning difficulties, and how these technologies have changed the way we teach students and the institutions they learn in. The third section argues for a redefinition of accessible technology and presents mobile learning as a case study of an inclusive form of educational technology. The fourth section draws conclusions.

The foundations of educational technology as a subject of study

The subject of educational technology is designed as a 'study and ethical practice of facilitating learning and improving performance by creating, using and managing appropriate technological processes and resources' (p24).[3] The first studies of technology in formal learning started in

Ancient Greece as early as 5000 BC[4,] although an understanding of the importance of technology in school education has only recently been realized. It took many years for comprehensive histories to be written on this topic, particularly those relating to electronic media in schools[5].

This is unfortunate as we now realize that technology often plays an important role in the delivery and assessment of teaching and learning, and has been involved in the understanding of learning processes from the earliest psychological and classroom experiments. For example, the earliest behavioral experiments devised to mimic learning, such as those of Ivan Pavlov[6], used devices such as bells and metronomes to provide stimuli. Similarly, Pavlov's contemporary Edward Thorndike[7] designed a technological innovation, the puzzle box, to mimic a complex form of learning behavior. Later Buhurus F Skinner[8] designed similar cages with levers to deliver punishment and rewards, and Martin Seligman[9], through instruments of punishment, incorporated technologies as a medium of learning in order to measure learned helplessness.

In his most popular work, *Beyond Freedom and Dignity*[10], Skinner took this notion of educational technology further still by suggesting that students could do away with traditional lessons and teachers, and instead learn in their own time through devices meant to provide positive and negative stimuli depending on whether students learnt a given piece of knowledge in a correct or incorrect way. Even modern studies of cognition refer to technologies, with Howard Gardner's[11] literature in particular referencing musical, artistic and physical technologies in the development and application of multiple intelligences. Yet despite the necessity of technologies to the development and application of all these learning theories, the *nature* and *role* of the technology that has been studied has too often been considered to be superfluous to the act of learning by school teachers in all but *high-tech* subjects.

Educational technology has, however, been established in other institutions for some time. In some universities in particular this attitude was different. Fifty years ago, for instance, educators in higher education started to realize that not only scientifically measurable behavior but the environment of education could be equally important to teaching and learning, and thus educational technology became of considerable value to new universities and colleges.

In 1966 the British Prime Minister Harold Wilson described the need to keep up with what he called 'the white heat of technology' through the delivery of lifelong learning for workers in Britain, in order to update their skills[12]. As it was impossible for these workers to attend universities full time, open and distance learning was developed and the Open University was created to train people in their own homes through communication technologies such as television, telephone and radio.

This was learning that had previously been delivered through more traditional routes of correspondence through paper files and weekend lectures in local colleges[13]. Consequently, the Open University developed considerable expertise through its Institute for Educational Technology in delivering learning and assessment materials via increasingly sophisticated and digitized technologies, including the earliest versions of the World Wide Web and social networking. Now Open University courses can be studied and research studies conducted entirely through web based technologies such as Second Life, the fantasized, virtual world in which human beings are represented through their own avatars, and can live life without gravity or geographical boundaries[14].

Despite this lack of balance in considering educational technology in schools and no unified theory of implementing and developing educational technology, a number of separate phases of the history of educational and learning technologies developed over the course of the 20th century, and still continue to develop separately at the beginning of the 21st century[15]. What is perhaps most important to identify in this chapter is that there are two particular phases that have transformed our use of technology in mainstream schools since the introduction of electronic technology into schools: the personal computer phase and the mobile computing phase.

The personal computer phase itself has two separate eras. The first is the introduction of general computing technology in the1960s: that is computing technology that did not take up a whole room and which, although it did not change mainstream teaching at the time, did introduce school students to the use of technologies in an educational environment. The second era came to bear in the 1990s and involved the use of computing technology in non-technical subjects and environments. This began with the introduction of teachers' computers, projectors and interactive computer-driven whiteboards – otherwise known as smart-boards.

Shortly after this phase students started to use computers for non-technical as well as high-tech subjects. With this second phase came a sea-change in teaching and learning, and an acceptance of digital technologies in lesson planning, curriculum development and assessments in education. This second era subsequently gave rise to new models of educational technology, models that included not just identifying technologies as they were in previous eras but classifying these educational technologies according to their pedagogical designs and needs.

One such is the SAMR model of classifying the use of technology[16]. This model categorizes the application of technology in lessons as either *Transformative* – *ie* one that transforms the subject of education and delivers a brand new topic to the curriculum; or *Enhancement* – *ie* the use of technology to enhance the teaching of traditional subjects and vocational skills during lesson periods. To enhance education through technology, teaching types are split into two further groups: the *Substitution* and *Augmentation* of mechanical tasks into digital tasks.

For example, instead of teaching students to type, as was required by many secretarial colleges and jobs in the past, digital technology has substituted the word-processor for this older technology, and required the teaching of a relatively similar set of skills in the same lessons. The introduction of digital technology has also led to the augmentation of tools that were once mechanical, such as the shredding or filing of documents, to digital equivalents, such as the use of electronic waste bins and folders on modern operating systems' desktops.

Similarly, to use technology as an *Enhancement* in education, teaching is split into two further groups: the *Modification* and *Redefinition* of mechanical tasks into new digital ones. For example, word-processors have not only substituted and augmented functions; they also have brand new tools that modify mechanical, physical ways of working to cognitive digital processes. Examples of these include the ability to save different versions of files, to email directly from a document, and to change a paper based document into a webpage.

Similarly, tasks once taught through the use of old fashioned technologies such as keyboards have been completely redefined, and are now possible through digital input devices such as voice inputs, or swiping and tapping touch screens; this requires a whole new skill set to be learnt by the students and trainees of the 21st century. This change in pedagogy is illustrated in Table 1.

Transformation		
Redefinition	Technology allowing for the transition of training in new tasks through AT/IT	Teaching students how to use their tablet computers, their operating systems, etc.
Modification	Technology allows for significant redesign of tasks	The inclusion of email functions within word processors, the integration of mail merge or hyper text editing within word processors
Augmentation	Technology substitutes as a direct tool, with functional improvements	Cut and paste functions, waste bin functions, spell checking functions, grammar checking functions within word-processing
Substitution	Technology acts as a direct tool substitute, with no functional change	The use of a word processor instead of a typewriter, or hot metal publishing processes.
Enhancement		

Table 1: An illustration of the SAMR model of technology driven education.

This raises two questions in relation to technology and disability:

How has technology changed the life and education of students with disabilities and learning difficulties?

Can the SAMR model of describing technologically enhanced teaching and learning be applied to the teaching of these students?

To address these questions, it is first necessary to look at what disabilities and learning difficulties in an educational context are.

Disability, learning difficulties and accessible technology

The word disability and the phrase learning difficulty have come to mean many things, although they were not used in education until the latter half of the 20th century[17]. The modern origins of these concepts date back to 18th century Europe when people who could not work or learn in the few schools available for able bodied students were increasingly marginalized by urbanization and resorted to begging in city streets, particularly those of port cities.

Although there were able-bodied beggars at the time, people with physical impairments were said to be resorting to begging in increasing numbers[18]. Indeed, people with what are now called disabilities were seen to be particularly successful as beggars or seen as a class apart deserving of charity, as Christian ethics determined that they needed assistance. However, this also stereotyped all people with disabilities as lazy and immoral, particularly as many of the causes of disabilities and learning difficulties were linked with diseases that were caused by immorality or prevalent amongst the 'lower classes', who were themselves often considered to be mentally subnormal.

As a consequence, a number of Christian institutions were founded in France, then Britain and then the rest of continental Europe, to institutionalize people with different forms of disability. These institutions were designed to educate people with disabilities and either provide an intellectual 'enlightenment' or to learn a trade that would discourage them from begging. Although initially developed for adults, these institutions also later adapted to cater for children, and took on a more formal educative role in the process.[19]

Although people with different conditions, such as blindness, deafness and mental illness, were kept in separate institutions from the 18th century to the first half of the 20th century, there was a tacit understanding that people with impairments, particularly physical impairments, had similar social struggles. This was recognised in many countries throughout Europe and from the 19th century North America too, with many countries passing laws for students with disabilities and appointing departments and experts to develop education for such students.

Perhaps the most respected of these experts was the educational psychologist Lev Vygotsky, who was appointed the director for students with 'defects' in the former USSR. In this respect Vygotsky[20] was the first theorist to acknowledge that social factors were at least as important as physical, sensory and learning impairments in education. As he stated on this matter:

Every physical defect, be it blindness or deafness, alters the child's attitude towards the universe and, primarily towards its fellow beings.

Let us take, for instance, the geometrical place of a human being in the social sphere, his part and his fate as partaker of life and all functions of social existence, and we shall all come to the conclusion that everything is to be entirely altered on the case of the human being with any defect. Any physical defect provokes a social sprain, with unavoidable consequences. (pp. 19-20)[21]

In concert with this evolving notion of disability was the development of inclusion into education and other social and cultural institutions for people with impairments. This was followed by the notion of a combination of cognitive, developmental, emotional and social impairments, such as dyslexia and behavioural problems that could lead to learning difficulties.

In more recent years, as equality and greater opportunities for people with disabilities have become the theme of politics in westernised countries, a debate on the equality of disabled people has also become a theme for national governments and quasi-international organisations and NGOs, such as the World Health Organisation (WHO) and the United Nations (UN). Consequently, these institutions have devised a series of definitions of disability that have increasingly incorporated the notion that social and cultural factors disabled people more than bodily or physical factors. This is particularly reflected in the UN's last definition of disability, which includes the notion of learning difficulty:

The term persons with disabilities is used to apply to all persons with disabilities including those who have long-term physical, mental, intellectual or sensory impairments which, in interaction with various attitudinal and environmental barriers, hinders their full and effective participation in society on an equal basis with others... Disability resides in the society not in the person. (Online)[22]

The technologies developed to assist inclusion of people with disabilities and learning difficulties in education have become known as assistive technologies and are broadly defined as 'any item, piece of equipment, or system, whether acquired commercially, modified, or customized, that is commonly used to increase, maintain, or improve functional capabilities of individuals with disabilities.' (P. 80504)[23] Historically, as soon as institutions for people with disabilities developed, technologies and adapted teaching methodologies evolved, articles were written and associations of teachers and innovators were incorporated to cultivate new pedagogies and technologies to overcome their impairments.

For example, special schools and institutions have become expert at teaching advances such as Braille – developed by a former student at the Paris institute for the blind, following on from touch languages developed from the 18th century[24] – magnifying lenses and devices to assist mobility such as crutches, white canes and later wheelchairs. With the advent of electronic audio devices also came the development of technologies such as hearing aids and amplifiers for deaf people, and radio transmissions for people who were blind or visually impaired. Later, digital technologies have also provided further help in making literature and knowledge available. Software in particular has helped to overcome barriers to learning through, for instance, audio descriptions of books and art works, enlargement or recolouring of text on screen, and the representation of sound as text[25].

In keeping with an SAMR model of classifying technology in education, training strategies have been developed to incorporate the use of these devices to *Enhance* learning. *Substitution* allows mainstream teaching to take place with technologies that can blend in with the pedagogy of the lesson. For example, students who have reading difficulties can record the teacher in class to play the lesson back through MP3 devices in lieu of note-taking, or can use enlarged or coloured type on computer screens to substitute for traditional reading materials[26].

Augmentation skills are taught through the use of software such as JAWS, Ruby on Rails, or other screen-readers that augment voices for blind computer users, or devices to augment voices for people with incapacitated facial muscles[27]. In addition to these enhancing technologies, there are more radical Transformations of syllabi through assistive technologies.

For example, software and hardware has *Redefined* how students are taught to read and produce writing through devices such as the Perkin's Brailler in schools for the blind. This tradition has continued with more contemporary technologies such as Braille readers to assist with tactile literacy for people who are blind[28]. Similarly, devices have been developed that can *Modify* the way that traditional skills in special schools are taught. For example, students with restricted movement in their limbs are taught mobility skills through virtual reality devices rather than traditional and potentially more dangerous equipment[29]. All of these categories are illustrated in Table 2.

Transformation		
Redefinition	Technology allowing for the training of new skills through	Customised technology that allows students to write or read using alternative technologies, such as the Perkins Brailler.
Modification	Technology allows for significant redesign of tasks	Customised technology that allows teachers and students mobility, writing facilities, reading facilities, hearing facilities
Augmentation	Technology substitutes as a direct tool, with functional improvements	Accessible settings, such as voice recognition
Substitution	Technology acts as a direct tool substitute, with no functional change	Tablet computers, smart phones, mp3 players and multimedia devices with differing inputs and outputs
Enhancement		

Table 2: An illustration of the SAMR model of assistive technology driven education.

However, there is a problem with the idea of traditional assistive technology as it has been applied in educational contexts – and arguably in other social settings too. In itself assistive technology too often separates students with disabilities from those without disabilities, and provides a reason not to include disabled students in mainstream lessons, curricula and schools. In many cases assistive technologies, and the skills needed by teachers to use and teach with them, require that they are installed in special schools, leaving no social inclusion at all in the lives of disabled students.

Furthermore, many schools, teachers, students and families have found that there are many economic problems with affording traditional assistive technologies, as their specialist nature and the fact that they are developed and manufactured in small numbers make them more expensive than mainstream, mass-produced technologies. In addition, although the name assistive technology is designed to signify the assistance of technology in lessons, this emphasis on difference often means that students with disabilities and learning difficulties are more often separated and taught skills necessary to use assistive technologies or modify existing tasks that separate students included in mainstream tasks than use technologies to support mainstream classes[30].

In relation to the SAMR model, what is often observable of many applications of assistive technologies in education is that they too often focus on *Transformative* education rather than provide an *Enhancement* to mainstream teaching and learning. This emphasis can be illustrated as an inverted pyramid, in which most teaching with assistive technologies occurs in the top half of the pyramid. This is illustrated graphically in Figure 1.

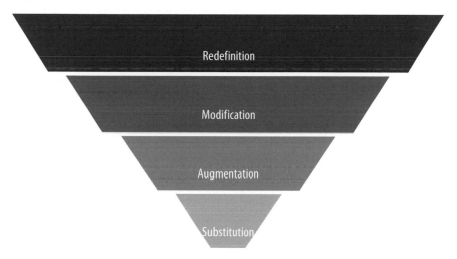

Figure 1: An illustration of the SAMR model of assistive technology, showing the traditional balance of teaching with assistive devices.

Redefining assistive technology as inclusive technology

It can thus be argued that traditional assistive technologies are some of the last cultural and social barriers to the full educational inclusion of students with disabilities and learning difficulties. This is a problem of assistive engineering and design as these disciplines are too often developed and written about by able-bodied people trying to imagine what it is like to have a disability.

Moreover, engineers and designers more often than not fall prey to the academic, social and cultural stereotypes that their imagination engenders. As a result, traditional assistive technologies often encompass highly immobile, awkward and physically restrictive devices which are bound to single classrooms and adapted environments. In addition, many assistive devices are also restricted to separate, special schools designed only for people with disabilities because, as has already been stated, they are also too expensive and uneconomical to install and maintain in mainstream schools and colleges.

There are also socially and culturally negative aspects of traditional assistive technologies that affect the self-esteem of students who have to use them. In particular, it has been observed that traditional assistive devices often identify a person as having a special need, which can stigmatize students with disabilities and learning difficulties among their able-bodied peers[31]. Academia itself also does not help in the *process* of developing methods to include students through assistive technology, as the largest body of literature targeting the use of assistive technologies in education focuses on the mechanical and electronic properties of hardware and software, rather than thinking about the aesthetics of their design, or the cultural and social acceptance of such devices in mainstream settings.

Moreover, despite the development of new forms of mainstream educational technology through innovations such as m-learning, there is little research on the use of this new technology with assistive devices, even though many modern mobile technologies now have assistive functions. This provides a problem in educational research and highlights the need for a re-philosophical evaluation of the pedagogy that accompanies assistive technologies. This re-evaluation can be summarized through the following two questions: what is inclusion in assistive technology? How can such technologies be inclusive?

In answer to the first question, it is argued[32] that inclusive technology is

> mainstream technology that can be used with either no or minimal adaption by a person with a disability as an accessible technology. It is also seen as technology that provides social inclusion, such as communication and interaction, for people with disabilities. (Online)

Thus, in order for technology and the design of technology for people with disabilities and learning difficulties to be wholly useful it needs to be driven by a mainstream social and cultural form in concert with the notion that students should not have a separate form of education. This brings the study of assistive technology in line with the educational philosophy of inclusion in education, one that states that all students should have social and cultural equality with each-other in all forms of teaching and learning.

In answer to the second question, it is argued that the existing understanding of what an assistive technology is needs to be reshaped, and the terminology used to describe such technologies and their accompanying pedagogies in mainstream environments needs to be redefined. The first method by which this can be done is to rename assistive technology in education as inclusive educational technology. This will help shift the focus away from the design and engineering of such devices as an engineered assistance to people who are disabled or who have learning difficulties, and move it towards the inclusiveness of the education that they support, and the social and cultural inclusion issues that they address.

The second part of this process is to redefine the process of engineering design itself, in order to make it fit for purpose for people with disabilities and learning difficulties, *ie* to not make the design and engineering process about perceived practical measures as defined by academics or engineers, and to make it customer led, focusing solely on the individuals for whom the technology is created.

This can be achieved by training and encouraging people with disabilities and learning difficulties to create their own technologies, or at the very least by including people with disabilities in the design process, and not just as end user testers. Furthermore, it is necessary that assistive technology should not signify inferiority, particularly in matters of intelligence. It must instead be emphasized that students with disabilities and learning difficulties still have human capital that is valuable to their societies.

If this is achieved, then we can invert the SAMR model's pyramid to show *Redefinition* of tasks as being the least important purpose of technologies in the education of students with disabilities and learning difficulties, and *Substitution* as being the most important role for these technologies. This is illustrated graphically in Figure 2.

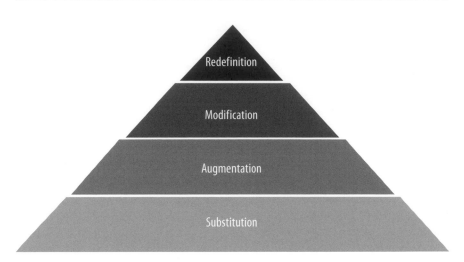

Figure 2: An illustration of the SAMR model of assistive technology, showing of teaching through technology that is truly inclusive.

For some engineers and designers, this process has already begun. As previously stated, mobile learning (m-learning) is a pedagogy employed in education with mobile devices, such as tablets, MP3 players and recorders, and mobile telephones – the latter most often through smartphones. This means that many aspects of education are controlled outside the traditional classroom and either resources become highly accessible in all learning environments – not just in the library – or that the classroom itself is less important to teaching and learning, allowing learning to happen in multiple locations at any time[33].

This form of learning lends itself to the education and training of students with disabilities and learning difficulties, as they can record mainstream classes, access extra data that they may need in mainstream classes, and even have access to specialist media such as Braille through the web. Apple devices in particular have been found to be noteworthy inclusive devices for use in m-learning as they are designed for multiple communication channels, multi-media and quick access to apps.

In addition, Apple has made a full commitment to accessibility in its mainstream devices. In its tablet devices, such as the iPad, iPhone or iPod, rather than engineering features for perceived individual problems of disability, features for use in special education are broken into the following four categories[34]:

Literacy and learning

Vision

Hearing

Physical and motor skills

For Apple, tablets in particular have a number of inclusive features fitted as standard, such as voice functions to identify objects for people who are blind or have reading problems: text on screen for people with hearing impairments; software and apps for reading to help students with learning disabilities; a zoom facility for users with low vision; and a function for changing colour to photo-negative – a function that can help people with low vision and also people with dyslexia and dyscalculia.

However, as has also been noted about this device, some elements still need improving. The cost of the iPad in comparison to other mainstream tablets, for instance, is relatively much higher. In addition, the amount of processing time is greater when using inclusive features, and it takes a large amount of time to setup the settings – which are described in a user manual that is inaccessible to many people who are blind, or who have many learning difficulties or visual impairments. Thus it is too early to say whether it significantly improves the prospects of students with disabilities and learning difficulties.

Conclusion

Assistive technology has helped many people, and has largely been perceived to be a force for good for students with disabilities and learning difficulties for over 200 years. However, unlike other aspects of education, it has failed to evolve to include all students in mainstream education. This is because the focus of the engineering and design of assistive learning technologies is largely on their technical capacities and perceived functions, rather than their form or their ability to include people with disabilities in all mainstream social and cultural settings.

Unfortunately, such design problems are often the result of a lack of understanding by the designers and engineers, who often over-intellectualise the problems of disability. The application of the SAMR model of learning with technology applied to assistive technology illustrates this point well. Thus what is needed, if we are to make technologies fully inclusive, is to consult and include users of assistive technology at every stage of the design process – not just the testing process – and in the long term train people with disabilities and learning difficulties to engineer technologies that best serve their own purposes.

More importantly, we must restate the aims and title of assistive technology as inclusive technology in education; technology that integrates students and others with disabilities and learning difficulties in all aspects of life. Although this process has started with mobile technologies and learning, there is still a long way to go.

References

2 Meurant, R.C. (2010) The iPad and EFL Digital Literacy. Communications in Computer and Information Science, 123, 224-234.

3 Richey, R.C. (2008). Reflections on the 2008 AECT Definitions of the Field. *Tech. Trends. 52/1/24-25*

4 Saettler, P. (1968). A History of Instructional Technology. New York: McGraw-Hill.

5 See for example, Reiser, R. A., & Dempsey, J. V. (2011). Trends and issues in instructional design and technology. London: Pearson., Anglin, G. J. (1995). *Instructional technology: Past, present, and future.* Englewood, CO: Libraries Unlimited., and Reiser, R. A. (2001). A history of instructional design and technology: Part I: A history of instructional media. *Educational technology research and development, 49/1/53-64.*

6 Pavlov, I. P. (1927). *Conditioned reflexes.* Mineola, NY: DoverPublications.

7 Thorndike, E. L. (1898). Animal intelligence: An experimental study of the associative processes in animals. *Psychological Monographs: General and Applied, 2/4/i-109.*

8 Skinner, B. F., Skinner, B. F., Skinner, B. F., & Skinner, B. F. (1972). *Beyond freedom and dignity.* New York: Bantam Books.

9 Seligman, M. E. (1975). *Helplessness: On depression, development, and death.* New York: Henry Holt & Co.

10 Skinner Op. Cit.

11 See for example, Gardner, H. (1985). *Frames of mind: The theory of multiple intelligences.* New York: Basic books.

12 Edgerton, D. (1996). The'White Heat' revisited: the British government and technology in the 1960s. *Twentieth Century British History, 7/1/ 53-82.*

13 Nasseh, B. (1997). A brief history of distance education. Adult Education in the News.

14 See for example a research project conducted on death in virtual worlds, r3beccaf. wordpress.com/2013/09/09/death-in-virtual-worlds/

15 Reiser Op. Cit.

16 Chell, G., & Dowling, S. (2013). Substitution to redefinition: The challenges of using technology. In Dowling, S., Gunn, C., Raven, J. and Hayhoe, S. (Eds.). eLearning in action. Redefining learning. Abu Dhabi. HCT Press.

17 Hayhoe, S. (2008a). God, money & politics: English attitudes to blindness and touch, from enlightenment to integration. Charlotte, North Carolina: Information Age Publishing.

18 (Hayhoe, 2008a), Ibid.

19 Hayhoe, S. (2011). How do we define ability? Keynote presentation to the National Association of Disability Practitioners Annual Conference and AGM, Warwickshire, UK, on the 27th June 2011.

20 Vygotsky, L. S. (1994). Principles of the social education of deaf and dumb children in Russia. In R. Van der Veer, & J. Valsiner (Eds.), *The Vygotsky reader* (pp. 19–26). Oxford, U.K.: Blackwell Publishers.

21 Vygotsky, Ibid.

22 United Nations. (Downloaded). Enable: Rights and dignity of persons with disability. Downloaded from www.un.org/disabilities/ on the 1st July 2012.

23 Architectural and Transportation Barriers Compliance Board. (2000). Electronic and Information Technology Accessibility Standards (36 CFR Part 1194). Federal Register, 65, 246, 80500-80528.

24 (Hayhoe, 2008a), Op. Cit.

25 Sultan, N. & Hayhoe, S. (2013) Assistive technologies for students with special needs at the Higher Colleges of Technology, UAE. In S. Dowling, C. Gunn, J. Raven, and S. Hayhoe (Eds.). eLearning in action: Redefining learning. Abu Dhabi. HCT Press.

26 Meurant, R.C. (2010) The iPad and EFL Digital Literacy. Communications in Computer and Information Science, 123, 224-234., Department of Education and Training. (2011). iPad Trial: Is the iPad Suitable as a Learning Tool in Schools? Queensland, Australia: Government of Queensland.

27 Hawking, S. (2013) The computer. Downloaded from www.hawking.org.uk/the-computer.html on the 29th September 2013.

28 Wong, M.E. & Tan, S. S. K. (2012) Teaching the Benefits of Smart Phone Technology to Blind Consumers: Exploring the Potential of the iPhone. Journal of Visual Impairment and Blindness, 106, 10, Downloaded from www.afb.org/afbpress/pubjvib. asp?DocID=jvib0610toc., Hayhoe, S. (2012). Using an iPad with a Blind Student: A Case Study at Sharjah Women's College, In Dowling S. et. al. (Eds.). eLearning In Action: Opening Up Learning. Abu Dhabi: HCT Press.

29 RivaetaL, G. (1998). Uses of virtual reality in clinical training: Developing the spatial skills of children with mobility impairments. Virtual Environments in Clinical Psychology and Neuroscience: Methods and Techniques in Advanced Patient Therapist Interaction, 58, 219.

30 Clarkson, J., Langdon, P., & Robinson, P. (Eds.). (2006). Designing Accessible Technology. London: Springer.

31 Hayhoe, S. (in press). An enquiry into passive and active exclusion from sensory aesthetics in museums and on the Web: Two case studies of final year students at California School for the Blind studying art works. British Journal of Visual Impairment.

32 Hayhoe, S. (2013). A review of the literature on the use of the iPad as an assistive devise for students with disabilities – with reference to the Gulf. Paper delivered at the Global Education Forum, World Trade Centre, Dubai, UAE, March 2013.

33 Ally, M. (Ed.). (2009). Mobile learning: Transforming the delivery of education and training. Athabasca, Canada: Athabasca University Press.

34 Apple. (2013). *Accessibility – Resources.* Downloaded from www.apple.com/accessibility/resources/ on the 12/2/2013.

Chapter 17

Thoughts of a digital immigrant

Yara Azouqa

In evaluating the effects that technology has on my profession as teacher, I want to share the experience beyond the initial glamour of the software, platforms and devices. I also want to look closely at the technology as an educator and active agent in my teaching and learning environment, not just as a passive recipient of any new gadgetry. Gurak argues that 'What we really need to understand is not just how to use the technology but how to live with it, participate in it, and take control of it' (Gurak, 2001, p. 11). In this respect, this chapter highlights some reflections and experiences I would like to share with you.

Since time immemorial we have discovered, manipulated, invented, and reinvented technologies to serve our needs. What is a common feature of technology today is its ability to permeate our lives. It is everywhere and perhaps a reason why we do not pause and contemplate this is due to its ubiquitous nature. It spreads throughout every aspect of our life, and we almost unconsciously surrender to its power. This seems to be the case as we enjoy, among other activities, listening to music, photoshop our favorite birthday pictures, polish our key-note or PowerPoint presentations for work, and check and update Facebook accounts.

As technology has been reshaping different facets of our daily life it is often claimed we are on the cusp of a new age. Suarez and Saltin-Bajaj argue that we are in the midst of an information revolution that may well surpass the industrial revolution in its impact and far-reaching consequences (2010, p. 27). I agree because it has certainly affected my lifestyle dramatically in the last decade or so. In particular, technology has become an inevitable part of our educational systems and there's an urgent need to take a closer look at how this process is affecting our teaching and learning environments and the daily activities of our students inside and outside of the classroom. Moreover, specific educational technologies may empower or disrupt the work of students, teachers, and administrators.

Today I am expected to teach by using some form of technology. I cannot function without using at least the internet at some point. I might use the internet before class, during, or after or a combination of all. The allure of the internet and what it has to offer is overwhelming. In order to better understand the internet, Gurak simplifies the key terms of speed, reach, anonymity, and interactivity. She explains that the internet is a powerful tool for learning (2001, p. 29) and I agree with her.

The kinds of technology I encounter on a daily basis can vary from connected classrooms, Wi-Fi throughout the school to complete online courses in which all teaching takes place virtually outside the regular confines of traditional classrooms. As a teacher who uses educational technologies on a regular basis, I think there are two areas which I need to address. First, there are the kinds of technology used, and secondly there is it functionality and practical application within a learning environment.

On a positive note most educational technologies have helped me break free from traditional classroom settings and from some of the more traditional forms of instruction. I have used it as a means to a higher end and not as a means in itself. For example, my thoughtfully-designed, technology-supported courses can 'foster higher-order thinking and 21st century skills and are now offered in the virtual worlds of education' (Cavanaugh & Hargis, p. 3). I have discovered that educational technologies may positively affect the function and delivery of the educational experience for both learners and teachers.

One specific type of technology interface I like is social media. I see this as a platform to extend my presence in both online courses and face-to-face courses. However, I acknowledge that not all my courses offer 21st century experiences or higher-order thinking skills, so to further develop them I am constantly upgrading my learning outcomes and skills sets to suit my learners' needs. For example, in addition to my online courses, my traditional classroom style is employing further technology elements as well. This has come about through ongoing reflection where I ask myself how and when to employ a specific technology or a particular multi-media interface.

It just isn't enough for me to know the definition, processes, and function of educational technologies in relation to the respective curricula I teach. I must know how to apply technology within a quite specific framework and in doing so discover what works, what doesn't work and what supports my students to achieve more successful learning outcomes. I find in my professional life there is a need for an ongoing review of my engagement with technology usage to avoid taking it for granted and turning such an important instrument and concept into ineffective practice when I treat technology as a mere tool rather than vehicle to implement creative teaching and learning.

My use of a technology interface is a measure of how technologically literate I am, and similar to learning and practicing a foreign language the conditions for my success as a digitally driven teacher are the frequent use and functionality of the medium I choose to use. To make my teaching more effective, I have to maintain a good standard of functionality when using a digital medium as my preferred method of delivery. As a digital immigrant, I am continually learning to become a multi-literate individual who can, as Anstey and Bull point out, 'interpret, use, and produce electronic, live, and chapter texts that employ linguistic, visual, auditory, gestural, and special semiotic systems.' (2006, p. 41)

As you can see I have a significant challenge ahead of me! But, in short, I think that educational technologies do facilitate the learning experience of my students and empower me as a teacher. They also become the bridge between school and life. My students will see that the tools they use in school, they will immediately use after school. At the moment I use a blog to comment on writing as part of peer review, and the blog is also used in a different social context for another purpose outside the classroom.

My students will no longer have to wait until the end of a school day to use knowledge learned in school for real life. The effect of our daily work in school will have immediate influence on the students in very much the same week, day, or hour! This merging of the classroom and the real world will create meaningful learning as students see the overall benefits of school beyond the school walls.

Yet, sometimes I do face a number of challenges with online learning and educational technologies. For example misinformation and wrong information and the fact that the internet has, in addition to knowledge, false knowledge sometimes presented in Wikipedia (Suarez & Saltin-Bajaj, 2010) concerns me. I have to teach my students to become critical thinkers and discerning users of the internet. Not only do I need to develop digital literacy competencies, I also need to support a critical digital literacy in order to filter what we see, hear, and read on the internet. As a teacher I always reflect on this issue and keep in mind that no tool is neutral, and that all digital tools have a specific use for a specific task and I have learned that I must act as the arbiter of how suitable any device is to carry out a task in the classroom.

Another important consideration for me is the quality of knowledge and the purpose of all the data we have available through the internet. In my day-to-day role as a teacher I emphasise to my students the importance of distilling the information they access online and make sure that it is useful, relevant and engaging to the purpose for which they need it. (Suarez & Saltin-Bajaj, 2010, p. 29)

Teaching and learning in the digital age requires all of us to learn from one another's experiences like never before, in order to engage in fruitful discussion and exchange best digital teaching and learning practices. To this end I foster an environment of co-teaching and co-learning with my peers. Results from these professional interactions reveal to me that I am not alone in migrating across to digital technology, nor do I feel alienated in adopting it, or having a set of new challenges in my classroom. I think that digital literacy will foster my professional development and empower me to engage more fully with my peers and become a dynamic teacher.

References

Anstey, M., & Bull, G. (2006). *Teaching and Learning Multiliteracies: Changing Times, Changing Literacies.* Kensington Garden: Alea.

Cavanaugh, C., & Hargis, J. (n.d.). Redefining School from Site to Service: Learning In and From K-12 Online Education. *Distance Learning, 7*(2), 1-5.

Ehrmann, S. C. (2012). Why Faculty Resist. *Distance Learning,* 60-67.

Gurak, L. J. (2001). *Cyberliteracy: Navigating the Internet with Awareness.* New Haven, CT, USA: Yale University Press.

Jin, Z. (2010). *Global Technological Change: From Hard Technology to Soft Technology* (2nd ed.). Bristol, GBR: Intellect Ltd.

Suarez, O., & Saltin-Bajaj, C. M. (2010). *Educating the Whole Child for the Whole World: The Ross School Model and Education for the Global Era.* New York, NY, USA: New York University Press.

Chapter 18

Through the looking glass: the transformational nature of digital learning in an EFL context

El-Sadig Yahya Ezza and Khaled Almudibry

Introduction

Ever since educational technology was introduced into the Saudi Arabian EFL context in the first decade of the 21st century, it has been (positively) affecting the teaching and learning processes in a variety of ways. For instance, Abdalla (2007) reports that, as a result of the use of the smart board at Majma'ah Community College of King Saud University the students, taken by this new prodigy, stopped complaining about the extension of classes into their class breaks and that precious time once wasted on silencing the students was fully used in covering course items.

In addition, Alebaikan (2011) informs that male professors, who are not allowed to be physically present to teach in female campuses, can do so through a variety of educational technology applications. Most importantly, customer satisfaction surveys administered to students each term have been producing positive feedback regarding teachers' performance.

The main impetus for the student satisfaction is given by the availability of courseware that teachers post on their web-pages and the possibility to communicate with teachers anytime by email or cell phones. Along these same lines, this chapter assumes that the introduction of the information and communication technology (ICT) into education has far reaching consequences for the degree of transparency in the classroom.

Support for this assumption comes partially from the view that teachers who were once considered educational authorities have recently assumed more moderate roles as facilitators as a result of the incorporation of ICT into the educational system. Other things being equal, this shift in the teachers' role is given impetus by the fact that 'a great deal of our students' learning takes place without our intention or sometimes even despite it' (Dowling, 2003).

Such a learning possibility is caused by the fact that students are conceived in the relevant literature to be 'digital natives', implying that they can be more digitally literate and thus more knowledgeable about the rich online educational resources than their teachers (Prensky, 2001). Yet, it is only in a transparent educational environment that such digital competence can be integrated into classroom activities. Now, given these facts about the role that ICT plays in the classroom, this chapter attempts to provide answers to the following questions:

1. To what extent does ICT literacy among the students impact EFL faculty's role in the classroom?
2. Do different aspects of the educational process trigger the same degree of transparency among EFL faculty?

Conceptual background

Generally speaking, the term 'transparency', being synonymous with 'openness', is conceived to be the process of (timely) delivery of information (Vught & Heijden, 2010) such that the lack of information is understood to be a clear symptom of bias, corruption and incompetence (Smith, 2004). Thus, 'transparency is fully expressed when there is lack of hidden agendas'. (Luba &Mahraj, 2013, para 10)

Speaking about transparency in educational contexts, many researchers approach it from different perspectives. One such perspective focuses on what Adnet *et al* (2011: 13) term 'transparent institution'. They maintain that for an institution to be so perceived, it must adhere to a number of criteria including selection of students who can complete courses based on educational achievement and potential, use of reliable and valid assessment methods and minimizing barriers to applicants.

Second, Vught & Heijden (2010, p 33) relate *transparency* to quality assurance as information delivery medium that aims at helping external stakeholders to 'form judgments and take decisions'. Third, according Offerman (2008, para 8), transparency is a characteristic of program-level learning outcome. In other words, transparency consists in the declaration and measurement of learning outcome in a way that is understandable to the students so that they can have an 'end-to-end view' of the relevant educational program.

However, it is stipulated that the program should represent 'a conceptual shift from curriculum as a collection of courses to curriculum as a strategic educational map that shows how and when developmental competencies are developed...' These perspectives focus on the aspects of academic transparency that relate to 'educational administration', 'management of financial resources', 'recruitment of academic personnel', 'admission to educational institutions', *etc.*

However, as shown in first question listed above, this study addresses a fourth ICT-generated transparency that centres on the teacher-student relationship, both inside and outside of the classroom. In particular it investigates the extent to which the doings, thoughts, interests, concerns *etc* of the teacher are visible to the student (Dalsgaard & Paulsen, 2009). The teacher's role is emphasized by the fact that it is the teacher who both facilitates and assesses learning. In that connection, there are two questions that this part attempts to answer: what is transparent teaching; and how can it be enhanced by the integration of ICT in the classroom?

To start with, Evans (2013) theorizes that transparent teaching represents a philosophical shift that requires courage, resolve and belief on the part of the teacher to share course information with the student so as to make the classroom an optimal learning environment for both of them. The relevant literature also shows that transparent teaching transcends mere information sharing to the reconsideration of 'some fundamental assumptions about course structure, content and instructor's role'. (Arvidson & Huston, 2008, p 4)

In other words, these assumptions were once peculiar to the teacher but can now be negotiated with the student in a transparent educational environment. Other practices and activities that render a classroom transparent include teacher's willingness to be candid, adventurous and self-critical (*ibid*) and engaging with the students, appreciating candid feedback and acknowledging contributions (Chang, 2002). Indeed, teachers should experience such behavioural changes to function properly in a transparent educational environment given the traditional view that 'teaching is normally a very a private activity, closed off from our peers by four walls of the classrooms, and also often jealously guarded behind the walls of academic freedom'. (Kelly, 2001, para 7)

Ezza (2012) reports that the teacher who was once considered 'an educational authority', 'a dispenser of knowledge' *etc* has recently assumed more moderate roles as, for example, a facilitator, an organizer, a guide, *etc* owing to the students' familiarity with digital technologies and hence rich educational resources accessed through them, among others.

There are at least two implications for the teacher that may result from this situation: students' ability to learn outside teachers' experience, and learning may achieve objectives other than those set by the teacher (Newhouse, 2002, p 38). As a result, the teacher has two extreme alternatives to choose from: resistance to the integration of ICT in education as it reduces his/her influence; or accept to acquire ICT-related skills and literacy to be able to function competently in the classroom.

Fortunately, research findings inform that there are strong tendencies among teachers to adopt more ICT-oriented roles that enable them to form learning communities with own students. (Fairman, 2004; Ezza, 2012)

Method
Participants

The study participants were 61 EFL faculty who were presumably in the service of 11 Saudi government-owned universities. In fact, the questionnaire was sent to 500 faculty whose email addresses were posted on the e-gates of their respective institutions but only 61 responses were received. Apparently there were unused/inactive email addresses as indicated by the 20 notices of delivery failure and subsequent apologies from some faculty who had not used their emails for a long time.

Since some e-gates did not include emails addresses of their EFL faculty, at least at the time of data collection (*eg* Prince Sultan University, Hail University, Jazan University, Northern Border University *etc*) they were excluded from this survey. The participants were targeted as a single group regardless of their gender, age, academic degree and academic status as the study intends to elicit general information about the degree of their teaching transparency.

Instrument

A five-scale, likert-type questionnaire (ranging from strongly agree to strongly disagree) was constructed to collect data, comprising 20 statements that centred on many practices that were assumed to enhance teaching transparency. They roughly fall into two categories: teaching practices; and communication practices. The first category formed the backbone of the questionnaire, both in terms of the number of statements (80% of the questionnaire), and the variety of teaching strategies included.

On the other hand, the communication practices focused on teacher-student communication outside the classroom to reinforce both teaching and learning. The instrument's face validity was verified by ten EFL faculty in a number of Saudi universities while Cronbach's alpha was used to calculate its reliability, resulting in the co-efficient of .834, thus indicating high consistency.

Procedure

The questionnaire was posted on Google Drive and then forwarded to the email addresses of the participants. In many cases it was sent to their institutional and general addresses when both were available on the e-gates of their institutions in case one of them was inactive. Yet, as shown in the participants' section above, a number of notices of delivery failure were received. Even worse, only about 13% of the study population completed the questionnaire despite the fact that it had been emailed twice to most of them. The questionnaire was posted on 1st September, 2013, and closed on the 30th September. It took a whole month to receive 61 responses.

Results

Descriptive statistics were used to analyse data to answer the first research questions: To what extent does ICT literacy among the students impact EFL faculty's role in the classroom? Table 1 below shows that the participants' responses are indicative of a high degree of transparency as can be substantiated by the high mean of their responses. This finding will be elaborated on further in the discussion section below:

Descriptive Statistics					
Std. Deviation	Mean	Maximum	Minimum	N	
8.66114	87.4262	100.00	66.00	61	VAR00001
				61	Valid N (listwise)

Table 1: Teaching transparency among EFL faculty in Saudi Arabia.

Regarding the data required to answer the second research question, it is important to point out in this connection that the questionnaire consisted of 20 statements that were assumed to reflect transparency in areas of teaching and communication. Thus the second research question sought to find out if practices pertaining to these two areas received equal attention from EFL faculty. T-test was used to analyse the difference between the responses in these sections (*ie* statements 1-16 and 17-20 respectively). Table 2 summarizes the finding:

One-Sample Statistics				
	N	Mean	Std. Deviation	Std. Error Mean
Transparency in Teaching	61	70.4754	6.76906	.86669
Transparency in communication	61	16.9508	2.52604	.32343

One-Sample Test						
	Test Value = 0					
	t	df	Sig. (2-tailed)	Mean Difference	95% Confidence Interval of the Difference	
					Lower	Upper
Transparency in Teaching	81.316	60	.000	70.47541	68.7418	72.2090
Transparency in communication	52.410	60	.000	16.95082	16.3039	17.5978

Table 2: T-test for the difference in transparency between teaching and in communication means.

Discussion

Table 1 indicates that transparent teaching has become a matter of heightened importance for the study participants. There are at least two reasons to explain the tendency to adopt a more open relationship with their students. First, Prensky (2001) argues that the new generations of learners (those who were born after 1983) have grown up amid digital technologies. And given the fact the internet has become a rich educational resource, it is possible to maintain that they not only access educational materials that could be richer than the textbooks prescribed by the teacher, but also learn over and above the relevant course objective.

In such an educational environment, it would futile to stick to the old roles of 'a dispenser of knowledge', 'an educational authority' *etc* as there are technology-based avenues of knowledge that could be more student-friendly than the traditional classroom where the teacher dominates the educational scene. It is natural, therefore, that teachers react positively to these changes by accommodating their students' digital competence to enrich the classroom activities. This explanation receives strong support from previous research findings.

For instance, Fairman (2004, p iii) reports that, as a result of the introduction of laptop in the educational system in Maine State, '[T]eachers have begun to see themselves as partners in learning with students and report more reciprocal relationship with students.' What is more, 'students are able to bring new content and information into the classroom, and are teaching technology skills to teachers and other students' (ibid).

Second, most Saudi universities urge their faculty to develop their personal web-pages where course materials and contact information are posted. Since this procedure makes the teacher and courseware available to students whenever need arises, it certainly renders the relevant educational environment transparent.

Regarding the second research question, Table 2 shows that there is a significant difference between participants' response to the two sections of the questionnaire: teaching practices (statements 1-16) and academic communication (statements 17-20). Analysis shows that the participants demonstrated more transparency in the former than in latter, despite the fact that they had posted their contact information, *eg* email addresses, mobile phones *etc* on the personal web-pages so as to facilitate communication not only with their students but also with members of academic communities nationally and internationally.

There is at least one piece of evidence emanating from data collection procedure that confirms teachers' tendency to favour teaching transparency over communication transparency. It was reported above that that there had been many notices of delivery failure resulting from the lack of use of email addresses to the extent that they were suspended. Therefore assignments could neither be submitted nor received electronically.

Conclusion and implications

Although educational transparency has been widely investigated, there is a paucity of data regarding its application in the classroom as most studies focused on transparency in academic administration, management of financial resources, recruitment of academic personnel, admission to educational institutions *etc*. It was only after the integration of ICT in education that teaching transparency has received more attention.

Relevant research has focused particularly, *inter alia*, on the possibility that learning might take place without teachers' intentions or even despite them. It is therefore proposed that educators should re-examine some dominating assumptions about a number of pedagogical principles and practice, including teachers' roles in the classroom (Dowling, 2003). In the light of these developments, the present chapter set out to examine the degree of teaching transparency in an educational environment characterized by techno-pedagogy in the Saudi tertiary institutions.

Overall, the findings indicated that teachers showed a high degree of transparency but that they demonstrated more transparency in teaching than in academic communication with their students. Each finding has an implication for classroom practitioners and researchers. Where the first finding is concerned, 'teaching transparency' does not seem to be an established concept as evidenced by the attempts made to report a working definition of it in the second question above.

The available literature provided a little help about what constitutes 'teaching transparency' to be employed to construct the data collection instrument for this study. This conclusion can be further substantiated by the fact that an intensive search on major databases such as EBSCO,

Sage *etc* using the keywords 'transparent teaching', 'transparent teacher' and 'transparency in EFL/ESL classroom' did not produce the required results. So, were it not for the articles accessed from free websites, this study would not have been completed.

Both teachers and classroom researchers are therefore strongly recommended to make greater efforts to develop this concept in theory and practice. The second finding seems to concern teachers *per se*. Apparently the study participants considered communication with their students when they are off campus a matter of secondary importance. Needless to say, the variety of learning management systems adopted by many Saudi tertiary institutions are meant to encourage continued collaboration between faculty and their students as it provides them with opportunities to enrich topics that they initiated in the classroom. Thus, a more positive attitude towards academic communication is required on the part of the teachers to facilitate both teaching and learning.

References

Abdalla, S. Y. (2008). The Role of Smart Boards in Enhancing students' Oral Presentations: The case of Al-Majma'ah Community College, King Saud University. *ATEL Journal, Lebanon*,17, 8-13.

Alebaikan, R. (2011). *A Blended Learning Framework for Saudi Higher Education.* A chapter Presented at the Second International Conference of E-Learning and Distance Learning, Riyadh, Saudi Arabia.

Adnet, N. McCaig, C. & Slack. K (2011). Achieving Transparency, Consistency and Fairness in English Higher Education admission: Progress since Schwartz. *Higher Education Quarterly*, 65/1, 12-33.

Arvidson, P. S. & Huston, T. A. (2008). Transparent Teaching. *Currents in teaching and Learning*, 1/1, 4-16.

Chang, R. K. C. (2002).*Transparent Teaching* [PowerPoint Slides]. Department of Computing, The Hong Kong Polytechnic. Retrieved August 4, 2013 from www4.comp. polyu.edu.hk/~csrchang/PolyU3.pdf

Dalsgaard, C. & Paulsen, M. (2009). Transparency in Cooperative Online Learning. *International Review of Research in Open and Distance Learning*, 10/3. Retrieved October 17, 2012 from www.irrodl.org/index.php/irrodl/article/view/671/1267.

Dowling, C. (2003). *The Role of the Human Teacher in Learning Environments of the Future.* IFIP Working Groups 3.1 and 3.3 Working Conference: ICT and the Teacher of the Future. Melbourne, Australia. Retrieved June 16, 2011 from

crpit.com/confchapters/CRPITV23Dowling.pdf.

Evans, C. (2013). *How transparent is your classroom?* Retrieved September 12, 2013 from www.guide2digitallearning.com/blog_chad_evans/how_transparent_your_classroom

Ezza, S. Y. (2012). EFL Teacher's Role in ICT-Oriented Classroom: The Case of Majma›ah University.

Proceedings of Imam University Symposium in English Language Teaching in Saudi Arabia, Riyadh, 31-53.

Fairman, J. (2004). *Trading Roles: Teachers and Students Learn with Technology.* (Research Report No. 3). *Main Education Policy Research Institute.* The University of Maine Office. Retrieved *January 20, 2010 from* libraries.maine.edu/cre/MEPRIP/MLTIResearchReport3.pdf

Kelly, T. M. (2001). Towards Transparency in Teaching: Publishing a Course Portfolio. Retrieved October 1, 2013 from www.historians.org./perspectives. issues/2001/0111/0111not1.cfm

Luba, E. W. & Mahraj, M. (2013). Enhancing the Learning Transparency through E-transparency. A chapter presented at the International Conference on ICT for Africa, Harare, Zimbabwe. Retrieved October 12, 2013 from www.ictforafrica.org/attachments/section/4/ict4africa2013_submission_3.pdf

Newhouse, P. (2002). The Impact of ICT on Learning and Teaching: Literature Review. Perth: Specialist Educational Services.

Prensky, M. (2001). Digital Natives, Digital Immigrants. On the Horizon, 9/5, 1-6.

Offerman, M.J. (2008). Transparency in Learning Outcomes: A refreshing Disruption in Higher in Education. Retrieved April 19, 2010 from www.clomedia.com

Vught, F.A. V. & Heijden, D. F. W (2010). Multi-dimensional Ranking: A New Transparency Tool for Higher Education and Research. Higher Education Management and Policy, 23/3, 31-56.

Appendix

Questionnaire

ICT as an index of transparency in the Saudi EFL classroom

Please tick the box that best describes your opinion, where:

5=Strongly Agree; 4=Agree; 3=undecided; 2=Disagree; 1=Strongly Disagree

No	Statement	5	4	3	2	1
1	Reconsidering one's role as a result of ICT literacy among students.					
2	Modifying teaching strategies as a result of ICT literacy among students.					
3	Asking students to propose online sources to enrich classroom activities.					
4	Asking digitally competent students to do some teaching tasks.					
5	Seeking students' help in dealing with ICT.					
6	Posting course materials on official websites.					
7	Recognizing and valuing the students as a source of knowledge.					
8	Accepting situations where teachers and students form a learning community.					
9	Encouraging information sharing between teachers and students.					
10	Understanding that learning can take place without teachers' intention.					
11	Visiting students online forums for feedback on teaching strategies.					
12	Accepting online sources suggested by students.					
13	Encouraging students to establish online forums to discuss class-related issues.					
14	Empowering students so that they develop personal confidence.					

15	Creating an environment characterized by increased collaboration.					
16	Training the students to be more autonomous learners.					
17	Accepting online submission of assignments.					
18	Sending feedback on the students assignments by email					
19	Communicating with students more frequently by email and cell phone.					
20	Participating in students' online forums.					

Chapter 19

What the brain says about digitally-driven education

Lawrence Burke

The insight for this reflective study came as I was driving along the Al Ain-Dubai freeway (Route 66) in the United Arab Emirates in the fall of 2011. Light traffic and good visibility didn't stop a vehicle ahead of me slowing down and weaving across the 4 lane highway like a driver under the influence of drugs or alcohol. I managed to overtake the car safely, and in doing so caught a glimpse of the driver interacting with a mobile device. Momentarily he would look up, scan the road ahead, and then return to the mobile device. Glancing through my rear vision mirror I could see that this unpredictable and dangerously erratic driving behaviour continued for some time.

Fitness to drive requires sound neuro-logical and cognitive competencies and it may come as a surprise to learn that attempts to describe and understand the full set of skills required of a driver and to define the psycho-cognitive process of the driving task within a general framework of driving theory have not resulted in an inclusive body of knowledge on the subject (Sanguen, 2008). Nevertheless we do know that driving competence relies on fine motors skills, visual perceptions, attention span along with working memory and the functional ability of long term memory. Research has shown that perceptual or memory impairment at any stage of driving a vehicle could prove catastrophic for driver and passenger (Anderson, Rizzo, Qian, Ergun, & Dawson, 2005). Yet under the guise of the somewhat flaky idea of multi-tasking, drivers around the world put their lives, those of their passengers and other road users at risk when they engage in any additional task which may tax their levels of functionality and undermine their cognitive ability to drive their vehicle safely and responsibility.

Theoretical Background

The capability of a human being to carry about more than one task at a time is reliant on his ability to hold tiny pieces of information in his working memory and retrieve these promptly before they fade away, because our working memory holds knowledge and information only for a few seconds or up to a minute (Sternberg, 1995) unless a strategy is developed in which the detail is coded and consigned into long term memory. Furthermore, we can only process several pieces of information at any one time in our working memory. Yet the caveat is that when this is achieved to any degree, we are required to focus all our attention on a primary task if we are to derive its full benefits or complete the task to more than a satisfactory degree.

Working memory ability is when a person is able to hold sustained attention on a primary task, while also maintaining relevant data in working memory and retrieving pertinent information from long term memory especially in the presence of distraction. In other words, working memory moves beyond a perfunctory operation of storing information however briefly to a procedure which involves storage and processing capability (Doolittle & Mariano, 2008).This capacity to store and process simultaneously occurs more often when there are internal distracters like emotions, impulses, thoughts and feelings and extraneous diversions like conversations, music, and other auditory and visual stimuli associated with a personalised digital lifestyle (Doolittle & Mariano, 2008). There is a wide body of research which argues that a person's innate ability to perform well on a variety of cognitive tasks ranging from their ability to remember previously learned information to their capacity to understand, apply, synthesis, evaluate and create new knowledge is determined by their working memory ability to function well notwithstanding internal or external distractors.

In addition, Daneman and Carpenter have shown how these distractors, along with individual differences in learner ability, have a significant bearing on what is remembered, retained, dwelt upon, recalled and processed between sensory memory, working memory and long term memory (Daneman & Carpenter, 1980).

We know that learning involves a multifaceted cognitive process, intricately linked to how we commit information and knowledge from our working memory to our long-term memory. Daneman and Carpenter further assert that previous research into how we transfer information and knowledge from short term memory to long term memory is flawed. (Daneman & Carpenter, 1980) Their key argument centres on the claim that researchers in the past perceived short-term memory storage ability as a largely one way, passive activity. They hadn't factored in the multi-functioning skills required of learners to process and store in their short-term memory. In brief, prior to the research of Daneman and Carpenter the theoretical approach was wrong.

Previously it had been argued that short-term memory played an essential role in developing the basic skills in linguistic literacies. Language learners had to develop the ability to construct the semantic and syntactical relationships of vocabulary into a coherent and cohesive narrative. Moreover, learners had to have access to previously integrated knowledge in order to assimilate new ideas into that learning. For example, using pronouns, objects and indirect objects in a sentence required access to previously taught knowledge about subjects and referents. In other words the successful transference of new knowledge was dependent on short term memory's temporary storage capacity, along with its functional ability to transfer this knowledge into the archives of long term memory, which in turn could be drawn upon at the appropriate time. This suggested that learners with a limited temporary storage capacity would have less relevant information on subjects and referents at their disposal at any given moment when called upon. More importantly, it assumed that short term memory was important for the successful acquisition of basic literacy skills including reading comprehension and vocabulary development. However, research conducted from 1939 up to 1979 indicated very weak correlations between the development of these basic literacy skills and short term memory storage capacity. (Daneman & Merkle, 1996) Daneman and Carpenter argued that the theory of short-term memory was inadequate to fully describe the functional process of how learners initially remember detail. (Daneman & Carpenter, 1980)

They claimed that far from being the passive recipients of new ideas and knowledge which are processed and subsumed into long term memory, learners engage in a functional and active cognitive process to remember. Daneman and Carpenter appropriated the term working memory from Baddeley & Hitch (1974) because learners are engaged in the parallel tasks of processing and storing ideas and knowledge simultaneously. Working memory is an active cognitive process. Furthermore, they argued that because of the individual differences in learners' ability to process and synchronize information into working memory, some learners would get caught up in process at the expense of synchronization and storage. The result would be fundamental weaknesses in their overall ability to function using the foundations of literacy. To illustrate their point they developed a simple, yet ingenious working memory test for college students. They were required to recall the last word of a set of increasingly lengthy complex set of sentences. It was hypothesized that those weaker in the functional process of comprehension would recall less final words, as they became enmeshed in the process of understanding the sentences rather than the storage of the final words. (Daneman & Merkle, 1996).

There is also widespread agreement among educational psychologists that rehearsal and practice is the key to the storage and retrieval of knowledge and information in our long term memory. (Sternberg, 1995).

Recent research suggests that the integration of content based educational informational technologies may undermine the development of cognitive processes which support the improvement of multi- literacy skills and the memorization of key material required for general and content based learning. (De Stefano & LeFevre, 2005). It is thought that while learners are sorting through more material online and via a plethora of multi-media platforms and tools, they are retaining less because of the multiple distractions embedded into web sites and their myriad web pages. (Rockwell&Singleton, 2007).

Burke argues that the research and evidence on the successful use of technologies in the acquisition of L2 literacy skills are inconsistent and lack convincing evidence that without them, an L2 student would not be as successful in becoming fully literate in an L2. (Burke, 2009)

Furthermore, there is on-going anecdotal evidence by teachers that students may become co-dependent on technologies to help them learn, and as a consequence lack the retention rates to recall knowledge successfully which is a fundamental requirement in their on-going studies and future careers. This observation isn't limited to a particular system in any specific country, but is to be found across learning institutions with a reliance on digital learning and online technologies designed as interfaces to facilitate and enhance teaching and learning in the classrooms of today.

There have been significant changes in how we learn since Daneman and Carpenter's original study in 1980. Most notably has been the impact of educational technology on methods and approaches to teaching and learning, much of it untested, yet utilized as an expedient, modern way to learn. Clarke (1983) argued that the use of multi-media tools and online learning processes is akin to a green grocer acquiring a new delivery van for his produce-it will have no impact on the dietary habits of a nation. Mayer & Moreno (Mayer & Moreno, 2001) counter-argued that the particular design of educational technologies may alleviate cognitive problems experienced by learners. They have shown the positive effects of Ed. Tech. tools and online learning in a controlled framework, which includes eliminating seductive distractors and positioning personalized text near visual aids to boost the transferable knowledge from working memory to long term storage.

Cognitive Learning Processes and Cognitive Overload

The ultimate goal of education is to create and impart knowledge and skills to recipients who in turn can transfer these into life skills which are developed, modified, adapted to circumstances over time and built on throughout one's life and career. To achieve this goal it is essential that the curriculum and pedagogical approaches to teaching and learning in all levels of the education sector are developed to maximize the intellectual growth of an individual which results in the acquisition of new knowledge and understanding, and minimize, and even eradicate those methods and processes within teaching and learning that disrupt this process.

Prior to the rapid introduction of educational technologies into teaching and learning a number of successful pedagogical approaches had been devised to facilitate student learning. These included, didactic teaching, rote and memorization and group based collaborative and cooperative learning. John Dewey's concept of Learning by Doing was also resurrected and rebranded as constructivism. In addition advances in understanding how we learn paved the way for different learning styles, differentiated learning methodologies along with pedagogies and theories which argued for multiple intelligences outside of a strict linear understanding of intelligence based upon cognitive development. Notwithstanding this fascinating variety in educational pedagogies, fundamentally teaching and learning still remains predicated upon our three memory constructs – visual & auditory sensory memory, working memory and long-term memory – an acquired attention span, and the complex interactions which move knowledge and information between them (Clark & Harrelson, 2002). Moreover, any one individual has a finite amount of thinking resources available to them at any given time, which they have to utilize in order for specific cognitive tasks to be performed simultaneously. When this limit is over-reached all manner of disruption occurs in the primary task leading to what is termed cognitive overload. The driver of the car weaving all across the Al Ain-Dubai highway cited earlier had lost the ability to perform the primary task of controlling a motor vehicle safely and effectively, and as his cognitive load increased due to his attempt to drive the vehicle and use the mobile device, he reached a point of cognitive overload.

The Study

Around 20 years ago the Jasper project (Cognition and Technology Group at Vanderbilt , 1990) showed that the ability of video to allow students to construct "rich, dynamic mental models of situations" far outweighed detail they could create from still pictures and texts" (Kozma, 2001). While more recent research confirms these earlier findings and argues for relevant, integrated and focused multi-media tools in education very few studies have been undertaken to look at the initial impact of cognitive overload on learners who are exposed to the prolific use of multi-media educational technologies in their day-to-day school and college lives. Most studies have focused on the added value of technology to facilitate learning, while few concentrate on the intrinsic effects multi-media have on cognitive processes and attention span, and how multi-media learning may be improved to maximise student achievement and create an experience in which learner's are empowered to monitor and self-regulate their own educational progress and achievements.

Primarily, this reflective study sought to establish a causal relationship between attention span, cognitive overload and working memory. In addition, retention rates of information, and the visual and auditory cues which enable a person to identify the key points in a narrative, spoken or written were considered too. Furthermore, the extraneous effects of seductive visual or auditory distracters, while secondary considerations, were also of particular interest in the study.

The 2012 Sixth Form cohort from Al Ain English Speaking School in the United Arab Emirates agreed to participate in the study. Three short BBC News (BBC News, 2010) clips of 60 seconds duration were used. The duration of the news clips and the length participants had to view and recall the content were based on the Precision Teaching Model of Lindsley (1991) which enables a teacher to observe and measure concrete behaviours that may be counted and recorded for the purpose of maximising a learner's capacity to self-monitor performance abilities in any discipline and in any classroom setting. Allowing learners to self monitor their aptitude to recall and remember detail has a significant number of value added learning outcomes in a lesson. Firstly, it contributes to increased intrinsic motivation, secondly, it promotes focus and expanded attention spans, thirdly, it facilitates the retention of data, information and knowledge in their working memory, and fourthly it is the catalyst to the process through which data, information and knowledge can be transferred into their long term memory (Binder, 1990) (Lindsley, 1999) (Binder, Haughton, & Van Eyk, 1990) (Hughes, Beverley, & Whitehead, 2007).

The news reader's commentaries, the news ribbon at the bottom of the screen, along with secondary audio and visual images were all retained in the original clip (BBC News, 2010). Moreover it should be noted that the visuals, news reader's spoken monologue, the news ribbon and the secondary auditory input were untouched and presented as they were broadcasts in an unsynchronised haphazard manner-as is often the case with televised news broadcasts- and did not correlate with the primary spoken cues being articulated by the news reader. Furthermore, the text ribbon ran from the right to the left across the bottom of the screen, counter to the left to right of the actual text. This pastiche of sensory input was chosen because it mirrored the kinds of barrage of sensory stimulation students may be exposed to in their day-to-day learning environments.

The first excerpt from BBC News (2010) was not altered and included the original audio and visual material. The second BBC News (2010) excerpt excluded the news ribbon at the bottom of the screen, but retained the news reader's commentaries and all other secondary audio and visual images. While the third BBC News (2010) excerpt retained all the features of first excerpt but was muted. After each clip was shown to 3 different groups (A, B, C) the respondents had 60 seconds to write down what they recalled from each clip.

Discussion

The whole cohort had to assimilate from the BBC news clip, multiple visual, auditory and textual cues into their working memory, hold it for 60 seconds, and devise a strategy to recall it later.

The news clip (BBC News, 2010) for group A was made up of 10 headline items with 25 news bites consisting of short, pithy visual, auditory and text ribbon announcements of events and actions often unrelated to the primary news items read verbally by the news reader.

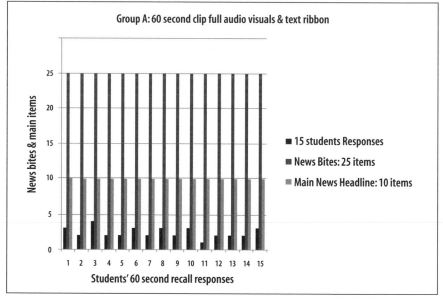

Figure 1.

The participants in Group A were unable to recall with any degree of accuracy main news headlines or the unrelated news bites. Most respondents recalled between 1-4 bits of unrelated information. These responses were often incoherent, illogical and in several instances illegible as it appeared the respondents subordinated accuracy of recall to completion of the task within the 60 second time frame. In addition to overloading their sensory and working memory, Group A respondents appeared to have manifested the effects of intrinsic stress on memory in which there's an inability to recall recent detail because of the immediate, urgent requirement to cognitively engage with multiple data and memory consolidation (Kuhlmann, Piel, & Wolf, 2005).

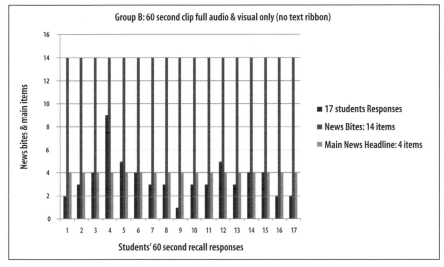

Figure 2.

Group B respondents viewed the full audio BBC news clip (2010) with the exception of one visual cue; the written left to right text ribbon which ran right to left across the bottom of the screen. Deleting the text ribbon reduced the number of news headlines by 6 and the number of news bites by 11. Although participants still responded to visual and auditory cues, it appears that the reduction in the amount of information to be processed and recalled significantly reduced the initial cognitive load on their sensory and working memory. Slightly fewer than 50% of Group B respondents were able to accurately recall the initial news headlines spoken by the news reader. This is significantly higher than Group A. However, only one of the respondents in Group B managed to partially recall the news bites relating to each news headline. In addition and similar to Group A, intrinsic stress on all memory processes may have been a factor which impacted on these respondents' working memory capacity to add additional recall details (Kuhlmann, Piel, & Wolf, 2005).

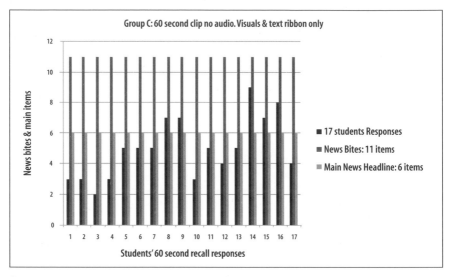

Figure 3.

Respondents in Group C viewed the excerpt from BBC News (2010) without any auditory stimuli. This reduced the main headline news to 6 items and the news bites to 11 items. Their sensory and working memory had to process visual stimuli in the form of images and text. The visual images changed regularly according to the BBC News (2010) reporter's delivery; and as the sound had been muted the images appeared as incoherent patterns and pictures unrelated to other sensory stimuli. However, the written text communicated in a left to right direction, yet travelling right to left across the bottom of the screen showed a clear, coherent pattern of readable and discernible language for the respondents. Furthermore, the bi-directional nature of the text enabled group C participants to read and comprehend the information without extraneous distractors and recognise familiar language and grammatical patterns (Willis, 2003). As a consequence 75% of Group C recalled slightly more than 4 of the main headlines, while 25% recalled all the main headlines. Furthermore, 25% of these respondents recalled between 6 and 9 of the 11 news bites. Notwithstanding any intrinsic stress indicators cited earlier

(Kuhlmann, Piel, & Wolf, 2005) it is evident that the overall attention span and recall capacity of Group C was significantly higher than groups A and B. Controlling the input on sensory and working memory appears to have reduced cognitive overload and allowed the respondents in Group C to select important aspects of the BBC News (2010) clip for further processing in their sensory and working memory.

Conclusion:

This study shows how learners' cognitive functions operate with multiple systems for processing material in their sensory and working memory. Moreover, it demonstrates that each system has a limit to the amount of material it can process at any one time. Furthermore, it illustrates that often a learner's expectation on the amount they think they can process at any one time may exceed their capacity to do so (Mayer & Moreno, 2003). At the same time it suggests that curriculum designers and educators who interpret the curricula and the medium, through which it is to be taught in the classroom, may over-estimate a student's ability to hold, process and synthesis data information and knowledge in their sensory and working memory. Moreover, Quas, Rush, Yim and Nikolayev (2013) argue that an additional factor to consider in the cognitive processes of adolescents is that any learning task may be perceived as more threatening because of the unique period of psycho-cognitive development the youngster is going through. Students may experience heightened sensitivity to the emotional and social evaluations of themselves amongst their peers and in the presence of their teachers.

It is argued today that meaningful learning includes not only subject content, but also trans- disciplinary approaches to learning, active enquiry based learning, learning by doing, peer and self-assessment, as well as a much greater emphasis on shaping the character and attitudes of learners through a values based education in which implicit principles and ideals are embedded in a curriculum. This multi-tasked approach to learning creates major cognitive obstacles and challenges for students today, just as driving a motor vehicle while using a mobile device provides major cognitive challenges and obstacles to a driver. In addition, the principles and practices which support multi-media education in the classroom are often promoted and supported without due care as to the effects and affects on a learners' psycho-cognitive and social and emotional development. The challenge in the 21st century for the educational, technology and educational book publishing sectors is to understand how we learn and to promote the usefulness of educational technologies in the teaching and learning environment through a sound historical knowledge of the theories of teaching and learning. It is to be remembered that fitness to learn requires sound neuro-logical competencies and that attempts to describe and map the whole process of learning within a digital-technological framework have not resulted in an inclusive and definitive body of knowledge on the subject.

References

Baddeley, A., & Hitch, G. (1974). Working Memory. In G. Bowen, *Recent Advances in Learning and Motivation* (pp. 47-89). Academic press: London.

BBC News. (2010, February 1). GMT with George Alagiah. London.

Binder, C. (1990). Precision Teaching & Curriclum Based Measurement. *Journal of Precision Teaching, Vol 7, No.2* , 33-35.

Binder, C., Haughton, E., & Van Eyk, D. (1990). Precision Teaching Attention Span. *Teaching Exceptional Children*, 24-27.

Burke, L. (2009). Towards an Empowering Pedagogy in Teaching ESL Writing. *Cultivating Real Writers: Emerging Theory & Practice for Adult Arab Learners*, 11-26.

Clark, R., & Harrelson, G. (2002). Desinging Instruction That Supports Cognitive Learning Processes. *Journal of Athletic Training, Vol 37, No.4*, 152-159.

Clarke, R. (1983). Multi media and learning processes. *Educational Technologies*, 31-33.

Cognition and Technology Group at Vanderbilt . (1990). Anchored instruction and its relationship to situated cognition. *Educational Researcher, Vol. 19, No. 6* , 2-10.

Daneman, M., & Carpenter, P. A. (1980). Individual Differences in Working Memory and Reading. *Journal of Verbal Learning & Verbal Behaviour*, 450-466.

Daneman, M., & Merkle, P. M. (1996). Working Memory & Language Comprehension. *Psychonomic Bulletin & Review*, 422-433.

De Stefano & LeFevre, J. (2005). Cognitive Load in Hypertext Reading: A Review. *Computers in Human Behavior*, 1616-1641.

Doolittle, P., & Mariano, G. J. (2008). Working Memory Capacity and Mobile Multimedia Learning Environments: Individual Differences in Learning While Mobile. *Journal of Educational Multimedia and Hypermedia, Vol 17, No.4*, 511-530.

Hughes, J., Beverley, M., & Whitehead, J. (2007). Using Precision Teaching to Increase the Fluency of Word Reading with Problem Readers. *European Journal of Behavior Analysis, Vol 8 No.2*, 221-238.

Kozma, R. (2001). Kozma Reframes and Extends His Counter Argument. In R. Clark, *Learning from Media: Arguments, Analysis and Evidence* (pp. 179-204). Connecticut: Information Age Publishing.

Kuhlmann, S., Piel, M., & Wolf, O. T. (2005). Imparied Memory Retrieval after Psychosocial Stress in Healthy Young Men. *Journal of Neuroscience, Vol 25, No.11*, 2977-2982.

Lindsley, O. (1999). Precision Teaching: Discoveries & Effects. *Journal of Applied Behaviour Analysis, Vol.25, No. 1*, 51-57.

Lindsley, O. (1991). Precision Tecahing's Unique Legacy from B.F.Skinner. *Journal of Behavioral Education, Vol 1, No. 2*, 253-266.

Mayer, R., & Moreno, R. (2001). Multi media tools and seductive distractors. *Educational Psychologist*, 56-62.

Mayer, R., & Moreno, R. (2003). Nine Ways to Reduce Cognitive Overload in Multi-Media Learning. *Educational Psychologist, Vol.38, No.1*, 43-52.

Quas, J., Rush, E. B., Yim, I. S., & Nikolayev, M. (2013). Effects of Stress on Memory in Children and Adolescents: Testing Causal Connections. *Memory*, 1-17.

Rockwell&Singleton. (2007). The Effect of the Modality of Presentation of Streaming Multimedia on Information Acquisition. *Media Psychology*, 179-191.

Sternberg, R. (1995). Memory-The Short Term Store. In R. Sternberg, *In Search of the Human Mind* (p. 277). Florida: Harcourt, Brace & Company.

Willis, D. (2003). *Rules, Patterns & Words:Grammar & Lexis in English Language Teaching.* Cambridge: University of Cambridge.

Acknowledgements

A special thank you to the 2012 Graduates from Al Ain English Speaking School, Al Ain, United Arab Emirates, who volunteered to participate in this study.

Afterword

Kasim Kasuri

Few things excite the human imagination quite like technology – perhaps because change and evolution are so intrinsic to our DNA. And technology certainly does change! I vividly remember my first Apple Macintosh computer in 1984 – a truly iconic machine, yet one so basic that its entire operating system (along with the software one was trying to use) managed to fit on a 3.5 inch floppy disk with a capacity of only 1.44 megabytes. The Macbook laptop I am using to write this afterword uses more space just to store a single photograph!

Indeed, technology has evolved beyond recognition in a few short years and, with it, so have our lives. Why then should we not expect technology to play an equally important role in the classroom?

In education circles, there is an old (and rather hackneyed) joke about a doctor, a scientist, and a teacher from the late nineteenth century who arrive in modern times (say 2014) in a space machine. While the doctor and scientist are confounded by the many innovations they see in hospitals and research centers and resultantly find themselves quite redundant, the teacher finds the nearest school, walks into an unattended classroom and starts teaching as if the last 100 years never happened! This little story has many variations but each is underpinned by the belief that the K-12 classroom has not evolved much in the last century or more. While seasoned educators like the ones reading this book may consider pedagogy to be at the center of this much-needed paradigm shift, a lot of 'regular people' with whom I routinely interact (administrators of K-12 schools or parents) automatically assume that the joke points to the lack of technology in the classroom. The truth is, most people believe that technology transforms learning – in fact, people take it as an uncontested truth in much the same way that they believe in the goodness of democracy.

Computers first made their way into the classrooms of Beaconhouse in the early 1980s – around the same time I was playing 'Ghostbusters' on my very first computer, a Commodore 64 (luckily I was not running Beaconhouse at the time)! I clearly remember that the focus in those days was the technology itself: there was much emphasis on learning about input/output devices, RAM and ROM and Logo and BASIC – the 'Beginners All-Purpose Symbolic Instruction Code'.

In the mid 1990s, there was a subtle but important shift at Beaconhouse from learning 'about' technology to learning 'with' technology through the launch of the 'Cross Curricular Computing' (C3) initiative aimed at enhancing the teaching of all subjects though the use of computers. Years later, as more and more technology entered our classrooms, 'C3' became the more inclusive 'ETAC' – Emerging Technologies Across the Curriculum – which embraced all technologies from the Internet to Lego Robotics to filmmaking, digital microscopes, Interactive whiteboards and more.

Since the 1980s, schools that have had computers have clearly had a perceived edge over those that have not. There is no doubt that computers have played a key role in the marketing of private/independent schools in many parts of the world. To have computers in one's classrooms automatically implied academic superiority, almost as if good computers could compensate for bad teaching.

Today, there is a quiet debate at Beaconhouse – one of the world's largest K12 school organizations educating a quarter of a million children – on the impact that all this technology has had on students' learning outcomes. The younger educators who are mostly digital natives along with the hard-core technologists take for granted that technology MUST have transformed learning. To them, it is as basic a reality as the air that we breathe: to question it is a sign of ignorance, of old-world thinking. On the other hand, there is a much smaller (and mostly silent) group of people – including those responsible for budgeting – who want to know if there is any empirical evidence that suggests that technology has improved student learning outcomes.

The reality is that there is no such evidence….but then we do not have evidence for a number of other things, either. For instance, we cannot prove beyond a doubt that professional development of teachers has led to improved student learning outcomes – simply because all our teachers are so different that it is impossible to determine what impact the 'pre-training profile' of a teacher would have had on her/his baseline – and subsequent – understanding of good teaching practice.

In the absence of any conclusive research, our conclusion is simple: the classroom cannot be isolated from the rest of the world. Children cannot play on iPads and smartphones at home but contend only with dusty chalk and heavy books in the classroom. As a result, more and more technology is introduced in our classrooms every year, the latest being tablet computing for the very young. While such devices are a source of much motivation and excitement for students, teachers and parents and undoubtedly enhance the school's profile in the community, the question regarding their ultimate impact on learning outcomes remains to be answered. One day in the not too distant future, we hope we will know and, as with most things in life, I suspect the answer will not be black or white.